WOMEN ACROSS ASIA

WOMEN ACROSS ASIA
Issues of Identities

Editors
Lipi Ghosh
Ishita Mukhopadhyay
Suchandra Chakraborty

GYAN

GYAN PUBLISHING HOUSE
New Delhi-110002

WOMEN ACROSS ASIA :
Issues of Identities

Rs. 625

ISBN : 81-212-0872-6

Published in 2006 in India by
Gyan Publishing House
5, Ansari Road, Darya Ganj, New Delhi-110002
Phones : 23282060, 23261060, Fax : (011) 23285914
E-mail : gyanbook@vsnl. com
Website : http : //www. gyanbooks. com

Laser Type Setting at : Master Computer's, Delhi
Printed at : Salasar Imaging System, Delhi

Contents

A few words to Begin with... 9

Editorial 11

List of Contributors 21

WOMEN, WORK AND PARTICIPATION

1. **Gender Stereotyping in South Asia** 25
Introduction • What the Story is • What Researchers Say • Problem of Quantification • As a South Asian Problem.
Ishita Mukhopadhyay

2. **Gender Disparity in South Asia : A Comparative Study of India, Pakistan, Bangladesh and Sri Lanka** 39
Introduction • Gender Disparity : Certain Conceptual Issues • Nature and Causes of Gender Disparity in South Asia • Education Outcomes • Employment and Economic Activity • Political Participation.
Smita Majumdar

3. **Whither the Women of Asia? An Exploration into the Trends in the Nature of Women's Engagements Visible in Asia** 63
A Bird's Eye–view of the First Regime Type: The Post-Colonial States in Asia • How do

the Women of such Regimes React? What is the Nature of their Activism? • The Second Regime Type : Myanmar • The Instance of Third Regime : The Case of Communist China • Concluding observations : A Reflection on the Trends in the Women's Activism.

Bonita Aleaz

4. **Women Participation in Panchayati Raj Institution in West Bengal** 77

Introduction • Status of Women in India and West Bengal • Political Participation of Women in India : Need for Reservation • Status of Women Panchayat Members in India and West Bengal • Participation of Women in Panchayat Activities • Kultikri : West Bengal's First All Women Panchayat • Conclusion.

Madhulika Mitra and Somnath Mitra

5. **Globalisation and its Impact on Women Workers : The Asian Experience** 99

Introduction • Women Participation in Work • Burden of Work on Women Workers • Economic Deprivation of Women Workers • Health Hazards among Women Workers • Other Exploitation at Work.

Suman Ray and Basabi Chakraborty

WOMEN AND POLITICS

6. **Quest for Identity : A Brief Sketch of the Palestinian Women's Movement** 113

Question of Identity • Palestinian Society • Women's Movement.

Aditi Bhaduri

7. **Between Secular Teaching and Islamic Preaching : Confused Identity of Soviet Central Asian Women** 141
History of the Process • Source of Problems • Impact of Religion.
Nandini Bhattacharya

8. **Between "Homeland" and Home : Russian Women in Uzbekistan** 163
Homelands and Identity • The Russian Dilemma • A Search for Homelands • Conclusions.
Anita Sengupta

WOMEN AND SEXUALITY

9. **Women's' (Non) Identity : the Case of the Bauls' Sadhansanginis** 183
Rajasri Basu

10. **Con (fused) Identity of a flying Woman** 195
Fusion of Roles : A flying Woman is a Housewife and a Whore in One Self • Confused Identities • Vulnerability Explored • At Work • At Home.
Swati Ghosh

11. **Identity–Women–Advertisement : Politics of Viewing** 209
The History of Advertisement • Women, the World of Advertisement and Her Identity.
Sarbani Guha Ghosal

12. **Religion, Sex and Issues of Identity: Women in Thailand** 225
Religion, Women and Sex Sector : Tradition to Modernity • Hinduism and its Resplen-

dent Influence • Buddhism, Society and Sex • Women, Monastery and Identity • Conclusion

Lipi Ghosh

WOMEN IN MIDST OF TRADITIONS

13. **Japanese Women : Mukoirikon to Modernisation** **249**

Mukoirikon and the Women-centered Society • Women in Politics and Religion in Ancient Japan • Change from Women-centered to Patriarchal form of Society • Impact of Warfare • Change in the Position in Edo or Tokugawa Period (1603 to 1867 A.D.) • Women and Modernisation.

Purabi Gangopadhyay

14. **Women in Bhutan : Aspects of their Status and Role** **257**

Introduction • Bhutan : Land and People • Bhutanese Women : A Socio-Cultural Profile • Changing Gender Relations in Bhutan • Conclusion.

Seikh Rahim Mondal

Index 285

A few words to Begin with...

Is there any Asian Women's Movement? Can we think of any Asian question of looking at identity? We were trying to address these questions when we held the two-day conference on Women Across Asia in Women Studies Research Centre, University of Calcutta on... The response to a general call for papers to the conference was diverse. The presentations were even more diverse. It was clear that the answer to the question of identity among Asian women particularly women's movement cannot be answered without respecting the diversity and heterogeneity among Asian women. The present volume was planned taking revised versions of some of the papers presented in the conference. A rearrangement of the papers across the themes of politics, economics, traditions, sexuality at least tried to locate some lines of identity. The book in this respect raises more questions than it answered. Debates are raised: can we at all address these themes as lines of identity? The point is not to win or lose debates. The point is only to raise the question, which is the need of the hour.

With global capital enforcing a process of development among countries of Asia, Africa and Latin America, the question of seeking identity has become significant both from global and local concerns. It is significant that this volume is coming out in a year when "Women's World: An Interdisciplinary Congress" is being held in Seoul, Asia. Understanding identity of world women's movement will also be one of the concerns there. In that sense, the volume raises questions which does not pertain to Asian countries alone. Certain world perceptions and major issues are also not perceived if we fail to address the specificities of local cultural ethnic traditions.

On the other hand we have macro questions of identity which can be tackled at economy, social and political respects. On the other hand we have micro traditions, culture, ethnicity binding us to the roots of identity. Combining both aspects leads to the world view, which the volume ultimately hopes to address. The volume is only a beginning. Debates are already there in the literature from the seventies regarding Asian question in defiance to 'end of history'. Neo-liberalism propagates in market being the emancipator. But it is an almost world consensus that market has failed to understand women's contribution to society. So we need an Asian question at identity which lacks at women's movement from an alternative angle, alternative to neoliberal and not to mention the hypotheses of 'end of history'. The volume is also a beginning to understand the politics of Asian women's movement in the new context of the global forces. The volume has raised more questions than it has answered. As knowledge builds on identifying major questions, the volume is an addition to the knowledge of Women Studies in this respect. The contributors to the volume have mostly based their opinions on extensive field work from the different countries. As they are mostly grassroot based researchers, some new issues are being raised which has the pulse of women from below. This makes the volume still more significant.

However, doubts still remain at the end how does one raises and resolves identity at grassroots combating both neoliberal version of global identity and indignity at the same time. Perhaps women's question is the best way to start raising issues and the volume rightly does so.

Editors

Editorial

Global development being the catchword today defines the question of identity in different ways. Identity was perceived earlier as national as well as international. There were various streams and various segments which used to harp on the question of identity historically. Asia has been one such segment where the issue of identity was felt very strongly. The countries do not differ vastly from the historical transition point and again countries of Asia are not widely divergent on the issue of culture and social characteristics. In other words the historical social, cultural and ethnic strings have always tended to bind the countries together. The economy and polity contextualises similar kinds of settings in this group of countries. The question then comes back in what sense is Asia a totality? The faces as follows are more than one.

The identity was a compulsion historically, a compulsion which is now felt economically and socially. Globalisation is a device that is advocating a pattern of identity in the name of unipolarism. But combating these efforts Asian people have upheld identities in the various ways perceived by them. Asia along with the global South has been a victim of the forces of globalisation, tending to divide communities and countries in terms of the effects of free trade, withdrawal of state and other economic evils. In this context, women have always been in a vulnerable position. The impact of globalisation on women have been widely discussed at all levels and more or less a consensus has been reached on the ground that the forces do discriminate along gender lines. In today's world identity along gender lines is a contested issue. Attempts have been made from the forces of globalisation to build walls of identity along many streams through gender lines. One can not deny the question of identity of gender, caste, class, ethnicity and others. But barring multiplicity of the question of identity that comes up, we have to confront the identity of the deprived, disadvantaged and displaced. This identity has to face the onslaught of globalisation the forces of. There is the need to construct identities and recognize existing identities across Asia.

Asia no doubt can take pride in its cultural, racial, religious diversity despite being a large geographical whole. Like climate, vegetation, animal life, its patterns of human adaptation are of varied forms which range from the nomads of Arabic and Central Asia to those of the crowned cities of the Yangtze basin and the Gangetic plain. Physically it is the largest of the continents, occupying 30 per cent of the world's land area.

In this land of varied society, the crucial question is distribution of role models acceding to sex, racial position, kinship etc.Women have selected rights and obligations as well as different behavior patterns according to social norms and exception in different social contexts. Usually the criteria for the division of labour between the sexes and deductively the feminine role does seem a bit arbitrary based on local customs and traditions rather than on their physical differences. Women's more petite stature does not prevent them from bearing heavy burdens or putting in exhaustive physical labour. However under the present twenty first century setting the connection between the social and biological roles of men and women are more thinly divided and may hereafter be just coincidental.

The present volume is the collection of papers presented in a workshop jointly organised by Indian Association for Asian and Pacific Studies and Women Studies Research Centre, Calcutta University on this agenda. Some selected papers coming out of the discussion are to be included in the book.

The volume takes us to the aspect of social identity of women in different parts of Asia. Gerard Duveen and Barbara Lloyd proposed that social identities be viewed as internalization of the social representations of the groups in which individuals participate. They have recognized and emphasized a need for methods appropriate to the investigation of culture and that implies investigation of the values beliefs and practices which characterise the categories– women and men. To Lloyd however the more important but most difficult issue is the definition of the social identity of women. The term social identity appears to be straightforward at first sight but how are appropriate comparison groups to be identified? Are they women and men, traditional and non-traditional women, women and mothers? The definitional problem no doubt does not end, rather increases at the emergence of several groups. This present volume serves it readers well by indicating the complexity involved in analyzing the social identity of women. The articles in the present volumes definitely provide an overview on the question of identity of Asian women as observed in a number of countries from South Asia, East and Central Asia. These include India, China, Japan, Uzbekistan, Iran, Palestine, Thailand, Bhutan and many others. The topics chosen are also varied, though one may observe strains of similarity or dissimilarity. The articles presented here provide pictures about different regions of Asia-South, Southeast, West and Central Asia and it takes up social, political and economic issues within its broad purview.

A significant domain to earmark the status of women in society is labour force participation and demographic variables which have causal links between both capital, work status, marriage, fertility, migration and mortality. Women's lives are actually more radically transformed by demographic and developmental changes than men's lives are. It is a general contention that modernization essentially involves the expansion of the 'masculine' public domain at the expense of the 'feminine' private domain of the family. Demography is basically concerned with changes that affect families and women's concern with development starts at the level of the family and expands from there. Similarly progress for woman can be facilitated by the governmental legislation but only spread when there is change at the level of the family. The idea of development from the grass roots up needs to be matched by a commitment by the government to economic and social structures which do not handicap women from the start at the level of the family.

However one important fact is that with economic changes over the past one and half decades, very significant social changes have taken place across Asia and so there is a resultant upward linkage in the general social status of women. In other words increasing educational and economic opportunities for women have brought important changes in the social and economic status of women in different parts of Asia. In this present volume we have presented a few articles, which examine the trends in women's labour force participation at different levels of development. The book is divided into the themes : Women, Work and Participation; Women and Politics; Women and Sexuality; Women in Midst of Traditions.

Ishita Mukhopadhyay's article entitled *Gender Styreotyping in South Asia* looks in to the question of women and work participation. Concentration of female employment in specific job types is the phenomenon associated with construction of gender stereotypes. They have been identified by many researchers in literature. Many occupations have also been identified with extreme gender stereotyping. The article tries to understand gender stereotyping in South Asia. The reasons for such stereotyping is also to be analysed from the evidences regarding women's work in South Asia. The article begins with the question of gender stereotyping from the point of view of women's work. It surveys the relevant literature on occupational segregation and reviews the existing measures on occupational segregation. In the final turn it analyses the different aspects of stereotyping of occupations in South Asia.

Gender disparity in South Asia : A Comparative Study of India, Pakistan, Bangladesh and Sri Lanka is the paper by Smita Majumder which analyses the nature and the common factor of gender disparity across four countries of South Asia in terms of political participation as well as related factors like health, education and earning. The central argument of Majumder's article is that women are most underrepresented in decision making positions and in an indirect way it has a repercussion on other developmental aspects of women's positions in society. To put it the other way, disparities relating to women pervades in the spheres of education, health and employment. The discriminatory practices towards women are nothing but hidden impacts of their subservient participation in politics. Majumder however also analysis the economic development and progress to women's status and position. To her, countries like Sri Lanka with higher per capita income will have better health, education and economic equality while gender disparity will be most predominant in an economically underdeveloped country like Pakistan.

Bonita Aleaz writes an analytical article named *Whither the Women of Asia? An Exploration into the Trends in the Nature of Women's Engagements visible in Asia.* When the question is raised "Whither the women of Asia?" we obviously refer to the conditions within which the women are embedded and the attempts, if any made by them to face/confront the same. Rather than using the frame of reference used so far and as indicated above we consider that women's activism in Asia, can be more clearly understood as a function of the state-structure they are ensconced in. At least four regime-types may be identified in the region : Beside the liberal democratic, the regimes of the region may be classified according to three other defining characteristics-the military dictatorships; the communist regimes; and the Islamic states.

The paper looks at the nature of women's activism in Asia as visible in at least one representative region reflecting each of the regime types indicated above and uses these as models for discovering trends visible in the other regions as well.

Women's Participation in Panchayati Raj : Institutions in West Bengal is an article by Madhulika Mitra and Somnath Mitra. With reference to the operational system of Panchayati Raj, the article makes a comparative analysis of women's position in West Bengal and India. The article claims to act as the *chef d'oeuvre* to study the grass-root level political institutions and role of women members therein with specific reference to *gram-sabhas* and *gram-panchayats.* It shows how the operational system of Panchayati Raj in west Bengal plays a role model for the rest of the country.

The article by Basabi Chakrabarti and Suman Roy relates to the issue of women and work during the process of globalization. *Globalization and its Impact on Women Workers : The Asian Experience* begins with a discussion on the characteristics of globalization and proceeds with a discussion on the specific impacts of globalization on women. To the authors, benefits of globalization are to be skewed towards the elite women of South Asia and not for the women of common genre. Marginalized and disadvantaged these ordinary women become vulnerable to a lot of injustices in society.

The commitment of the political right to transfer existing social structure and process has became more transparent in recent years because of changes which have take place in the language used by political groups. The identification of the 'right' with value for changes is apparent in the way in which they characterize their opponents as resisting 'progress' and 'seeking to turn the clock back'. That way extension of political powers and rights reflects empowerment of women and this also happens to be an important variant of the identity of women in a society.

It is an accepted fact that the history of women's rights is still dominated by the stay of the long and dramatic struggle for the vote which reached its climax in the early decades of this century. By concentrating upon male opposition to votes for women and by couching its polemics in terms of war between the sexes, feminism put too much emphasis upon the political aspect of emancipation. In the present volume we present four articles taking to the question of women's political rights across Asia.

Quest for Identity : A Brief Sketch of the Palestinian Women's Movement is the article by Aditi Bhaduri she shows how politics imbibed with religion shaped the history of the women's liberation and also brought about an evolution in Palestinian women's identity. Ms. Bhaduri took up the history of organized politics of the1920s and 1930s. It was with Israeli take over of Palestine in 1967 a turning point arrived in women's of Israel as may disasters submerged the questions of women's developments. The late 1970s however saw the revival of women's organization and gradually it shaped out as the *Intifada* against Israeli occupation and that marked the 'golden age' for the Palestinian women. To Bhaduri it was with *Hamas* (radicalization and Islamization of intensive Palestinian authority) that women's role in society became subservient and female political activists were looked down upon. The author concludes with her belief that existing political awareness might bring in time liberal changes in the life of the Palestinian women.

Nandini Bhattacharyya writes on socialist secularism of USSR in Central Asia and the question of women's identity, in her article titled *Between Secular Teaching and Islamic Preaching : Confused Identity of Soviet Central Asian Women*, the author speaks on traditional orthodox ideologies as propounded by Islam and its derogatory impact brought on society and women. Campaign against the use of *parendzha* (veil) was a direct challenge to authoritarianism as shown by the author. The interesting point about the article is the inner contradictory role of women's belief and faith in progressive propagandas on the one hand and magical power symbols on the other, while the anticipated conclusion of the author is that the final resort might be that the women would take emotional anchorage in the lap of Soviet rule. She apprehends a tremendous chaos in the country's scenario at the end of the Soviet regime. To her this turns the social structure upside down and brings forth nothing but a 'confused identity' of many central Asian women.

Between Homeland and Home : Russian Women in Uzbekistan is an article by Anita Sengupta which reviews the status and political stature of Russian women in the post-Soviet era. Taking to the history of Russia migration to Central Asia she has shown how Russians are now the 'New Minorities' in the post Soviet scenario. Sengupta's article talks about the dilemmas in the political sphere as well as dualities in women's identities.

Sexual orientation has a very important role to play in the evolution of social identity of women. In other words, one of the dominant paradigms within which identity of women are to be judged is the matrix of sex. This treatment of sex within gender varies with cultures. Age, region, country, social class, educational level, ethnicity and religion–are the factors which influence and the attitude towards gender diversity. Significant cultural variations also occur in what is considered appropriate sexuality.

Women's (non) identity : The Case of Baul Sadhansanginis is the article presented by Rajasri Basu which explains utilization of the female sex of the specific Baul Community of Bengal in terms of philological interpretation of religion and the female sex. The history of the Baul implies that conjugal meditation and bodily pleasure are treated as the highest level of Baul spiritualism. Thus, Baul women's identity are important because they act as the stooges of the Bauls for achieving their spiritual truth. To Basu, it is a kind of exploitation, loneliness and deprivation of women. The novelty about the article is that the author has touched upon the issue of individual reidentification of the *Baul Sadhansanginis* who have developed a distinct identity for the female singers.

Swati Ghosh's article *Confused Identity of a Flying Woman*, explores the dimension of twofold identities of a flying woman. A flying woman's identity is dubious-she is a housewife as well as a whore. To Ghosh, within domesticity, she has a primary role to play as a housewife and a mother while her sex is utilized in a lustful manner while whoring in the world of sex-service. These multiple identities no doubt are fragmented and at different levels leave her vulnerable and confused.

Advertising is one of the most important areas of public life in which gender is displayed in images as well as in language. Advertisements often make lavish use of women's bodies to draw people's attention and in that way it shows how advertising has a considerable literal and figurative investment in the appropriation and display of female bodies. Sarbani Guha Ghoshal's article entitled *Identity, Women, Advertisement : Politics of Viewing* emphasises the role of sex in the visual medium. She gives importance to proliferation of the electronic media and delves into the issue of identity of women vis-à-vis the advertisement world and its socio-political implications. To the author the world of advertisement is a perpetuating male domination in any kind of modern patriarchal social system. The article with reference to several television channels shows how the entire gamut of events become a very interesting field of social science analysis. To Guha Ghoshal female the body is a focal point of commercial buying and selling. Exploitation of their sexual identity and advertisement virtually becomes the melting pot of indigenous and global advertisement themes and thereby contributes actively to the image of "modern" women.

The aspect of multiple and fragmented identities are revisited while we read the article by Lipi Ghosh entitled *Religions, Sex and Issues of Identity : Women in Thai Society*.

The article shows how in patriarchal Thai society relationship between religious values, patriarchy and women's sex can be combined together to explain the dual identity of Thai women. It is social *mentality* which combines itself with religious sanctions to evolve a 'new' identity of woman in Thai society. It is again exploitative, oriented towards serving the interest of the patriarchy.

The book identifies two articles which deal with the question of evolution of women's status from the traditional phase to the modern age. Purabi Gangopadhyay's article *Japanese Women–Mukoirikon to Modernization* represents the history of gradual evolution in the status of Japanese women. While the Tokugawa period showed a kind of parental supremacy, the *Mukoirikon* was a female centric marriage system which contributed to political, social and religious supremacy of women in Japanese society. The article takes us to the question of women's elevated role in politics and religion through the ages and in the final round shows the existing dichotomy between constitutional/ legal prosecution and factual reality.

Seikh Rahim Mandal's article entitled *Women in Bhutan: Aspects of their Status and Role* is a remarkable attempt to present a socio-cultural and economic identity profile of the women of Bhutan. Women do not hold a homogeneity in the heterogeneous society of Bhutan. Mondal's article speaks about economic activities and related status of women in different sectors of village activities like agriculture, weaving, animal husbandry, cottage industries etc. Women perform a better entrepreneurial role in rural economy as well as in family economy. The article takes further note of women's marital as well as educational position. The overall situation confirms a superiority of female folk over the male.

List of Contributors

Aditi Bhaduri, Independent Researcher and Columnists in Leading Newspapers, Kolkata.

Anita Sengupta, Fellow, Maulana Abul Kalam Azad Institute for Asian Studies, Kolkata.

Bonita Aleaz, Reader, Dept of Political Science, University of Calcutta, Kolkata.

Ishita Mukhopadhyay, Director, Women's Study Research Centre, University of Calcutta, Kolkata.

Lipi Ghosh, Reader, Dept of South and Southeast Asian Studies, University of Calcutta, Kolkata.

Madhulika Mitra and Somnath Mitra, Institute of Social Sciences, Eastern Regional Office, Kolkata and Department of Geography, Midnapore College, West Bengal.

Nandini Bhattacharya, Senior Lecturer, Calcutta Girls' College, Kolkata.

Purabi Gangopadhyaya, Lecturer, Department of Japanese Studies, Visva-Bharati, Santiniketan.

Rajasri Basu, Senior Lecturer, Department of Political Science, Rabindra Bharati University, Kolkata.

Sarbani Guha Ghosal, Senior Lecturer, Bijoy Krishna Girls College, Howrah.

Seikh Rahim Mondal, Professor, Centre for Himalayan Studies, University of North Bengal.

Smita Majumdar, Senior Lecturer, Surendranath College for Women, Kolkata.

Suman Ray, Associate Researcher and **Basabi Chakraborty**, Research Associate, Centre for Urban Economic Studies, University of Calcutta.

Swati Ghosh, Senior Lecturer, Department of Economics, Rabindra Bharati University, Kolkata.

WOMEN, WORK AND PARTICIPATION

1

Gender Stereotyping in South Asia

Ishita Mukhopadhyay

Introduction

Occupations can be differentiated between those with disproportionately female labour forces and those with disproportionately male labour forces. This phenomenon is well known as the phenomenon of occupational segregation into gender types. During the last decade, much research on employment trends of women focused on occupational segregation into gender types. The paper attempts to look into the phenomenon of stereotyping of jobs into gender types in South Asia. The paper starts with looking into the question of gender stereotyping from the point of view of women's work and then surveys the relevant literature on occupational segregation. Then it reviews the existing measures on occupational segregation. The paper ends with an analysis on the different aspects of stereotyping of occupations in South Asia.

What the Story is

Women's work has been an issue of discussion in women's studies and women's movement due to the peculiar notion of this kind of work. Women of all ages work or rather have to work. Irrespective of the caste, class identities women work. Some may work more and some less. It is a universal truth that a non-working female is rare to find. But a part of the work is paid and a part unpaid. The proportion of unpaid work done by women is very high compared to that of the paid work. So, when we discuss women's work, we have to realize that most of it is either supplementary or invisible, and total information of this kind of work is practically impossible. Women work as unpaid household maids, as home based workers, as informal sector workers and workers who are mostly unrecognized and uncared. Work outside as well as home based work can be documented, but the unpaid work cannot be accounted. The unpaid work can be analysed through time-use surveys, which estimate the time required to perform each job by women. But time use surveys are not always available and we get less and less information about women's work.

Inquiry into women's work is also essential from the point of assessing women's empowerment. According to UNDP guidelines, construction of Gender Empowerment Measure has women's economic participation as an important element in the construction of the index. Hence the contribution of women's paid work towards empowerment constitutes economic empowerment of women. Unpaid work does not contribute to women's economic empowerment. Home based work provides earnings for women but as earnings here do not correspond to working hours this also is not a good contributor towards economic empowerment. There has been much criticism on these and various other grounds on the applicability of this measure in developing countries like South Asia. In developing countries, where poverty of a large section of the population is a burning issue, any question of economic empowerment cannot be dealt with without the programme of poverty eradication intertwined with the question of earning opportunities. In fact, there is a consensus among many that employment of women is the prime mover of poverty eradication and empowerment. It is around work participation and employment opportunities that the process of social empowerment and lessening of gender inequality can be understood.

Globalisation has set in enormous amounts of changes in work conditions and working patterns of both men and women. In this context, the question of gender related deprivation in employment in the Third World countries has been one of the most discussed questions of the last decade. The massive scale of unemployment and informalisation of the existing scope of employment in the Third World countries have taken the form of a gendered dimension in each issue relating to development. The different aspects of female employment have raised different questions regarding :

(a) shifts in occupational and job pattern during the last decade and the much debated issue of feminisation of labour force

(b) stereotyping of female employment in specific occupations and jobs

(c) feminisation of informal sector activities

All the questions are interrelated and linked to the broader question of feminisation of poverty and gender deprivation achieved through employment. Gender stereotyping is a result of feminisation as well as informalisation of the labour force. The question of stereotyping is linked to the question of economic empowerment of women in developing countries through economic participation in the labour force.

What Researchers Say

Evidence of occupational segregation into gender types have been obtained by Blau, F and Jusenius, C (1976), Elia,

P (1988), Hakim, C (1979), Reskin, B and Hartmann, H (1986), Watts, M and Rich, J (1993), Anker, R (1998) and many others. All of them have stated several reasons why the phenomenon of occupational segregation is important for the discussion of labor market as a whole.

Occupational segregation occurs when different people participate in different kinds of occupations and there exists rigidity in the mobility of groups or people from one occupation to another. Such occupational segregation often occurs along gender lines. We often find occupations which are termed 'male' or 'female'. The observation is that women are excluded from the 'male' occupations and males are not preferred in the 'female' occupations. The employers extend the logic of differential of efficiency in the case of male and female workers. It is stated that relatively less efficient and low skilled jobs are assigned to women and skilled and efficient jobs are for men. This particular type of occupational segregation if it persists sets in a process of gender stereotyping. The process is itself self-reinforcing. This has an important negative effect on how men see women as well as women see themselves by reinforcing and perpetuating the process. The process of gender stereotypes is generated and maintained by persisting occupational segregation. Women who are repeatedly engaged in less or unskilled jobs develop a preferential 'skill' in those unskilled jobs and this reality is felt by both the employers and the workers. Although this has a general negative effect on labor market conditions, this is hardly felt by the participants in the labor market. The stereotyping along gender lines in the workplace can be due to various reasons. One basic reason behind the phenomenon has been the perception of women's work as an extension of housework. What a woman should do is what she is used to do. So there is a process of 'housewification' of the work done by woman outside her home. Since women perform the marginal duties, it is perceived that they would also perform similar types of duties outside their home. The other perception is the fact that the underlying gender dimensions in the socio-economic set up calls a job 'marginal' if it is done by women and there is marginalisation of women's occupations. It is also obvious why women are lesser paid than men. The less or unskilled jobs fetch low wages and we have a male-female wage differential. Although there exists male-female wage differential within occupations, but the differential is more pronounced due to occupational stereotyping. Even if it is possible to eliminate occupation-wise male female wage differential, the differential persists due to gender stereotyping. As men and women do different kinds of jobs, they fetch different wages. It is also clear why women are given cheaper wages than men. The process of stereotyping strengthens the rigidity in the labor market. Persisting occupational segregation can generate and accentuate several important impacts upon the labor market in general. To understand these impacts, it is necessary to identify areas or occupations where stereotyping is being generated. The difference between the concept of occupational segregation and the concept of persisting and reinforcing occupational segregation is also to be spelt out.

Thus, we observe a subtle difference between segregation and stereotyping. Occupational segregation exists when men and women are differently distributed across occupations to a degree greater than is consistent with their overall shares of employment, irrespective of the nature of job allocation. Stereotyping is the phenomenon when the occupational segregation persists, maintains itself, and strengthens over time. Stereotyping is a dynamic concept, whereas segregation is a static one. There may be occupational segregation at two different points in time, but the patterns may be different. Stereotyping is said to exist when men and women continue to do the same type of work in the job market so that labor mobility across gender types is prohibited. Occupational segregation is thus necessary, but not sufficient for creation of gender stereotypes. So clearly, we have two dimensions of any measure of stereotyping—the segregation and the intensity of segregation along the same direction over time.

The measure of segregation can also be used for finding the extent of displacement or shifting of workers from existing jobs. If the pattern of segregation changes direction, then we may conclude that workers have shifted from one type of occupation to the others. However, this shift can also take place without substantial occupational segregation. Since we are discussing the aspects of gender stereotyping, the paper does not consider the pattern of shift that can occur without occupational segregation.

Occupational segregation hence can be measured and the overtime changes in the pattern of this measure can be observed. The overtime pattern can be continuation of the pattern in the same direction or in different directions. If the pattern reinforces itself in the same direction, we claim that stereotyping has occurred. If the pattern moves over to different directions, then we claim that shift has occurred. When occupational segregation occurs at a particular direction, or in other words, either males or females are continuously repeatedly employed in the same occupation over a fixed time period, we say that stereotyping has emerged.

The discussions on globalization policies in the third world have yielded the consensus that this has devalued the traditional areas of female work, such as subsistence agriculture, agro-based small scale production. This has shifted female laborers from the mentioned occupations into certain newly created job types. Empirical observation relates to the fact that female specific income generating and employment projects have not received the same level of resources and attention. Hence this led to the concentration of women in marginal economic sectors. Concentration of female workers has become higher in ill-paid and low-skilled jobs, and we find occupational segregation of female laborers in such areas.

Displacement from original spheres of activity of both male and female laborers have combined with an increasing concentration of female labor force in marginal activities. It is the female with little or no skill who is then employed at the tail end of the production process. Thus globalization has brought in the indirect effect of occupational segregation into gender types.

There exists several theories in the literature explaining gender stereotyping. According to the neoclassical theory of human capital, we have the twin theories supported by demand and supply forces. The labor supply theory stresses on lower levels of human capital of women. Since women are lesser educated and trained, they are pushed to ill-paid jobs. The labor demand theories push forward the argument that there are direct and indirect costs of labor in the case of female laborers. The labor market segmentation theories base their arguments on the concept of dual labor market. They stress the existence of segregated labor markets and occupations. Gender theory makes a contribution to explaining occupational segregation by sex by pointing out how closely the characteristics of female occupations correspond to typical stereotypes of women and their supposed abilities. Traditionally women are endowed with caring nature, skill at household related work, greater manual dexterity, greater honesty etc. and these characteristics push women to ill-paid jobs.

However, none of these fully explain the phenomenon of emerging stereotypes. The reason for persistence of the phenomenon of stereotyping is due to existence of a vicious cycle in the process. Women are generally specialized in some marginal jobs, which are the ones which need unregulated hours of work, piece-rate of payment and seasonal pattern of employment. Working in any of these jobs can thus by themselves not sustain any individual. The individuals are forced to participate in multiple jobs consequent in longer working hours and low wage rates. These are mostly unskilled labor but due to persistence of stereotyping, individuals who are stereotyped in this unskilled labor market attain a level of specialization in these jobs. Stereotypes are 'specialized' in these jobs and the cycle goes on and on. The cycle gets support from the demand as well as the supply side. The employers gain maximum profit by maintaining a backyard of marginal unskilled and semi-skilled laborers, who are to be paid the minimum. The suppliers of this type of labor are willing as the absence of regularity and labor laws fits in well with the unpaid labor market in the household. But as they participate in any one of them, they cannot sustain themselves without participating in the other. This develops the participation in the multiple labor markets. So the process gets reinforced by itself. Multiple labor markets reinforce a process of working in unregulated markets, which means occupational segregation. Figure 1 illustrates the above Vicious Cycle.

Multiple jobs
↓
Ill-paid jobs
↓
Occupational segregation
↓
Stereotyping
↓
Multiple jobs Gap

Figure 1

Globalisation policies have reshuffled the employment-production structure of the economy. This has increased informalisation and piece-rated job types. These involve lesser pay and longer hours of work, which necessitates multiple jobs done by women to make both ends meet. These are all ill-paid jobs and involves significant amount of stereotyping.

Problem of Quantification

The present section presents the existing measures on occupational segregation into gender types and then decomposes the existing measures into both the effects of existing stereotyping and emerging stereotyping.

The simplest measure of occupational segregation has been the sex-ratio of the workers employed in the various occupations. If there exists n occupations indicated by 'i'. M_i and F_i indicate respectively the number of male and female workers in the ith occupation, then $S_1 = F_i / M_i$ indicate occupational segregation ratios. Higher S_1 means that the particular occupation 'i' has more concentration of females relative to males. Scott (1994) defined degrees of gender segregation in order of ascendance of the measure $=S_1$. Higher values and lower values of the indicator helps to categorize the occupations as exclusively men (EXM), mainly men (M), mixed (MF), mainly women (F) and exclusively women (EXF). This measure has been used by a number of researchers successfully (Hakim, 1979; Reskin and Hartmann, 1986) to estimate the extent of segregation in different countries across occupations and also across jobs. Occupations are defined as aggregates over the cluster of jobs belonging to the occupation. Empirical data has shown that occupational segregation can smoothen out the extent of segregation across job types. So sometimes segregation across job types reveal the intra-occupational segregation. Whatever may be the extent of desegregation, this measure of segregation suffers from the absence of relativity as this does not measure relative concentration of females compared to males in the occupations.

Karmel and Maclachlan (1988) defined an index of occupational segregation where the aspect of relativity was included. Segregation in each occupation should be measured relative to the overall segregation. An occupation employing more females relative to males is not alone sufficient to claim segregation. The occupation becomes an F or M occupation if the occupation employs proportionately more females relative to the overall sex-ratio of the employees. Karmel and Maclachlan index (K-M index) is presented below.

$$S_2 = (1/T)\Sigma \mid F_i - a(M_i + F_i) \mid = (1/T)\Sigma \mid (1-a)F_i - aM_i \mid \quad (1)$$

where T and a stand for total employment and female share of total employment.

This index can be split up into constituent Composition and Mix effects, where the latter can be split up into Occupation, Gender and Interaction effects. The Composition effect looks at the change after excluding the change in the occupational structure and the associated change in the male and female employment. The Occupation effect looks into the change after excluding the change in the total employment and the proportional change involved in the respective occupations. The Gender effect is based on comparison after including the changed gender shares of the occupations. Since the change in the occupational structure and the change in the growth rates of both the female and male employment across occupations are related, there is an Interaction effect composed from both the effects. The K-M index have been developed further by Watts and Rich (1993). As an alternative to the above index, Blackburn, Siltanen and Jarman (1993, 1995) presented the marginal matching index (M-M) and index of dissimilarity (I-D). I-D may be interpreted as the sum of the minimum proportion of women plus the minimum proportion of men who would have to change their occupation in order for the proportion of female to be identical in all respects.

$$I - D = 1/2\Sigma \mid F_i/F - M_i/M \mid$$

Here the symbols indicate the number of females and males in female and male occupations and the total female and male occupations.

Siltanen, Blackburn and Jarman (1995) expressed I-D in terms of a basic segregation table where the measure clearly equals the proportion of women in female occupations minus the proportion of males in female occupations. However, this value is sensitive to the changes in occupational structure of labor force and the extent to which the occupations are feminized. The marginal matching index (M-M) intends to correct this disadvantage by measuring changes in occupational segregation by sex resulting exclusively from changes in the sex compositions of occupations.

$$MM = (F_f * M_m - F_m * M_f) / F * M$$

The subscripts 'f' and 'm' indicate the occupations categorized into female and male categories. I-D and M-M are the same when half of the labor force is female. But if it is not so the measures yield different results of stereotyping. However the measures show very clearly that even if stereotyping does not appear to exist in apparent terms, the data might show its existence in terms of these measures.

As a South Asian Problem

In South Asia, evidence of informalisation and home-based work done by women is borne by documents and records. South Asia is a place where women's identity is not expressed through her contribution to productive work in the nation. Women identify herself not through work, but mostly through her contribution in the family. Hence most of the work is unpaid, unrecognized and unaccounted. Stereotyping is a phenomenon which is mostly visible in this invisible work. Women are stereotyping in marginal workforce and the works where women are stereotyped are called marginal. This becomes clearly a hen and chick problem. This feature of stereotyping is evidently borne by Human Development Report in South Asia (2000) (2003).

According to the 2000 Report, South Asian women are invisible national economic accounting systems. When they are counted as workers, the figures come to 33 per cent of the total official labour force. As women are engaged in ill paid jobs, their total earnings are only half as much as men. The share of women in administrative and managerial positions during 1992-97 is 2.7 per cent compared to 10 per cent in developing countries. The share of women in professional and technical occupation is 21 per cent during the same period. This again speaks of severe stereotyping in the work force with minimal bargaining power over wages. Obviously these are the informal sector and agriculture.

The situation hardly improved when we consider the 2003 report. It is specifically mentioned in the report that women are mostly concentrated in the low productivity segments of all three sectors–agriculture, industry and services. Hence the figures will show a rise in female employment, which has been much advocated as feminisation of employment. But a more disaggregated sectoral occupational classification of data will depict a stereotyping in low-end jobs. 2003 Report identify these jobs as self-employed or wageworkers or free contributor to family labour or home-based work for global production chains.

Lack of gender-disaggregated data at lower levels of production is a problem in calculating the extent of stereotyping according to the measures suggested above. Much of the wage discrimination between male and female workers exists as they are unequally paid for unequal work. Unequal wages for equal work also exists but they can be combated through legal infrastructure, political and civil society movements. But what cannot be combated in this mechanism is unequal wage for unequal work. Stereotyping is a phenomenon, which implies unequal wage for unequal work. Low-end jobs will always fetch low wages and women will continue to be the victims of stereotyping. Absence or silence of data does not allow us to measure stereotyping in accurate details. What can be measured is occupational sex ratios. A consideration of these ratios is thus relevant to understand the gender development and gender empowerment of the country. As a large part of stereotyping occurs in the agricultural sector, this is a special problem for South Asian women. The only way for working women, whether visible or invisible to get out of this trap of stereotyping is participating in more programme for skill training and technical education.

References

Anker, R *: Gender and jobs : Sex segregation of Occupations in the World,* ILO, Geneva, 1988.

Blau, F and Jusenius, C : 'Economist's approaches to sex-segregation in the labour market', in M. Blaxall and B. Reagan (ed) *Women in the Workplace* : Chicago : University of Chicago Press, 1976.

Elias, P : "Family formation, occupational mobility and part-time work" in Hunt (ed) *Women and Paid Work,* London, Macmillan, 1988.

Hakim, C *: Occupational Segregation,* Research Paper 9, Department of Employment, London, HMSO, 1979.

Human Development Report in South Asia (2000) : Mahbub ul Haq Human Development Centre, Oxford University Press, Oxford, 2003.

Karmel and Maclachlan : Optional sex-segregation : increasing or decreasing, *Economic Record,* Vol. 64, 1988.

Mukhopadhyay, I and Mitra, N : *Gender bias of Marketisation : A Study of Informal Sector in West Bengal* (mimeo) : presentation in a national seminar on Market vs. planning in the honour of Prof. A. K. Dasgupta held in Viswabharati University, West Bengal, 1995.

Reskin, B and Hartmann, H *: Women's Work; Men's Work : Sex-segregation on the Job.* Washington D. C. National Academy Press, 1986.

Scott, A, M : *Gender Segregation and Social Change : Men and Women in Changing Labour Markets.* Oxford University Press, 1994.

Vickers, J : *Women and the World Economic Crisis.* Zed Books, London, 1991.

Watts, M and Rich, J : "Occupational sex-segregation in Britain, 1979-1989; the Persistence of Sexual Stereotyping", *CJE,* Vol. 17, 1993.

2

Gender Disparity in South Asia : A Comparative Study of India, Pakistan, Bangladesh and Sri Lanka

Smita Majumdar

Introduction

South Asia is a land of many countries. Its landscape extends from the mighty peaks of the Himalayas in the North, through vast plains and arid deserts, to tropical forests and palm-fringed beaches in the South. More than one-fifth of the world's population live here. South Asia has experienced several foreign invasions which has left a mosaic of different cultures, religions and traditions and thousands of languages and dialects.

South Asia, which constitutes about 22 per cent of the world's population, is the poorest, the most illiterate and most malnourished region of the world which is least sensitive to the needs of the women. In South Asia more than 500 million people live in a state of severe deprivation, lacking sufficient access to adequate nutrition, health, housing, safe drinking water, sanitation, education and employment. Women in South Asia are often denied basic human rights and they continue to struggle against prejudice and discrimination due to certain social, economic, political and legal factors.

Gender disparity–between men and women and between boys and girls is a large problem in South Asia. The main objective of this paper is to analyze the nature and causes of gender disparity across four countries in South Asia namely, India, Pakistan, Bangladesh and Sri Lanka at the dawn of the 21st Century.

At the outset we shall discuss certain conceptual issues regarding gender disparity which will be followed by analysis of nature of the gender disparity in four countries in terms of health, education, earnings and political participations.

Gender Disparity : Certain Conceptual Issues

In a very narrow sense gender disparity can be defined as the purely descriptive observation of different outcomes between males and females. The major causes of gender disparity are discrimination (which is differential treatment of individuals because of their gender), biological differences, individual and society's belief and attitudes about appropriate gender-specific roles etc. These factors are causally correlated and it is very difficult to differentiate between underlying causes and proximate indicators or symptoms.

In a more broader sense gender disparity can be defined as unequal sharing of the burden of adversities between women and men. The prevalence of gender disparity in society is manifested in the intensification of women's work, discontinuation of girl children's education, increases in the time spent by women on home maintenance and higher levels of mental stress, abuse and violence of women in society.

Gender inequality exists in most parts of the world. However they are manifested in many different forms. So gender disparity is not a homogeneous phenomenon but a collection of heterogeneous and interlinked problems. Amartya Sen (2001) has analyzed seven types of gender inequality. They are described as follows :

Firstly, *mortality inequality* is the most prevalent gender inequality found in South Asia. It involves matters of life and death and is manifested in most of the countries in South Asia by unusually high mortality rates of women. This results in preponderance of men in total population as opposed to preponderance of women in societies where there is no or little gender disparity in health, education and nutrition.

Secondly, *natality inequality* is emerging as an important phenomenon in India and South Asia. It is true son preference and unfavourable female male sex ratio is prevalent in male dominated societies but with the availability of modern techniques to determine the gender of the fetus sex selective abortion has become common in many countries. This results in sex ratio becoming even more adverse illuminating the existing gender bias.

Thirdly, *basic facility inequality* : Even if where there is not much mortality and natality inequality, there are certain basic facilities like health care, education, schooling, nutrition where women can have less than a square deal. Gender inequality in access to education and health care is a very important issue in South Asia.

Fourthly, *special opportunity inequality* includes opportunities of higher education encouragement to women to cultivate one's natural talent etc. is less prevalent among women than men. The traditional preference for boys over girls leave girls at home to do household work and help in rearing children. Girls generally tend to have higher opportunity cost of going to school than boys resulting in discouraging investment in their higher education. It is a common perception that parents would for go return from investment in girl's education because as soon as they get married they move out of parent's household. So all these results extreme gender asymmetry in areas of education, training and professional work.

Fifthly, *professional inequality* is prevalent both in developed countries and developing countries for different reasons. In developing countries since girls are deprived from higher education and training in terms of employment as well as promotion in work and occupations they are handicapped. However, in more equalitarian societies where there is much less prevalence of basic facility and special opportunity inequalities progress to higher levels of employment and occupation is much more problematic for women than for men. In terms of opportunities in the labour market, the possibility of girls finding a more lucrative job, given the same education and ability and professional skill as boys is likely to be lower. All these results in professional inequality of women.

Sixthly, *ownership inequality* is quite prevalent in South Asia where basic assets such as home and land is unequally shared. This is one of the reasons why women have less bargaining power and lower status at home and society on the one hand and cannot flourish in commercial, economic and social activities on the other hand.

Seventhly, *household inequality* : There are certain basic inequalities in gender relations within the household in terms of unequal sharing of burden of housework and childcare. This results in higher dropout and enrollment in school. Women and girls are typically the last to eat in a family, thus if there is not enough food they are the ones to suffer most from malnutrition. The malnutrition among women are compounded by heavy work demands, by poverty on the one hand and by childbearing and rearing on the other hand. So it has been taken it for granted that men will naturally work outside the home as bread earners and women could do it if and only if they combine it with household duties which is unequally shared.

Though we have discussed seven types of gender inequality separately, yet they are very much interrelated.

There are certain non-conventional indicators of gender disparities. These are greater prevalence of mental distress and of abuse and violence among women. The main reasons behind higher level of mental distress are poverty, violence, sexist discrimination, women's lack of power and autonomy and nature of roles that women are expected to fulfill etc.

Different efforts have been made to conceptualize different forms of gender inequality. In 1995 United Nations Development Programme [UNDP] brought out the Gender Development Index [GDI] as a tool to capture gender inequality. GDI is a composite index based on the same variables as human development index. The index is based on three indicators : longevity, as measured by life expectancy at birth, educational attainment, as measured by a combination of adult literacy [two-third weight] and the combined gross primary secondary and tertiary enrolment ratio [one-third weight] and standard of living, as measured by GDP per capita [PPP US$]. Gender Development Index adjusts the average achievement of each country in life expectancy, educational attainment and income in accordance with the disparity in achievement between men and women [Human Development Report 2000].

However there are certain disadvantages of GDI as measure of gender inequality. It fails to take into account many important dimensions such as the quality of community life, access to basic amenities like human rights, safety and security, household allocation of resources, unpaid labour and constraints imposed on mobility and on sexual and reproductive freedom etc.

Again recognizing the centrality of gender-based political imbalances the UNDP has clearly identified the movement towards gender equality as a political process. So its Gender Empowerment Measure [GEM] attempts to reflect this and consists of variables that reflect women's political participation, their access to professional positions and their earning power. So Gender Empowerment Measure [GEM] is a composite index using variables constructed explicitly to measure the relative empowerment of women and men in political and economic spheres of activity. Three indices-for economic participation and decision making, for political participation and decision making and for power over economic resources–are added to derive at the final GEM value.

Now GEM is also criticized on the ground that it is based on only three variables on the one hand and it is based on the very narrow conception of empowerment without including legal and human rights.

So GDI unfolds the relative capabilities attained by men and women and GEM seeks to throw light on the extent to which they participate in the economic, political and professional arenas of their respective countries. Now greater the gender disparity, the lower a country's GDI compared to HDI. The maximum value of GEM like GDI and HDI is one. *While the GDI focuses on expansion of capabilities, the GEM is concerned with the use of three capabilities to take advantage of the opportunities of life [UNDP, Human Development Report 1995, p. 73].*

According to the recommendation of the International workshop on Building a Framework for Measuring Gender Equity [1996], it is necessary to incorporate three variables namely ownership of wealth and assets by women, consumption of food by women and domestic violence in GDI/GEM to conceptualize gender disparity in a more realistic way.

So these in a nutshell are some conceptual issues regarding gender disparity. Against this backdrop we shall analyze the nature and causes of gender disparity in the four regions of South Asia namely India, Pakistan, Bangladesh and Sri Lanka.

Nature and Causes of Gender Disparity in South Asia

South Asia has made considerable progress in various aspects of economic and human development in recent decades. South Asia's GNP per capita has increased from US$ 126 in 1973 to US$ 437.9 in 1999. Its Human Development Index [HDI] has increased from 0.204 in 1960 to 0.554 in 1999. Now the average annual growth rate of GNP per capita in 1998-1999 is 4.3 per cent. Among the South Asian countries Sri Lanka and India belong to medium human development countries whereas Bangladesh and Pakistan belong to low human development countries with HDI being 0.47 and 0.498 in 1999 respectively. Sri Lanka is the most prosperous among the countries in terms of economic development where per capita GNP has increased from US$ 230 in 1973 to US$ 820 in 1999 and Bangladesh is one of the poorest South Asian countries whose GNP per capita has increased from US$ 80 in 1973 to US$ 370 in 1999. In India and Pakistan GNP per capita behaved in the similar way (Table–1).

Table-1 : Trends in GNP Per Capita and Human Development in South Asia

	South Asia	*India*	*Pakistan*	*Bangladesh*	*Sri Lanka*
GNP per capita (US$) 1973	126	130	130	80	230
1999	438	440	470	370	820
Human development index					
1960	0.204	0.206	0.183	0.166	0.475
1999	0.554	0.571	0.498	0.47	0.735

[*Source* : Human Development in South Asia 2001].

If we look at Gender related development index [GDI] we find that in South Asia it has increased from 0.415 in 1995 to 0.535 in 2000. At the individual country revel DGI was the highest for Sri Lanka (0.732) followed by India (0.563), Pakistan (0.468) and Bangladesh (0.459) in 2000. In 1995 GDI for Sri Lanka (0.70) was much above the region average followed by India (0.424), Pakistan (0.399) and Bangladesh (0.342) [Table 2].

Table-2 : Gender Related Development Index in South Asia 1995-2000

		GDI	*Rank*
South Asia	1995-2000		
	1995	0.415	70
	2000	0.535	
Sri Lanka	1995	0.700	105
	2000	0.737	

(Table-2 Contd.)

		GDI	*Rank*
India	1995	0.424	120
	2000	0.560	
Pakistan	1995	0.399	121
	2000	0.468	
Bangladesh	1995	0.342	121
	2000	0.459	

[*Sources* : (i) Human Development Report on South Asia 1999 and 2002].

What is revealed from (Table 2) is that gender disparity is very much prevalent in South Asia. Through its intensity has decreased from 1995 to 2000 in South Asia as a whole and the four individual countries yet it is most prevalent in Bangladesh and least in Sri Lanka.

Despite considerable progress in recent decades, gender disparities remain pervasive in many dimensions of life in South Asia. Gender disparities between men and women– and between boys and girls exist as a consequence of differences in the opportunities and resources available to them. Inequalities in the allocation of such resources as education, health care and nutrition is the main reason behind this gender disparity and this affects an economy's well-being, productivity and growth.

Though women and girls bear the most direct brunt of these inequalities, yet this ultimately extends to the entire society. The severity of gender inequalities is best reflected in the fact that although female infants have a biological advantage at birth, men out number women in this region, with the exception of Sri Lanka. The sex ratio (number of females per thousand and males) is 939, 917 and 955 for India, Pakistan and Bangladesh respectively. Whereas it is 1022 for Sri Lanka in 2000. If we look into South Asian countries in the world where women and men have nearly the same life expectancy at birth. So in these countries the typical female advantage in life expectancy is not seen. However in Sri Lanka life expectancy at birth (in years) in 2000 for males in 69.5 year whereas for females it is 75.3 years and Pakistan life expectancy at birth for males is 60.2 years and for female it is 59.8 years. So the biological advantage of females at birth is not seen in most of the South Asian countries due to gender disparity.

Against this backdrop we shall discuss certain broad indicators of gender disparities related to health, education, employment by economic activity and political participation.

Health and reproductive health : Generally girls have a greater chance of surviving childhood than boys–except where sex discrimination is greatest. Though female disadvantage in access to health services is diminishing in the developing countries yet the female disadvantage in mortality and morbidity is carried into adolescent and reproductive years. Health conditions related to sex and reproduction (reproductive health) have been estimated to account for 25 per cent of the global disease burden of women. Reproductive health, which is a state of physical and mental well-being in relation to the reproductive system and its functions and processes, can be achieved through education, services during pregnancy and childbirth, provision of safe and effective contraception and prevention and treatment of sexually transmitted diseases [World Development Indicators 2001].

We shall first consider the child mortality rate and adult mortality rate of females to analyze gender disparity in the four countries of South Asia namely India, Pakistan, Bangladesh and Sri Lanka. The ratio of female to male child mortality, defined as the chance of a child dying after turning one but before turning five is 1.46 for South Asia in 1988–

1999. At the individual country level it is highest (1.05) and Sri Lanka (0.9). So gender disparity is most prevalent in Pakistan and India is slowly inching towards gender equality. In Sri Lanka child mortality is higher for boys than for girls because here parental gender preferences are absent. Due to economic prosperity and human well-being child mortality at absolute level is very low in Sri Lanka both for male (10 per 1000) and female (9 per 1000). So gender disparity is not uniform within South Asia. The main reason behind higher female child mortality in some counties of South Asia is likely that girls have unequal access to resources. It is true that female disadvantage is best reflected in differences in child mortality rates because it captures the effect of preferences for boys due to adequate nutrition and medical interventions particularly for the age group 1-5. ,Now because of natural female biological advantage, when female child mortality is higher than male child mortality, there is good reason to accept the fact that girls are discriminated against. This is exactly what happens in South Asia excepting in Sri Lanka though the dimension is different for different countries.

Adult mortality rate which is defined as the probability of dying between the ages of 15 and 60 i.e., the probability of a 15 year-old dying before reaching age 60, affects both men and women. In the developing and underdeveloped countries one of the major reason behind increase in adult mortality rates is the increase in AIDS-related mortality that affects both men and women. Adult mortality rates of female of South Asia is 212 per 1000 female. In the individual country level it is highest in Bangladesh (290 per 1000 female) and lowest in Sri Lanka (96 per 1000 female) in 1999. Excepting Bangladesh this mortality rate is higher for males in all other countries of South Asia. Though this indicator does not directly reflect gender disparity yet it really indicates the status of women's health particularly reproductive health in South Asia.

One of the important indicators of the status of women's reproductive health is *maternal mortality rate* (per 100, 000 live birth) which is highest for Bangladesh (600) followed by India (440), Pakistan (200) and Sri Lanka (60) in 1995 [World Development Indicators 2001]. If we look into the birth attended by skilled staff we find that during 1996-99 only 14 per cent of total birth is attended by skilled staff in Bangladesh whereas in Sri Lanka it is as high as 95 per cent. Again analyzing total fertility rate (births per woman) what is revealed that in Sri Lanka it has fallen from 3.5 in 1980 to 2.1 in 1999, in India it has fallen from 5. 0 in 1980 to 3.1 in 1999, in Bangladesh it has declined from 6.1 in 1980 to 4.8 in 1999. Pakistan in 1999 could not even attain Sri Lanka's nineteen eighties total fertility rate (Table 3).

Another interesting indicator of reproductive health is the percentage of *pregnant women receiving prenatal care.* While in high income countries women have universal access to health care during pregnancy, in developing countries it is estimated that 35 per cent of pregnant women–some 45 million each year–receive no care at all (United Nations 2000). Prenatal care is essential for recognizing, diagnosing and promptly treating complications that arise in pregnancy. According to 1996 estimates 100 per cent of pregnant women receive prenatal care in Sri Lanka, followed by 62 per cent in India, 27 per cent in Pakistan and only 23 per cent in Bangladesh. So female disadvantage in child mortality is carried into reproductive years in most of the South Asian countries excepting Sri Lanka (Ref. Table 3).

One of the most tragic elements of reproductive health status of women in South Asia is the maternal deaths which is highly preventable with proper care. Infections, blood loss and unsafe abortions account for the majority of deaths. This is highly controllable in the developing countries of South Asia because it neither requires high technology nor

Table-3 : Female Health and Gender Disparity in South Asia

	India	*Pakistan*	*Bangladesh*	*Sri Lanka*	*South Asia*
(a) Child mortality rate					
(i) Male (per 1000) 1988-89	19	22	37	10	26
(ii) Female (per 1000) 1988-99	20	37	47	9	38
(b) Ratio of female to male child mortality	1. 05	1.68	1.27	0.9	1.46
(c) Adult mortality rate					
(i) Female per 1000 in 1999	206	153	290	96	212
(ii) Male per1000 in 1999	218	186	276	150	223
(d) Maternal mortality rate (per 1000, 000 live birth in 1995 adjusted)	440	200	600	60	
(e) Total fertility rate (births per women)					
1980	5. 0	7. 0	6.1	3.5	
1999	3.1	4.8	3.2	2.1	
(f) Percentage of pregnant women receiving prenatal care 1996	62	27	23	100	

[*Sources* : (i) World Development Indicators 2001 ii. Human Development of South Asia 2001]

expensive drugs. Trained health workers with midwifery skills increases the safety of childbirth on the one hand and by spreading information about family planning increases the awareness of women on the other hand. It is exactly what Sri Lanka has done in South Asia and Nepal, Bhutan and Bangladesh are lagging far behind.

What is revealed from analyzing the general health and reproductive health profile of women in four countries of South Asia is that gender disparity is highly prevalent in some countries of South Asia, like in Bangladesh and Pakistan, moderately prevalent in India and least prevalent in Sri Lanka. It is revealed from Gender related Development Index (GDI), life expectancy at birth, different mortality outcomes particularly child mortality rates. Again the prevalence of inequitable gender relations in the society definitely determine reproductive and general health status of women in the country. The countries where reproductive health status of women is good, gender disparity is also much less. So gender disparity indirectly influences reproductive health status of women in South Asia. So an over all strategy for improving female health status would improve gender disparity automatically.

So Sri Lanka is performing best in all the indicators relating to women's health, human development and gender development.

Education Outcomes

In South Asia the literacy gaps between men and women are narrowing down slowly from 1980 to 1999. In 1980 the percentage point difference between male and female adult literacy rates is 27 which has fallen to 24 in 1999 [World Development Indicators 2001]. Though the enrollment has improved more for girls than for boys yet gender gap in favour of boys continues to malve disadvantages for girls in South

Asia. In this region girls access to primary to secondary education is still limited in rural regions excepting Sri Lanka and some states of India like Kerala on the one hand and girls are more likely to drop out of school on the other hand. Beyond improving the number of schools, special measures are also necessary encourage girl's enrolment including subsidies and other financial incentives to girls and improving the relevance of education in the society so that returns to investment on education also increases.

The first indicator we have chosen to analyze gender disparity in education outcome is the Literacy Gender Parity Index (LGPI while) (is the ratio of the female literacy rate to the male rate), If this ratio is one then we can infer there is gender equality in literacy and if it is less than one then there is gender bias (in favour of males). One thing is very clear from Table 4 that gender disparity has declined from 1970 to 1999 in all the countries of South Asia. However gender disparity in literacy rate is most prevalent in Pakistan and least prevalent in Sri Lanka where literacy gender parity index has increased from 0.79 in 1970 to 0.94 in 1999. One interesting feature to notice is that the literacy gender parity index of Sri Lanka (0.79) in 1970 is much higher than this index of 1999 in all the other three South Asian countries namely India (0.66), Pakistan (0.51) and Bangladesh (0.57). Sri Lanka is very fast moving towards gender equality in literacy.

If we look at *adult female literacy rate* at the dawn of the twenty first century (2000) we find it is as high as 89 per cent in Sri Lanka and as low as 27.9 per cent in Pakistan. India lies in between with an adult female literacy rate of 45.4 per cent in 2000 (Table–4).

Now the differential access of female and male children to schooling is reflected in variations in enrolment rates. To measure relative access we estimate what may be called a

Table-4 : Female Education and Gender Disparity in India, Pakistan, Bangladesh and Sri Lanka

	India	*Pakistan*	*Bangladesh*	*Sri Lanka*
1. Literacy gender parity index				
1970	0.40	0.12	0.19	0.79
1999	0.66	0.51	0.57	0.94
2. Adult female literacy rate (percentage of age 15 and above) in 2000	45.4	27.9	29.9	89. 0
3. Combined primary, secondary and tertiary gross enrolment ratio in 1999				
Female (%)	4.9	28	33	71
Male (%)	6.2	51	41	68
4. Ratio of female enrolment rate to male enrolment rate in 1999	0.79	0.55	0.80	1. 04
5. Female primary school gross enrolment (as percentage of male)				
1970	64	37	48	92
1995-1999	82.8	69.6	96.9	98.2

[*Sources* : (i) World Development Indicators 2001; (ii) Human Development Report of South Asia 2001; (iii) Human Development Report 2002]

"equality coefficient" which is the ratio of female gross combined (primary, secondary, tertiary) enrolment to male enrolment rate, so that this ratio may be equal, less than or greater than one. There would be equality between male and female when the coefficient is unity, gender bias against women when it is less than unity. The lower the coefficient, the wider the female-male gap : the higher the coefficient the narrower gender disparities. What is revealed from Table 4 is that there is gender bias in favour of women in combined primary, secondary and tertiary gross enrolment in Sri Lanka (1.04) in 1999. So there is no gender disparity in enrolment ratio in Sri Lanka. Gender disparity in enrolment is most prevalent in Pakistan (0.55). India and Bangladesh have similar equality coefficient of around 0.80 in 1999. Though there is a wide gap between literacy gender parity index and adult female literacy rate between India and Bangladesh, yet Bangladesh has improved to a great extent in female enrolment rates in the nineties both at combined level and primary level.

Another interesting feature is that in Bangladesh female primary school gross enrolment as percentage of male has improved from 48 per cent in 1970 to 96.9 per cent in 1995-99 whereas in India it has improved from 64 per cent in 1970 to 82.8 per cent in 1995-99 and Sri Lanka it has improved from 92 per cent in 1970 to 98.2 per cent in 1995-99 (Table–4).

Though the access to education of females has improved to a great extent in South Asia yet gender disparity in education still exists in South Asia except in Sri Lanka. Social and economic factors seem to account for lower enrolment rates for girls than boys in South Asia. In some places caste or *sharia* based societies subordinate women to men and in some other places class based societies are responsible for gender bias. In Sri Lanka one of the immediate effects of introduction of universal suffrage in 1931 was the stimulus it gave to a broad impulse towards social welfare especially in the last decade before independence. There was a massive investment of resources on education, health and food subsidies. Together with it most of the governments in Sri Lanka since independence narrowed the gap between male and female, rich and poor much more effectively than in most Asian and African states. As a result of this though Sri Lanka is one of the poorer nations of the world, yet it provides its citizens with a quality of life which much wealthier nations have yet to achieve.

However for India there is gender bias due to certain economic and social factors. There is traditional preference for boys over girls at home to do household works and look after children. Girls would tend to have a higher opportunity cost of going to school than boys which results in lower investment in girls' education. Again there are lower returns on investment in girls because employees are reluctant to hire girls for fear that once they get married they would leave their jobs. Parents are also reluctant to invest in girl's education because they would forgo returns from investment in girls education as soon as girls got married and integrated into the families of their husbands. However, the boys would continue to send remittances to parents even after they moved away.

All these led to lower female literacy rate and lower enrolment ratio among females in India. In Pakistan and Bangladesh along with these factors religious and certain social inhibitions may explain the relatively lower female enrolment.

Employment and Economic Activity

Since girls are allowed less education by their families than boys are–a disparity is reflected in lower female

Table-5 : Employment and Economic Activity of Women in India, Pakistan, Bangladesh and Sri Lanka

	India	*Pakistan*	*Bangladesh*	*Sri Lanka*
Estimated earned income (PP US$)				
Male 2000	3383	2884	2026	4724
Female 2000	1267	916	1151	2270
Earned income share (female as percentage of male in 1995)	34	26	30	55
Labour force participation ratio (female to male ratio in 1999)	0.5	0.4	0.7	0.6
Administration and managers (percentage female in 1992-97)	2.3	4.3	4.9	17.6
Maternity leave benefits (percentage of wages paid in covered period 1998)	100	100	100	100

[*Sources* : (i) World Development Indicators 2001; (ii) Human Development Report of South Asia 2001; (iii) Human Development Report 2002.]

enrolment and lower female literacy. As a result, women have fewer *employment opportunities*, especially in the formal sector. They also earn less income than men (Table-5).

A labour force participation ratio (is the ratio of the percentage of women who are economically active to the percentage of men who are) of less than one (1.0) shows that women's labour force participation in the formal sector is lower than men's (a ratio of 1.0 indicates gender equality). As far as labour force participation ratio is concerned gender disparity is least in Bangladesh (0.7) and highest in Pakistan (0.4) in 1999.

But it is a well known notion that women who work outside the home continue to bear disproportionate share of the responsibility for housework and child-rearing. They also face discriminatory practices in the workplace especially relating to equal pay and maternity benefits. As far as maternity leave benefits (i.e. percentage of wage paid in covered period) in South Asia is concerned what is revealed that in all the four countries hundred per cent of the wages i.e. full wages is paid as compensation provided to women during maternity leave (Table 5). Though this apparently points out that there is no gender disparity, yet this data only relates to legalized benefits and does not include contractual benefits negotiated through labour union contracts. Again these benefits only apply in the formal sector, leaving out the vast majority of working women in informal sector in developing countries of South Asia.

Women also face discriminatory practices in the workplace especially relating to equal pay. Female in South Asia earn 33 per cent of what male earn in 1995. At the individual country level female in India, Pakistan, Bangladesh and Sri Lanka earn 34 per cent, 26 per cent, 30 per cent and 55 per cent respectively of what their male earn in 1995 (Table 5). So as per as earning is concerned gender disparity is most prevalent in Pakistan and least prevalent in Sri Lanka. We get a slightly different picture if we look at the estimated earning of male and female in 2000. The ratio of female income to male income in 2000 is highest in Bangladesh (0.57) even higher than Sri Lanka (0.48) and lowest in Pakistan (0.32).

If we look at the job profile of women in South Asia we find that only 2.3 per cent of female is engaged in administration and managers in India during 1992-97 which is as high as 17.6 per cent in Sri Lanka. In Pakistan 4.3 per cent of female is engaged in administration and managers and in Bangladesh it is 4.9 per cent (Table 5). So gender disparity is very much prevalent in South Asia as far as economic activity, income and employment scenario is concerned.

Political Participation

Women are vastly underrepresented in decision making positions in governments. Although the scenario has changed to a certain extent with 6 per cent of the world's cabinet ministers being women in 1994 which has increased to 8 per cent in 1998.

It is well known that India along with Bangladesh, Pakistan and Sri Lanka has had female heads of governments. In the case of Bangladesh, where both the prime minister and the leader of opposition are women we naturally can expect a higher role of women in decision making. But here the percentage of women ministers has fallen from 8 per cent in 1994 to 5 per cent in 1998. However in Sri Lanka it has increased from 3 per cent in 1994 to 13 per cent 1998. India is most grossly underrepresented in decision making positions both at political level and administration and managerial level.

Table-6 : Women in Decision Making in India, Pakistan, Bangladesh and Sri Lanka

	India	*Pakistan*	*Bangladesh*	*Sri Lanka*
Gender empowerment measure (GEM) in 1997	0.24	0.176	0.304	0.321
Women in decision making position percentage ministerial level				
1994	3	4	8	3
1998	—	7	5	13

[*Sources* : (i) World Development Indicators 2001, (ii) Human Development Report of South Asia 2001; (iii) Human Development Report 2002.]

Gender empowerment measure (GEM) which is used to measure the relative empowerment of women and men in political and economic spheres of activity is quite low in most of the countries in South Asia. It is highest for Sri Lanka (0.321) and lowest for Pakistan (0.176).

So what is revealed from the above analysis is that among the South Asian countries gender disparity is most prevalent in Pakistan and least prevalent in Sri Lanka. This cross country analysis supports the conclusion that economic development provides an enabling environment for gender equality. Countries with higher per capita incomes have better health, education and other related outcomes which help in fostering gender equality. This is basically the reason why Sri Lanka has much less gender disparity in life expectancy, primary, secondary school enrolment, political representations than other South Asian countries.

Gender disparity is neither uniform within South Asia, nor more importantly within the countries in South Asia. There are much greater differences in gender disparity among the states of India with Kerala in one extreme and

Uttar Pradesh on another extreme. So we shall get a more realistic picture of gender disparity in South Asia if we can make this study at a more disaggregate level which is beyond the scope of the present analysis.

References

Robinson, F. (ed.). *The Cambridge Encyclopaedia of India, Pakistan, Bangladesh, Sri Lanka, Nepal, Bhutan and The Maldives*, Cambridge University Press, Cambridge, 1989.

Sen Amartya, "Many faces of Gender Inequality", *Frontline*, October 27 November 9, 2001.

The Mahbub ul Haq Human Development Centre, *Human Development in South Asia* 2001, Oxford University Press, New Delhi, 2001.

United Nations Development Programme (UNDP), *Human Development Report 2002*, Oxford University Press, New Delhi, 2002.

World Bank, *World Development Indicators*, 2001, World Bank, 2002.

3

Whither the Women of Asia? An Exploration into the Trends in the Nature of Women's Engagements Visible in Asia

Bonita Aleaz

Women of Asia have emerged into the limelight only in the last two and a half decades or so. The major concern, which has guided query so far, has been whether the development achieved in the particular regions has percolated down to the women as well. In other words concerns about women have been expressed in the by now well discussed modernization frame work which has reflected the following three dimensions–first, the understanding on the one hand is : modernity and tradition are mutually exclusive phenomena, under the 'trickle down' concept of modernization, the bedrock of tradition would disappear once large doses of the modern is firmly rooted. Secondly, it suffers from the "silence and omission" syndrome–while women's movements in the western world receive attention, they are ignored in the erstwhile colonial world. Third, the scholarly literature perusing women's activism in these parts of the world generally fail to consider women as agents and activists in their own right. The traditional epithets of the political process framework presuppose certain levels of organizational strength, resources of the activists, participants consciousness and subjectivities, in other words prefixed notions are perpetually applied to assess the state of readiness of the women. On all these points Third world women fail to exhibit the predetermined indicators of activism.

When the question is raised "Whither the women of Asia" we obviously refer to the conditions within which the women are embedded and the attempts, if any made by them to face/ confront the same. Rather than using the frame of reference used so far and as indicated above we consider that women's activism in Asia, can be more clearly understood as a function of the state-structure they are ensconced in. At least four regime-types may be identified in the region : Besides the liberal democratic, the regimes of the region may be classified according to three other defining characteristics-the military dictatorships; the communist regimes; and the Islamic states. The paper looks at the nature of women's activism in Asia as visible in at least one representative region reflecting each of the regime types indicated above and uses these as models for discovering trends visible in the other regions as well.

A Bird's Eye–view of the First Regime Type : The Post-Colonial States in Asia

(The HDR of 2002, on the basis of income in aggregate indicates a total of 27 'developing' countries in the region including 8 countries of South Asia, Iran is included with South Asia, and 19 of East Asia and the Pacific, Japan has not been included in the region. The post-colonial state in Asia has had to expend rigorous efforts in two major dimensions : internal rapid socio-political and economic restructuring, and also to face the onerous all-inclusiveness of the global economic system; and secondly, to face the combined impact of the innumerable interest groups which asserted themselves in the post-colonial period. In such a situation, the vulnerable state-structure, subjected to internal dissension and external pressure may resort to "command capacity building" to legitimize its existence. This may be visible in all the states indicated above; those ruled by excessively religious fundamentalist groups, the military dictatorships, the state sponsoring democratic-communist regimes, or even the state having liberal democratic moorings. By "command–capacity of the state" we mean its ability to formulate laws affecting equal conditions of work; discriminatory family laws or conditions governing political affairs, all of which are found to be intensely discriminatory against women.

The specific questions raised in the paper would thus be: (a) what is the context of the women of the different regime-types indicated above and how do they engage with / countenance the same? and (b) what if any are the general trends that emerge from the same as reflective of the future prospects of their activism.

While, the Asian women who venture into public space, to earn a living, as a whole, confront all the principal forms of ideological control rife in society, as articulated by the state, the community and the family, it is in the case of the women of the Islamic regimes of the region where, exclusion is most rampant as a result of the complex mesh of cultural norms and practices, through which the ideologies are articulated.

The women in the Islamic regimes, in Asia confront the paradoxical situation of state-sponsored "traditional protectionism". On the one hand, the cultural norm prevalent throughout the region, is the dependence of the women on the men. Religious texts are invoked to highlight the need for protection and dependence of the women, both economically and socially. The desired condition for women is thus domesticity and the instrument through which the desired form of exclusion is achieved, is that of purdah. This illusion is sought to be retained even in contexts where the male income is grossly inadequate for the family's survival. Traditional protectionism contravenes the low productivity and harsh economic conditions to which most of the population is subject to, and the burden of which is invariably borne by the women. The women therefore, in these countries are subject to the paradox of a work front hostile to the female work force, and yet, have to shoulder the burdens of life and livelihood for their families.

Shaheed gives a graphic portrayal of the situation prevailing in Lahore, which represents the situation prevailing in the urban areas of Pakistan. Economic survival and male honour (linked to men's ability to provide for the family, as well as keep women within the home) has resulted in women taking up 'chardewari work'-that is home-based piece work, which virtually renders the fact of their working invisible to the world. It has all the semblance of a purdah. Apparently, those who venture outside, may be better off than those who are ensconced within chardewari work, yet, the former are subject to other tendencies which have kept alive the sex-segregated labour market (assigning women lower paid jobs; limits on their on–the-job training and other delimiting factors). They are also physically isolated from one another and also from information about market rates, virtually excludes all categories of women venturing into the work front.

Afshar similarly shows how Iranian women are subject to the paradox of seclusion subscribed through religion. The visibility/ invisibility of the purdah or hejab in Iran has been negatively correlated with the attitude of the prevailing state structure. The Shah regime with its perspectives on modernism had rendered it invisible and apparently freed the women from its confines, but, on the other hand conscious of its modernist clean image, resorted to a rampant clean-up operation of all slums and shanties–ousting the destitute women, without any alternate provisions for them, thus whatever shelter the bisarparastan, or the destitute had managed for themselves was taken away, this had resulted in tremendous public outcry leading to the revolution.

The Islamic post–revolutionary state, true to its Islamic dictate and in its zeal to curb what it interpreted as a growing religiosity, launched the most serious Islamification, which resulted in the reactionary interpretations of Islamic dictum. Under the paternalistic interpretations women, once again were the prime symbols through whom the reversal back to orthodoxy could be most observable. The hejab was mandatorily re-instituted, in recent times we get reports of a team of surveillance staff deputed primarily to warn women against bad-hejabi (not wearing the hejab properly) in public. The Sharia made its re-emergence, in place of civil justice through family law courts, and along with it all the necessary components essential for women in order to access public space were removed, (such as abolishing creches, cutting down on welfare protection, non-recognition of maternity leave). On the other hand, male unemployment, conscription and polygamous marriages leads to abandonment of women, making it imperative for the women to find independent sources of earnings within an environment which is totally hostile to their welfare. 59.1 per cent of Iran's women in the 80s did not enjoy the benefits of 'protected domesticity' but are bisarparastan.

The paternalistic discourse 'male as protector' was never voluntarily followed up by the government to build up support structures for destitute women. Whatever measures had been initially undertaken were abandoned to pay for Iran's war efforts. The regime has of today never been willing to accept that for many women 'immoral' occupations such as prostitution are a necessity and not a carefully planned western-inspired wicked plot to lead upright Muslim men astray.

In the case of Bangladesh, besides the strictures of the purdah, we get the image of women confronting two other paradoxical extremes. On the one hand a perusal of the Five Year Plan documents indicate escalating efforts for specific inclusion of the women in the comprehensive developmental strategy of the Government. On the other, the startling picture of the incapacity of the state to settle its priorities by itself in its plan processes also emerges, which leaves the women at the mercy of a decision-making process which intrudes very violently into an extremely private area of their lives.

The country today is the world's 8th most populous country and has the world's highest density, barring some city states. It is also a country excessively dependent on foreign aid, In 1992, its total external debt was 53 per cent of its GNP and the total net official assistance (ODA) received was 5.3 per cent of its GNP. Aid creates a situation of patronage and this is nowhere clearer than in the area of women's issues. The donor community has been openly critical of Bangladeshi society. Its clear mandate being to lessen the intensely high fertility rate in order to raise economic standards. This has resulted in a form of interventionism in the lives of the women which has not been visible elsewhere in the rest of Asia.

"Crash Programme" for family planning was introduced in 1982, under the military regime, the programme has continued with varying degrees of intensity. On the one hand, the intensity of the national concern is visible from the totally unrealistic targets set by the government to please the donors and on the other outmoded and unsuitable forms of sterilization techniques imposed upon the women, regardless of her consent. Reaching targets become more essential than the total health of the women.

The women are not in a position to exercise their autonomy since sterilization becomes almost compulsory through its linkage with other schemes essential for existence, such as the micro-credit scheme.

In such a scenario the efforts made for the first time by the Fourth Five Year Plan for empowerment of women are totally falsified. None of the developmental plans by the government can be independently developed, they become functions of the donor agencies prioritizing allocations and plans in terms of their assessment of the same.

How do the Women of such Regimes React? What is the Nature of their Activism?

The women do not question the dictates of Islam as religion. It is from within this realm that the women of Iran for instance find the source of their activism. If post revolutionary Iran has reinstituted the Sharia, then true equality in the work place and in the domestic sphere for women can also emerge through correct interpretation of the composite Koranic verses they feel. The Koran does not sponsor destitution, it only liberates. Correct interpretation of its verses had liberated from a previous state of bondage (contractual marriage as against proprietary marriages, proscription of female infanticide; abolition of women's status as chattel). Reinstitution of the veil similarly is empowering for the women. It provides respectability when working outside.

There has been no unilinear response by the Muslim women to their oppressive structures. While Iran's higher GNP, allows better access of the women to education, even a change in the extremely oppressive divorce laws have been seen. The same quantum of reforms influenced by women in the either Pakistan or Bangladesh is not visible.

In the case of the Bangladeshi women for instance, consciousness about interventions in their bodies remains a totally alien concept. Rights relating to reproductive choice of the women, or controls over their own bodies has no meaning to them, or for that matter for the majority of the women of Asia. Therefore agitation around these issues have not really taken off. The history of women's development in Bangladesh is too short to provide a definite answer to the question what is the desired level of autonomy of the women. The organizations of the women reflect lack of homogeneity, participation seems to be a fad rather than consciousness of real issues. The real issues affecting development concerns have yet to be tackled by the women.

The Second Regime Type : Myanmar

It represents a state under siege. Since 1962, it has been under military occupation. Despite the extremely closed conditions prevailing in the country for more than forty years, the response of the women to the prevailing conditions are very remarkable. They may be categorized under two heads: the influence of tradition; and the reasons governing reality. The transition from village economy to urban life took place under the impact of modernization for the Burmese people under the impact of colonialism yet, terms of the state-society discourse remained bound by the prevalence of the earlier structure–subservience to the dominant political authority whatever might have been its nature. The Burmese claim there has never been a basis for the growth of a healthy civil society-monarchy was replaced by the British centralizing rule and the demolition of the quasi-autonomous institutions (such as the Buddhist Sangha, the indigenous land–owning elites), preventing the growth of a critique of any kind. The military merely replaced such absolutist control. The growth of civil society and progressive critique of the dominance of the military might have been effective if the dissension existing among the large numbers of non-Burman people included in the economy had been curtailed, and they had rallied behind the anti-regime protesters.

The voice of Aung San Suu Kyi remains, but without a valid test of the numbers supporting her it would not be correct to say that she commands majority support. Even if she did at one point of time, mere facts of dealing with the reality of existence draws a different response from the women today. Analysts find a growing climate of conformism among the women and their families in Burma today. Fear of the future security of their children draws such a response from the women particularly. Thus rather than rebellion,"collective amnesia" about the past was developing and this was handed down to the children as a learned process. Not that women's organizations do not exist, The very few that do exist have been wholly appropriated by the state. Thus the women find "complementarity" towards the regime a better way out rather than participating in any prolonged resistance, since this might mean seclusion, and abject poverty.

The Instance of Third Regime : The Case of Communist China

It is possible only in the case of the PRC to specifically chart the method adopted by the women in response to the conditions affecting them. In 1956 PRC declared that the transition to socialism was complete, for women this effectively meant issues such as the equality of women were essentially resolved. Although the All-China Women's Federation (ACWF) did not agree with this position of the CCP yet, it was pressurized to adopt the resolution that socialism had brought women's liberation and equality between men and women. Despite the acknowledgement of "factual inequality" existing between the sexes, the period between 1966-78 saw the ACWF being abolished, which effectively left no national organization to speak on behalf of the women.

It is since 1979, when a new phase in the political climate of socialist China started that one can relocate the efforts made by the women as well. The ACWF was re-instituted.

Since this period it is possible to look at two strains clearly visible in the women's movement which remain dominant even today. We label these as the 1) consciousness–raising and efforts at autonomy and on the other as 2) indications of conformism.

1. The gains of the new women's movement started being visible since 1993 when, under the aegis of the ACWF a new law of 57-articles was brought into effect concerning the rights and interests of women-even though the power of the new legislation is still debated yet, it could gain symbolic victory, so far as consciousness raising and committing the state to justice for women was concerned. Similarly, a coordinating committee on women and children in the State Council was established in1990-enabling greater resources mobilization towards women than the ACWF could ever command. Such acts proceeded along with the realization that practical 'empowerment of the women' was needed and to that effect skills development particularly of the rural women was undertaken.

Chinese women's studies which developed at this stage undeniably was influenced by western feminism. Yet, the writings which emerged were at pains to emphasize the "national character" of the women's movement in China. In other words, efforts have ranged from denouncing the too political concept western concept of 'feminism' (*nuquan zhuyi*- or women's rightism) to the more agreeable *nuxing zhuyi* (female-ism). The shift in terminology is significant since it indicates the Chinese women's desire to express their own points of view (but without any fierce political movements) rather than wresting their rights form the men and attempting to follow men's standards.

2. Western feminism has always been regarded as liberal, bourgeois and radically anti-sexist, seen as divisive to working class struggles. This analogy brings us to the second strain visible in the new Chinese women's movement-that of conformism. The ACWF, interestingly rejects critiquing the CCP and its approach to the women question as symbolizing "public patriarchy" as has been done by those who perceive its top-down approach as distinctly anti-feminist. Chinese criticism is on women themselves. The AWCF developed a four-fold slogan (self-respect, self-confidence, self-reliance, and self-improvement) based on the assumption that women's own weaknesses prevents them from becoming full members of society. Differences in interpretation about the gains of the women's movement during the different periods of its existence continue today between the ACWF and the women research scholars in the various women's research centers in different Chinese universities. The response emanating from both however, amount to this on no account western standards of assessment are to be applied to evaluate the women's movements in China since, their response is contextual and located within the larger problem of socialist achievements for the whole society. One point however, remains unresolved, while economic reform and gender remain the primary concerns, the women are yet to realize the rapid infiltration of the negative inputs of a market-economy in society. Thus, escalating cases of aids-positive patients, homosexuality, the still unresolved problems of kidnapping and imposed marriages of women and a host of other issues need prioritization, before socialist controls and discipline are completely thwarted.

3. Our final diagnosis concerns the state of women in a liberal democracy, South Korea. South Korea represents the paradoxical effects of the modernization process, which almost all liberal democracies in their penchant for rapid advancement have undergone. While an apparent inclusion of women in the work force was undertaken to meet the changes in the production sphere yet, today, the prime engagements of the women vis a vis the state concern, equal weightage for skills and equal pay for equal work remain unequal. Despite apparent changes in society, the Confucian precepts of exclusion of the female from the public sphere remains a prominent underlying norm and the discrimination indicated above.

Concluding observations : A Reflection on the Trends in the Women's Activism

Women's activism in Asia is shaped and moulded in an environment, where the regimes reflect "command capacity"– the women's conformity with the regime type or their distancing from the same can on no account be a measure of the nature of activism of the women. Rather, their varied attempts to access means of livelihood in extremely stringent circumstances in the respective regimes reflects upon their intense engagements with the state.

There is obviously no sign yet of the women of Asia appearing to speak in one voice/or any generalist trend appearing from their activism. Women of each regime type have their own modes of engagements with the state. Whether it is "collective amnesia" or erasing from memory events in the past, in an effort to construct a safe future for their progeny (as in Burma); or accepting chardewari work as a better option than mere dependence on the male under the state-sponsored norm of "traditional protectionism" for the female.

There is no attempt to wholly thwart tradition. Rather, tradition is the bedrock from which consciousness about rights emerges, or even the foundation from where the renewed expressions for equality and gender just laws may be made, (as is visible in the PRC or in Islamic Iran).

A fourth trend, in one sense a continuation of the 3rd is also visible. There is almost a fierce resistance against universal definitions of what constitutes feminism-the desire very explicitly is to interpret feminism in their own terms, or to write history with their own pens rather than the pen of the western feminist, using her terminology.

Their common confrontation is obviously with patriarchy. However, despite the realization of the same, neither a radical restructuring or headlong confrontation with the visibly patriarchal state is attempted, rather the preferred mode is dialogue with the state.

Finally the question whither the women of Asia? They neither succeed nor do they fail, they proceed on the slow yet measured road to consciousness, followed by attempts at access.

References

Haleh, Afshar, ed. *Women and Politics in the Third World.* London and New York, 1996.

"Women in the Work and poverty trap in Iran" in Haleh Afshar and Bina Agarwal ed. *Women, Poverty and Ideology in Asia* London : Macmillan, 1989.

Akhter, Farida, *Depopulating Bangladesh, Essays on the Politics of Fertility,* Dhaka : Narigrantha Prabartana, 1996.

Carey, Peter ed. *Burma-The Challenge of a Change in a Divided Society* London : Macmillan, 1997.

Duza, Asfia, "Bangladesh Women in Transition" in K. Mahadevan ed. *Women and Population Dynamics, perspectives from Asian countries,* New Delhi : Sage, 1989.

Fink, Christina, *Living Silence : Burma under Military Rule.* London : Zed Books, 1988.

Giddens, A.. *The Consequences of Modernity.* Cambridge, Polity Press, 1990.

Hom, Sharon, "On the translation of special terms of Women's studies" in Centre for women's studies at Tianjin University ed. *Chinese Women and development : Status Health and Employment,* Zhengzhou : Henan People's Press, 1994.

Khaing, Mi Mi, *The World of Burmese Women,* London : Zed Books, 1984.

Kuumba, M. Bahati,. "You've stuck a rock." Comparing Gender, Social movements and transformations in the US and S. Africa. *Gender and Society,* Vol 16 : 4, August, 504-23, 2002.

Mathur, Deepa, *Women in Transition in South Asia* Delhi : Kalinga, 2001.

Meulen, van der Yana, (n. d.) *A Reversal of Fortune for Korean Women : Explaining 1983's Upward Turn* in Relative / Policy Research Working Papers, World Bank.

Rehman, Sobhan, *Planning and Public Action for Asian Women,* Dhaka : University Press. 1992.

Shaheed, Faridaq. "Purdah and Poverty in Pakistan" in Afshar and Agarwal, 1989.

Silverstein, Josef, *Burmese Politics : The Dilemmas of National Unity,* Rutgers Press, Rutgers 1980.

Tsai, Kellee S. "State Ideology and Women in rural China" in Rekha Datta and Judith Konenberg ed. *Women in Developing Countries. Assessing Strategies for Empowerment.* London : Lynne Rienner Publishers, 2002.

Yoon Hoo-jung, "The nature and directions of Korean women's Issues" in Chung Sei-wha ed. *Challenges for Women, Women's Studies in Korea,* Seoul : Korean Women's Institute, Ewha Women's University, 1986.

Zhang, Xiaodan "Creating a Space for Women : Women's Studies in China in the 1980s" in *Signs,* 20 : 1, 1994.

4

Women Participation in Panchayati Raj Institution in West Bengal

Madhulika Mitra and Somnath Mitra

Introduction

According to Census of India 2001, the total population of the country is 102.7 crores of which, 49.57 crores are women. Since independence, a number of measures have been taken up for upgrading the status of women but their political empowerment was not really thought of, restricting women to get opportunities of bringing improvement in their status. Though women, were involved in the freedom movement of India, their involvement in political activities was not appreciated in Indian society.

With the improvement in socio-economic conditions, Indian women were gradually getting exposed to the outside world and their political exposure was also increasing, but their participation in political activities remained an unrealized dream. A small number of women, who came into politics, were from urban areas. In rural areas, women could not think of it in spite of having good capability in some cases. A statutory support was necessary to break this barrier, which materialized in 1992 with the 73rd amendment of Indian

Constitution. The reservation of one-third seat in all the three tires of *Panchayat* have provided an opportunity to the Indian women to get a foothold in the political sphere. Women for the first time in India contested and got elected in a large number. West Bengal was the first state to hold the *Panchayat* election in 1993 just after the enactment of this amendment in the state. Ten years have passed after this revolutionary change has taken place in the country. It is expected that by this time, a preliminary leadership has grown among the women in political sphere and they have been able to motivate the Indian women to take active part in the local affairs. As the operational system of Panchayati Raj of West Bengal plays a role model for the rest of the country, it is expected that in this state, women's involvement in the Panchayati Raj Institution (PRI) is satisfactory.

In the above background, the present paper seeks to study whether any significant change has taken place in the gender aspect of the political scenario of the state. Reservation ensured women to occupy one-third seats in of the *Panchayat*. However, the question remains whether they are playing the role of titular heads or they are taking active part in the decision making process.

Status of Women in India and West Bengal

There are a host of demographic information, which could provide a handful of socio economic indicators in relation to the status of women. To keep our analysis simple only a few of them have been gleaned out in order to get some basic insight into our point of concern. The indicators taken are sex ratio, literacy rate, and percentage of school going children in the age group of 6-17 years and a few other indicators on women's health and decision making.

In terms of sex ratio there is marked improvement during the last decade of the twentieth (1991-2001) century both at the national level as well as in West Bengal (Annexure 2.1). In fact West Bengal has shown a marked improvement in sex ratio during this period, from 917 (1991) to 934 (2001). The position of the state, during this period, has also improved from below the national average (927) to above the national average (933). In fact the state has improved its position in terms of sex ratio, from 22nd (in 1991) to (in 2001) among the Indian states and Union Territories during the last decade of twentieth century.

The sex ratio figure of the Indian states and UTs reveal that the top ten states in 2001 are Kerala, Pondichery, Chhatisgarh, Tamil Nadu, Manipur, Andhra Pradesh, Meghalaya, Orissa, Himachal and Uttaranchal. It is also notable that Kerala and Pondichery are the only two states where female population is more than the male population.

In West Bengal Medinipur stands first in terms of sex ratio followed by Bankura, Purulia and Murshidabad, forming the top five whereas, Kolkata, Howrah, Bardhaman, North 24 Parganas and Uttar Dinajpur are among the bottom five districts in this respect (Annexure 2.2).

A look into the literacy scenario reveals that the state of West Bengal has shown an increase of about 14 per cent in female literacy during the last decade of the twentieth century (Annexure 2.3). The female literacy rate for the state stood at 46.6 per cent in 1991 and reached to 60.22 per cent in 2001. The literacy rate for the rural female remained lower (53.82 per cent) than the overall figure of 2001. However, the state remained ahead of the national average on both the counts as during 2001 overall female literacy and rural female literacy rate of India was 45.74 per cent and 36.83 per cent respectively.

Apart from the literacy figures the available information on the population in the age group of 6-17 years attending school by age and sex provides an interesting insight (Annexure 2.4). Of all the females in the age group of 6-17 years 68 per cent attend school in West Bengal compared to 66.2 per cent in India. The corresponding figures for the males in the same age groups remain higher 73.7 per cent in West Bengal and 77.6 per cent in India. A close look also reveals that with the increasing age school attendance for females falls significantly. In the age group of 6-10 years only 68.7 per cent and 36.9 per cent females attends school respectively, compared to 75.4 per cent and 51.4 per cent of males in the corresponding age group.

The information on state of women's health especially at the reproductive age provides valuable insight into the status of women in any society. Two aspects of women's health–prevalence of anemia and antenatal care is taken in the present analysis. The available information (Annexure 2.5) reveals that in India 51.8 per cent of ever-married women suffer from iron-deficiency anemia, which is even higher in West Bengal 62.7 per cent. In terms of antenatal care West Bengal shows much better result. In India where 48.6 per cent of women at reproductive age group receive antenatal care form a qualified doctor outside home, in West Bengal such care is available to about 75.8 per cent of women in the same category. The detailed figures for various categories are shown in Annexure (2.6).

Finally some of the observations on ever married women involved in household decision-making Annexure (2.7) clearly reveal that in West Bengal, as in India, the decision making power of women mainly revolve around her kitchen. About half or more have no power to decide on their own health care, purchase of jewelry or household items and staying with their parents or siblings. Moreover, about half of the ever married women in West Bengal have no access to money, which is even lower than the national average of 59.6 per cent.

Political Participation of Women in India : Need for Reservation

Though Indian women joined the freedom movement and a large number participated actively, but the political activity, by and large has remained a field for males. In 1950, when the question of reservation of seat for women was raised by the members of the Constituent Assembly, it was totally rejected (Mohanty, 2003). As a result, after the independence, again the women of the country were relegated to the four walls of domesticity. Even after the passage of more then 50 years, women could not find adequate space in national politics. After the first Lok Sabha election in 1952 women members constituted only 2.8 per cent of the total strength of the Lower House. The representation of women in the parliament continued to remain significantly low till date. The following table reveals the proportion of women in Lok Sabha since 1952.

Table-3.1 : Proportion of Women in Lok Sabha since 1952

Year	*Total Strength*	*Women*	*% of Women*
1952	489	14	2.8
1957	494	18	3.6
1962	494	30	6. 0
1967	520	31	6. 0
1971	520	20	3.8
1977	542	19	3.5
1980*	529	28	5.3
1984	542	42	7.7
1989**	523	23	4.4
1991	536	39	7.2
1996	543	40	7.3
1998	543	43	7.9
1999	543	49	9. 0

* Election not held in 12 constituencies of Assam and one in Meghalaya.

** Election not held in J & K and Punjab.

Source : Santha E. K. Political Participation of Women in Panchayati Raj, 1999.

In 1957, when the Panchayati Raj Institution was first recognized, Balwantrai Mehta Committee Report recommended the co-opting of two women in all the three tiers of the Panchayat, "who are interested in work among women and children". The recommendation influenced Maharashtra Zilla Parisad and Panchayat Samiti Act of 1961, which provided for "nomination of one or two women" to the Panchayat bodies "in case women were not elected". Moreover, the West Bengal Panchayat Act, 1973 also provided for co-opting 2 women. In 1974, the Committee on the Status of Women in India (CSWI) recommended the representation of women in Panchayat and also the establishment of an all-women Panchayat at village level. The Committee said "We therefore recommended the establishment for statutory women Panchayats at the village level to ensure greater participation by woman Panchayats at the village level to ensure greater participation by women in the political process. We recommend it as a transitional measure to break the traditional attitudes in rural society which inhibit most women from articulating their problems or participating actively in the existing local bodies. In 1977, Asoka Mehta Committee recommended for the automatic co-option of two women in Zilla Parishad who would get the maximum vote in Zilla Parishad elections. The Committee also recommended the co-option of two women in case where no women had contested. It would be noted that prior to 73rd Constitution Amendment, women mostly were brought into politics only through co-option, which was very much undemocratic. As a result, women representation in PRI remained very low. In 1978, in Maharashtra Panchayat, only six women were elected. In 1988, elections were held for 74, 000 village sabhas in former U. P. where less than one per cent of women came through. Provisions were made for the co-option of only one woman. In 1983 for the first time in the country, Karnataka Panchayat Act made provision for the reservation of 25 per cent of seats for women in all the three tiers of Panchayat but due to some reasons election was held in 1987. The National Perspective Plan for women 1988-2000 strongly recommended 30 per cent reservation of seat for women in local government. Their argument was that even after passing 40 years of democracy, the representation of women in Parliament could not reach eight per cent.

This gap has been tried to be filled up in the 73rd Amendment, which in 1992, introduced mandatory reservation of one-third of seats for women at all the levels of PRI. Today, every five years, about one million women are elected in PRI. About 200-district Panchayat, more than 2000 Block Panchayats and about 85,000 Gram Panchayats of the country are headed by women.

Status of Women Panchayat Members in India and West Bengal

Several studies have been conducted on women Panchayat members from which three important studies have been used for the present paper to observe the socio-economic background of the women Panchayat members of different states of the country, (a) Nirmala Buch Study on Madhya Pradesh, Rajasthan and Uttar Pradesh (former), (b) Sushila Kaushil's Study on Tamil Nadu, Haryana, Madhya Pradesh, Orissa, Rajasthan and Uttar Pradesh and (c) E. K. Santha's Study on Tamil Nadu Kerala and Haryana.

All the studies have observed that majority of the women Panchayat members are illiterate or barely literate. The exceptions are Kerala, Tamilnadu, Orissa and the Garhwal region of UP, what is now called Uttaranchal. In Kerala the general as well as female literacy rate is high, which is also reflected at the Panchayat level none of the women Panchayat leaders interviewed, were illiterate (Santha, 1999). Regarding the age, both Buch and Kaushik studies report that approximately 70 per cent of the women Panchayat members are below the age of 45. Santha has observed that in Haryana most of the elected women are above 40 years of age, whereas, in Kerala and Tamil Nadu, the picture is totally opposite i.e. most of them are less than 40. Both Buch and Kaushik studies have found more or less similar patterns in occupational structure. According to Kaushik, 50 per cent of them elected are even if the number is marginal.

Table-4.1 : Age-wise Distribution of Female GP Members (1993–98)

District	*Age (years)*			
	< 30	30–45	46–60	60+
Uttar Dinajpur	58.6	37.1	3.7	0.6
Dakshin Dinajpur	56.9	40.2	2.9	0
Bardhaman	55.4	39.2	5.1	0.3
Birbhum	57.7	36.5	5.1	0.7
Nadia	52.8	42.7	4.3	0.2
Jalpaiguri	49.2	46. 0	4.6	0.2
Hugli	44.9	48.2	6. 0	0.9
S. 24 Parganas	53.7	41. 0	5. 0	0.3

In West Bengal, State Institute of Panchayat and Rural Development (SIPRD) conducted a study on the socio-economic profile of Panchayat members 1993-1998 of eight districts (Table 4.1). It is revealed that in all the districts studied, about 45 per cent-60 per cent of the women Panchayat leaders were below 30 years of age and about 36 per cent-48 per cent of them were in the age group of 30–45. A marginal proportion of them was in the age group of 46-60 and above that there were very negligible share of female leaders.

Table-4.2 : Educational Status of Female GP Members

	Education							
District	1	2	3	4	5	6	7	8
Uttar Dinajpur	8.82	16.36	11.95	40.52	21.05	0.71	0.28	0.28
Dakshin Dinajpur	2.69	6.95	14.80	37.89	33.86	3.36	0.45	0.00
Bardhaman	1.83	17.40	10.08	31.71	33.49	4.07	1.10	0.31
Birbhum	4.87	16.70	15.08	31.77	27.86	2.67	0.95	0.10
Nadia	1.06	4.63	6.76	35.99	41.84	6.91	2.51	0.30
Jalpaiguri	1.39	5.09	8.51	36.68	43.51	3.91	0.84	0.35
Hugli	0.75	8.56	9.51	28.20	42.57	7.94	2.33	0.14
S 24 Parganas	1.44	5.82	10.05	34.87	40.21	39.78	1.59	0.67

1. Illiterate; 2. Neo-literate; 3. Literate; 4. Primary, 5. Secondary; 6. Graduate; 7. Post Graduate; 8. Technical
Source : Socio Economic Profile of Panchayat Members : 1993; SIPRD

Table 4.2 shows the educational status of the women Panchayat leaders during the term 1993-1998. No doubt, most of the female Panchayat leaders were literate but majority of them did not cross the school level education. In Uttar Dinajpur, Dakshin Dinajpur and Birbhum, maximum number of women Panchayat leaders had education up to the primary level whereas in case of other districts, majority of them had secondary level education. It is interesting to note that in South 24 Parganas, a substantial number of the women Panchayat leaders were Graduate. In all the districts, some of them, though in marginal proportion, were postgraduate and from the technical field. The districts showed varied proportion of illiterate women Panchayat members being highest in Uttar Dinajpur and lowest in Birbhum.

Participation of Women in Panchayat Activities

The 73rd Amendment has created an opportunity for a large number of rural women to take part in political institutions. A number of instances are there across the country where women Panchayat members are taking active part in the village Panchayat members attend the meeting regularly. Their knowledge about the functioning process of Panchayat has increased. Now they not only take up the issues relating to basic needs like drinking water, health and education but also general developmental activities for example, augmentation of income of the Panchayats, irrigation facilities etc. There are instances of women Panchayat members supervising eye camps, leasing out ponds and managing orchards. At the same time, there are a large number of proxy women who depend on their men folk for conducting the Panchayat activities. Whatever the same is, participation reason should not be confined to the Panchayat members only. The empowerment should penetrate into the other women also to take active part in the village affairs. The most important platform of participation is the *Gram Sabha,* through which the rural women can attach themselves with Panchayati Raj system but the question arises how much participation do women have in Gram Sabha? Before coming to this point, the concept of Gram Sabha and its powers should be made clear.

Gram Sabha is the basic institution of decentralized government and has always been an important part of Gram Panchayat. It is the only forum which can ensure direct democracy offering equal opportunity to all the adult inhabitants of a village to discuss, criticize and approve or reject proposals of the Panchayat executives and assess its past performance. It is a watchdog of democracy at the grass roots level. There is one or more Gram Sabhas under a Gram Panchayat consisting of one or few villages. The voters of these villages become the members of Gram Sabha. The Gram Sabha is supposed to conduct discussions on the annual statement of accounts, administrative reports, selection of beneficiaries for anti-poverty programmes and drawing up annual plans. Another function of Gram Sabha is to suggest remedial measures for economic and efficient functioning of the Panchayats, which can be fulfilled by Social Audit, which has the right to check the accounts of the Gram Panchayat (Mohanty, 2002).

In West Bengal, as the Gram Panchayats are very large, the 1994 amendment of the State Act introduced a two tier structure of grass roots democracy–1) *Gram Sansad*, which is the constituency based body and 2) *Gram Sabha*, which consists of all the voters of the Panchayat area. The Gram Sansad meetings take place twice a year, in May and in November. On the other hand, Gram Sabha meets at least once a year, generally December after all the Sansads have been held.

Our concern is women's participation in the Gram Sabha. The Seventy-third Constitution Amendment Act made it necessary for the women to be present both in Panchayat and in Gram Sabha. It is also interesting to note that the government of West Bengal, Madhya Pradesh and Kerala, has made provision for hiving a sub quorum for women (Mohanty, 2002). Still after passing ten years from the 73rd amendment even in West Bengal, which plays a role model for the rest of the country, women's participation in Gram Sansad meeting remains very low. In a study of 20 villages of the state, Ghatak and Ghatak (2002) analysed that while women constituted 46 per cent of the total voters, their share in the total attendance in the Gram Sabha meeting of May, 1999 remained only 9 per cent. Again, in seven out of 20 villages, none of the women voters attended the meeting. Table 5.1 shows the attendance in Gram Sansad meetings held in May, 2002 in different districts of the state. It reveals that in spite of government emphasis on people's participation, attendance of voters in Gram Sansad meetings was very poor. In no district, even 20 per cent of the voters were present and women's attendance presented a very sad picture. In five districts such as Kuchbihar, Darjeeling Hill Council, Siliguri Sub-division Council, East Medinipur and Barddhaman, only three per cent of women voters were present in the meeting. In some districts, the attendance was two per cent, while in rest of the districts; only one per cent women voters attended the meeting. Murshidabad presented the saddest scene where not a single women voter came to attend the meeting. The situation improved only when some women groups or organizations working at the grassroots level took initiative to convince the women about the necessity of their participation in village affairs (Swanirvar, 2001).

Table-5.1 : Attendance in the Meeting of Gram Sansads of West Bengal, May 2003

District	*% of total voter attended meeting*	*% of women voter attended meeting*
Kuchbihar	17	3
Jalpaiguri	18	2
Darjeeling Hill Council	12	3
Siliguri Mahakuma Council	11	3
North Dinajpur	9	1
South Dinajpur	7	1
Malda	9	1
Murshidabad	18	-
Nadia	10	2
North 24 Parganas	10	2
South 24 Parganas	8	2
Howrah	6	1
Hugli	11	2
East Medinipur	12	3
West Medinipur	11	2
Bankura	9	1
Purulia	11	1
Bradhaman	12	3
Birbhum	8	1
Total	12	2

Source : Directorate of Panchayat and Rural Development, Government of West Bengal.

Kultikri : West Bengal's First All Women Panchayat

Kultikri Gram Panchayat is one of 10 Gram Panchayats under the Panchayat Samity of Sankrail Block under Jhargram subdivision, located in the southeastern corner of the West Medinipur district. The Panchayat office revealed form their knowledge that the 2001 population of the Gram Panchayat is about 9700. The composition of population reveals that the proportion of SC and ST population is about 12.1 per cent and 34.5 per cent respectively i. e. about half the population of the Gram Panchayat belongs to SC/ST category. 70 per cent of the total main workers depend on agricultural and allied activities of which 30 per cent are agricultural labourers. There are eight Gram Sansads in the Gram Panchayat area.

The most striking feature of this Gram Panchayat is that it is the first all women elected Gram Panchayat of West Bengal. In fact, during the 1993-98 term it was the only Gram Panchayat run by an all women body, which added a new dimension to the democratic decentralization of power at the grass root level in West Bengal. Moreover, the Gram Panchayat continued to be run by an all women body even after the 1988 Panchayat election. It is a remarkable feat towards the realization of the goal of 73rd Constitutional Amendment. There were 13 members during the 1993-98 term and after the reorganization of the Gram Sansads during 1998 poll, 8 women were re-elected.

During the early 1990s the National Literacy Mission (NLM) was launched with an objective to achieve full literacy among the people of India. After the launch of NLM, a large number of local volunteers were involved to realize the goals and objectives of the programme and motivate people to join the literacy campaign. It was observed that during the early days, the women volunteers of the Kultikri were more active and sincere than their male counterparts. It was, primarily, due to their sincere effort, a large number of illiterate masses particularly women joined the literacy centers all over the Gram Panchayat area. Another factor which drawn a large number of women of the Kultikri area into prominence was their active part in the drive against alcoholism. Tapati Sing, the Gram Pradhan, a tribal women herself admitted that uncontrolled alcoholism among the village men has been checked to a large extent due to their sustained campaign since the early nineties.

All these factors brought a large section of the women of the village, especially, from the tribal and other poorer sections, into the forefront of the village society and greatly influenced local CPI (M) leaders to choose 13 women for their candidates in the 1993 Panchayat poll. After the end of the first term and reasonable performance of the Gram Panchayat Kultikri continued to be an all woman Panchayat.

Present Pradhan also cited another example of good work of the woman workers of the Kultikri–during the recent survey on the identification of BPL families, women volunteers met the deadline and whatever the pending work remains of BPL family identification, belongs to the male surveyors.

Development Activity of Kultikri Gram Panchayat deserves separate discussion at this juncture. Under the women leadership, Kultikri Gram Panchayat made much progress in development activities in the following sector:

> The Gram Panchayat aims to bring all the villages within its area under full coverage of sanitation. One out of eight Gram Sansads has already been covered fully and work is in progress in the other seven Sansad areas. In 2003 the Gram Panchayat would achieve cent per cent coverage in sanitation.

- As major part of the Panchayat area falls into the literate tract of West Medinipur district, installation of tube wells or dug wells is not easy and often a costly affair. The Gram Panchayat has initiated a piped water supply scheme, which is partially complete.

- From 1993, the Gram Panchayat took much initiative to improve the educational status of the villages. The Panchayat authorities distributed a large number of books free of cost among the students of primary, high and higher secondary schools. There are 9 primary schools in the Gram Panchayat area. One of those was set up during the previous term of the Panchayat. Apart form these formal educational facilities there are 12 'Sishu Siksha Kendras' run by the Panchayat and 8 ICDS centers. Under the 'Sarbo Siksha Abhiyan' Panchayat has already identified the residual illiterates of the area. At present Panchayat is running 8 centers and 62 sub centers for those residual illiterates.

- The Panchayat has prepared 145 schemes under various category of SGRY scheme of which 54 are completed by the end of November.

- 84 SHGs have been formed so far in the village though of them only 14 have received financial support after gradation. The main activities of the SHGs revolve around making baskets and ropes, plate making from Sal leaves (used mainly in community feasts), goat rearing, mushroom cultivation etc.

Table-6.1 : Attendance in Gram Sansad Meeting

Gram Sansads	*Total Voters*	*Attendance in November 2001*			*Attendance in May 2002*		
		Persons	*Male*	*Female*	*Persons*	*Male*	*Female*
Kultikri-I	635	103	73	30	71	50	21
Kultikri-II	935	112	81	31	115	85	30
Mukundapur	484	82	54	28	72	45	27
Amjhatia	1025	151	108	43	92	70	22
Phulbani	980	104	85	19	90	65	25
Charar	493	68	66	2	112	95	17
Baligeria-East	577	63	46	17	92	55	37
Baligeria-East	686	63	46	17	92	55	37
Total	**5185**	**775 (14.9%)**	**—**	**212**	**834 (16.8%)**	**—**	**248**

Source : Kultikri Panchayat Office

People's Participation in Kultikri is also significant. Participation in the Panchayat activities is satisfactory in Kultikri. It can be aptly supported by the sanitation and literacy activities in the Panchayats discussed earlier. Sri Motindranath Debnath, BDO of Sankrail block also stated that Kultikri is the most active Gram Panchayat among the 10 Panchayats of the area. There is a tendency to gauge participation level from the attendance in the Gram Sansad meeting. The attendance record of the two meetings for all the Gram Sansads is shown in the following table :

The average participation in the said meeting during November 2001 and May 2002 was 14.9 per cent and 16.8 per cent respectively, which is higher than the average participation in the State (12 per cent) as well as in the district (11 per cent). However, being a drought prone mono-crop area, there is a lack of employment opportunity in the region, and many from the village have to go out of the village in search of livelihood. As financial position of the rural household rotates with the crop cycle, summer is the season of financial hardship resulting in substantial out migration of the rural labour. Thus the attendance in the May meeting of the Gram Sansad remains lower. The Pradhan, Tapati Sing has cited all these as principal reason for lower attendance in the Gram Sansad meetings. A remarkable aspect of the Kultikri Gram Panchayat is that women constituted about 28 per cent and 30 per cent of the total turnout of the Gram Sansad meetings in November 2001 and May 2002 respectively.

However, the more striking fact in terms of women's participation emerges if the women's turnout in the Gram Sansad meetings is compared with the State and district average. During the May 2002 Gram Sansad meetings all over the districts of West Bengal, only 2 per cent of the women voters were present. In the West Medinipur district average turnout was also 2 per cent. However, in Kultikri Gram Sansad meetings during the same period about 10 per cent of the women voters were present. This is a clear indication that the all women leadership of the Panchayat has been able to induce gradual change in the attitude of village women in terms of participation. Rebati Das, Pradhan in the previous term and presently a member of Panchayat samiti of Sankrail block has cited that in terms of literacy campaign and SHG formation response from the village woman has been quite encouraging.

Conclusion

The reservation of one-third seat in the 73rd Constitution Amendment Act, 1992 in all the three tiers of Panchayat have provided an opportunity to the Indian women to get a foothold into the political sphere. Women for the first time in India contested and got elected in a large number. It is expected that by this time, a preliminary leadership has grown among the women in the political sphere in the country and specially, in West Bengal which plays a role model for the rest of the country. In the present paper, an effort has been made to understand whether the actual decentralization has taken place to include the women in the Panchayati Raj Institution. It is observed in the paper that though in some cases, women Panchayat leaders are taking active part in the decision making process but they could not motivate rural women in large numbers to participate in the village affairs. The attendance of female voters in the Gram Sansad meetings in all the districts is very low. At the same time, it is observed that when women are getting the opportunity their interest in village development is also increasing and their attendance in Gram Sansad meetings is also increasing (as has been observed in Kultikri). Finally, we may say that the disadvantageous position of women in the country is only a matter of some time.

A statutory support was necessary to overcome the problem that has been provided by the 73rd Constitutional Amendment but ten years time is not enough to realize the full potential of it. Now the women members of the Panchayat are performing the role of change agents and they have to go a long way to bring about a remarkable change.*

Annexure 2.1 : Sex Ratio of the Status and Union Territories

State/UT	*1991*	*2001*	*State/UT*	*1991*	*2001*
1. India (927)**	927	933	19. Assam	923	932
2. Jammu and Kashmir	896	900	20. West Bengal**	917	934
3. Himachal Pradesh	976	970	21. Jharkhand	922	941
4. Punjab	882	874	22. Orissa	971	972
5. Chandigarh	790	773	23. Chhatisgarh	985	990
6. Uttaranchal	936	964	24. Madhya Pradesh	912	920
7. Haryana	865	861	25. Gujarat	934	921
8. Delhi	827	821	26. Daman and Diu	969	709

(Annexure 2.1 Contd.)

State/UT	1991	2001	State/UT	1991	2001
9. Rajasthan	910	922	27. Dadra and Nagar Haveli	952	811
10. Uttar Pradesh	876	898	28. Maharashtra	934	922
11. Bihar	907	921	29. Andhra Pradesh	972	978
12. Sikkim	878	875	30. Karnataka	960	964
13. Arunachal Pradesh	859	901	31. Goa	967	960
14. Nagaland	886	909	32. Lakshadweep	943	947
15. Manipur	958	978	33. Kerala	1036	1058
16. Mizoram	921	938	34. Tamil Nadu	974	986
17. Tripura	942	948	35. Pondichery	979	1001
18. Meghalaya	955	975	36. Andaman and Nicobar	818	846

Source : Census of India 2001, Provisional Population Totals.

Annexure 2.2 : Sex Ratio in West Bengal

Districts	1981	1991	2001	District	1981	1991	2001
1. Bankura	964	951	953	11. Medinipur	951	944	955
2. Bradhaman	897	899	921	12. Murshidabad	959	943	952
3. Birbhum	962	946	949	13. Nadia	946	936	947
4. Darjeeling	888	914	943	14. N. 24-Parganas	891	907	927
5. Haora	873	881	906	15. Purulia	957	947	953
6. Hugli	909	917	947	16. S. 24-Parganas	927	929	938
7. Jalpaiguri	910	927	941	17. Dinajpur (D)	946	944	950
8. KochBehar	935	935	949	18. Dinajpur (U)	931	921	937
9. Kolkata	741	799	828	West Bengal	911	917	934
10. Malda	949	938	948				

Source : Census of India, 2001.

Annexure 2.3 : Female Literacy in West Bengal

Districts	1991	2001	Rural 2001	District	1991	2001	Rural 2001
1. Bankura	36.6	49.80	47.92	11. Medinipur	56.6	64.63	63.63

(Annexure 2.3 Contd.)

Districts	1991	2001	Rural 2001	District	1991	2001	Rural 2001
2. Bradhaman	51.5	61.93	57. 08	12. Murshidabad	29.6	48.33	46.37
3. Birbhum	37.2	52.21	50.35	13. Nadia	44.4	60. 06	55.50
4. Darjeeling	47.8	63.92	56.14	14. N 24-Parganas	58. 0	72.13	61.71
5. Haora	57.8	70.93	65.13	15. Purulia	23.2	37.15	33.91
6. Hugli	56.9	67.72	62.58	16. S. 24-Parganas	40.6	59.73	56.89
7. Jalpaiguri	33.2	52.91	47.97	17. Dinajpur (D)	27.9	55.12	31.43
8. KochBehar	33.3	57. 04	54.49	18. Dinajpur (U)	-	37.16	51.16
9. Kolkata	72.1	77.92	-	West Bengal	46.6	60.22	53.82
10. Malda	24.9	41.67	38.85	India	-	45.74	36.83

Source : Census of India, 2001, West Bengal, R-U Distribution.

Annexure 2.4 : Percentage of the Household Population Age 6-17 Years Attending School by Age and Sex (West Bengal)

Age	Male	Female	Total
6-10	83.7 (85.2)	82.1 (78.3)	82.9 (81.9)
11-14	75.4 (80.2)	68.7 (67. 0)	72.2 (73.9)
15-17	51.4 (57.7)	36.9 (40.3)	44.5 (49.3)
6-14	80.2 (83.1)	76.7 (73.7)	78.5 (78.6)
6-17	73.7 (77.6)	68. 0 (66.2)	70.9 (72.1)

Figures in parenthesis show the corresponding national figures.
Source : NFHS-2, West Bengal, 1998-99; p-23.

Annexure 2.5 : Per cent of Ever-married Women Classified as having Iron-deficiency Anemia

State	% of women with any anemia
India	51.8
West Bengal	62.7
Lowest (Kerala)	22.7
Highest (Assam)	69.7

Source : NFHS-2, West Bengal, 1998-99; P-252.

Annexure 2.6 : Antenatal Check up in West Bengal

	Antenatal Checkup only at home from health worker	Antenatal Checkup only at home: Doctor	Other health Professional	Traditional birth attendant other	No Antenatal Checkup	Missing
Urban	0 (2. 0)	87. 0 (74.8)	9. 0 (8.8)	0 (0.2)	3.6 (13.6)	0.4
Rural	3.2 (6.6)	73.4 (41.2)	11.5 (11.5)	0.6 (0.3)	10.8 (39.8)	0.5
SC	0.9 (5.9)	74.2 (41.7)	17.9 (13.3)	0.9 (0.2)	5.7 (38.2)	0.4
ST	1.5 (10. 0)	65.3 (34.7)	18.7 (11.5)	0 (0.3)	11.6 (43.1)	2.9
OBC	2.7 (5.9)	85.5 (48.9)	9. 0 (9.6)	0 (0.2)	2.8 (34.8)	0
Others	3.2 (4. 0)	77.2 (56.5)	7.7 (10.6)	0.5 (0.2)	11.1 (27.9)	0.3
Total	2.6 (5.6)	75.8 (48.6)	11.1 (10.9)	0.5 (0.2)	9.5 (34. 0)	0.5

Figures in parenthesis show the corresponding national figurers.
Source : NFHS-2, West Bengal, 1998-99; p-46.

Annexure 2.7 : Percentage of ever Married Women Involved in Household Decision-making

State	Per cent not involved in any decision making	Per cent involved in decision making on: What to cook	Own health care	Purchase of jewellery etc.	Staying with her parents	Per cent who permission to: Go to the market	Visit friends/ relatives	Per cent with access to money
India	9.4	85.1	51.6	52.6	48.1	31.6	24.4	59.6
W. B.	8. 0	87.4	45.1	48.4	46.7	17.8	14.1	51.4
High-est	Naga-land	Naga-land	H. P.	H. P.	H. P.	T. N.	Mizoram	Goa
	(0.4)	(97.4)	(80.8)	(93.4)	(91.4)	(78.5)	(59.5)	(82.4)

Source : NFHS-2, West Bengal, 1998-99; p-70.

References

* The study on Kultikri Gram Panchayat by the authors is supported by Institute of Social Sciences.

Census of India-Provisional Population Totals *Distribution of Rural-Urban Population* Series 20 West Bengal.

Ghatak Maitersh and Ghatak Maitreya-Recent Reforms in the Panchayat System in West Bengal : Toward Greater Participatory Governance, *Economic and Political Weekly,* January 5-12, 2002.

International Institute for Population Sciences-*National Family Health Survey (NFHS-2) 1998-99 India* Mumbai

International Institute for Population Sciences-*National Family Health Survey (NFHS-2) 1998-99 West Bengal* Mumbai.

Jain Devaki–Panchayat Raj *: Women Changing Governance,* Gender in Development September 1996 www. undp. org/gender/resosurces).

Jayal Nirja Gopal–*Development or Empowerment? Women's Participation in Panchayati Raj Institutions* Presented in the International Seminar on Local Governance in India and China, Kolkata, January, 2003.

Mathew George-*Status of Panchayati Raj in the Status and Union Territories of India,* Institute of Social Sciences, New Delhi, 2002.

Mathew George–*Local Governance System in India and China : Learning from Each Other,* Paper Presented in the International Seminar on Local Governance in India and China, Kolkata, January, 2003.

Mohanty Bidyut (Ed)–*Women and Political Empowerment* 1998, Institute of Social Sciences, New Delhi.

Mohanty Bidyut (Ed)–*Women and Political Empowerment* 2000, Institute of Social Sciences, New Delhi.

Mohanty Bidyut–*Women and Local Government in India and China : A Mission Link for Empowerment,* Paper Presented in the International Seminar on Local Governance in India and China, Kolkata, January, 2003.

Santha E. K.–*Political Participation of Women in Panchayati Raj Haryana, Kerala and Tamil Nadu,* Institute of Social Sciences New Delhi, 1999.

Swanirvar-*Annual Report,* 2000–2001.

5

Globalisation and its Impact on Women Workers : The Asian Experience

Suman Ray and Basabi Chakraborty

Introduction

It is well known that liberalization, privatization and economic reforms–these three are considered as the pillars of globalisation. During the last decade of 20th century globalisation has brought enormous changes in the working patterns and conditions of both men and women of the Asian countries. As a result working men and women have faced severe problems and constraints in the employment sector. But in patriarchal social set-up, men and women experience poverty in different ways. As a result after the implementation of the economic reforms the working women have become poor to poorer and a large number of women have lost their jobs due to privatization. The advent of globalisation brings with it a marked change in our outlook as far as management of national economy is concerned. Under economic globalisation, country after country has opened up their economies to free flow of finance capital technology and goods. The '*death of distance*', as globalisation is often referred to, heralds a change in the role of service sector with less developed economies to such an extent that geography and levels of industrialization are no longer the ordinary determinants of the location of productive services. Thus, the 'death of distance', the services revolution and the mobility of capital-the three pillars of globalization-present tremendous opportunities for less developed countries.

However, the transition from a close lethargic economy to a vibrant, globally integrated economy cannot be painless. It has led to the reduction in the role of the state and a shift from welfare to a market friendly system of governance. Thus, globalisation brings with it a set of advantages as well as disadvantages. Accordingly the outcome is either starkly visible affluence or starkly visible poverty. With globalizations, the affluent sections of the cities find the opportunity to grow and expand. The poor on the other hand, are unable to take advantage of the globalisation process as even in the closed economy, they have been excluded. It is because of these dynamics, that the disparity between the affluent and the poor rise, manifesting a wide disparity in the quality of life of the two. This disparity has also been widened for men and women, especially when they are working in different producing sectors. When the globalisation process began in some countries of South-east Asia it showed a dream of miraculous change in socio-economic conditions of working men and women. But after few years 'myth' and 'reality' differed. In 1991 India had also taken globalisation process to change her the then existing economic structure. On the backdrop of this situation the present paper intends to highlight the socio-economic plight of the working women of South-Asian countries with special reference to Nepal, Bangladesh, Pakistan, Bhutan, Sri Lanka and India. In order to explore the conditions of other Asian countries the paper also seeks to present the scenario of Maldives, Malaysia and Thailand. Moreover, an attempt has been made in this paper to address the health status of working women, because due to extreme poverty, a large number of women are left with no other option than to engage themselves in such jobs, by which they are very much exposed to occupational health hazards. Discrimination among the male and women workers is found in the payment of wages and in case of other facilities and this discrimination is rising over the years throughout the world. Such discrimination is also present in U.S.A., which is also evident from the issues selected for Women's Equality Summit held in 2002 in Washington.

Working women all over Asia share the same experience. Even in the industrially developed countries the condition of working women living below poverty line is not better. In this paper we have tried to highlight the follwing issues :

1. Women participation in different sectors of production in the post globalisation period;
2. Burden of work on the women worker;
3. Economic deprivation;
4. Health hazard among women workers;
5. Other exploitation of women at work.

These issues are discussed in detail in the following paper.

Women Participation in Work

We have tried to focus on women employment as compared to the percentage of male in the globalisation period. The following table shows the status of women workers' participation in the selected Asian countries.

Table-1 : Women Participation in Different Sectors of Production (as Percentage of Male rate)

Country	*Agriculture*	*Industry*	*Service*
India	124	48	67
Pakistan	164	46	50
Bangladesh	144	82	40
Nepal	n. a.	n. a.	n. a.
Sri Lanka	129	96	74
Bhutan	n. a.	n. a.	n. a.
Maldives	55	67	172
Malaysia	68	85	126
Thailand	95	85	119

Source : Human Development Report (2004).

From this table we can see that in the Indian sub-continent women participation in agriculture is more than that of male workers, but the countries where reform measures have been taken earlier like Thailand, Maldives etc. women participation is more in the service sector. The major reason behind this is that the Indian sub-continent countries the major economic activity is agriculture which is mostly based on family farming. On the other hand the East-Asian countries are more developed in service oriented economic activity. In industrial sector also we can find the same trend. This clearly demonstrates the informalisation of women worker because in most of the cases agriculture sector is generally informal. Women's involvement in agriculture is extensive both in terms of labour and farm management decisions. The already heavy workload of women in the agriculture sector is increasing as women become responsible to a greater degree for agricultural production in addition to household activity. In South Asia women spend a lot of time looking after livestock. But unfortunately due to existing patriarchal social structure women are excluded from decision-making. They are not even recognized as labour. Even women workers in industrial activity are engaged as informal workers.

Table-2 : Women in informal sector (%)

Country	*1982-83*	*1994-95*
India	93	97
Bangladesh	44	75
Nepal	56	77
Thailand	46	71

Source : Human Development Report (1984, 1996)
(Note : Percentages of women workers in this sector are the percentages among working women.)

In most of the countries in Asia women are involved in informal activities. Throughout South-Asia, the informal sector has grown more in relation to formal sector both in absolute and relative terms. In all South Asian countries women's participation in informal sector is gradually increasing over time. The requisite data on women's participation in informal sector are not available for all countries mentioned in our paper. The scenario regarding informal sector for four countries are mentioned in Table : 2.

Table 2 depicts that in the course of globalisation women's participation in informal sector is gradually increasing and this change is comparatively less in India but for other countries this rises by almost 50-60 per cent. This phenomenon is also true for Thailand which has started the globalisation process earlier. Actually what happens is that due to globalisation new firms enter the market but they employ persons on hire-and-fire basis. In these new firms women have an opportunity to join in the workforce. The entrepreneurs also encourage women workers to enter because they can pay lower wages to the workers involved in production.

We found that liberalization, which is part of globalisation, has caused an increasing inequality in employment opportunities and incomes. Economic opportunities created by the liberalisation are highly unequal. Those better endowed, with more access to skills, to markets, and with more resources or better links internationally have been able to benefit. For women at the upper income, upper skill end, the quality as well as opportunities for employment have improved. For most women workers however, the quality of employment is poor, without opportunities either for skill development or moving up the ladder, or with very low income returns. If we examine the impact of globalisation on employment and income of women workers, four distinct trends are visible : (i) is loss of existing employment without creation of new employment; (ii) changes due to new technologies and skills; (iii) informalisation of work and (iv) creation of new employment opportunities.

Women are most affected by changes due to mechanisation. The employment of manual workers is reduced and is displaced by workers who run the machines. In these cases the total number of jobs is reduced drastically. Moreover, women are generally replaced by men, although the income earned may actually increase. There are many examples of this.

In the agricultural sector men have taken over from women those activities in which technology has substituted machinery for manual labour. All other labour intensive tasks are still left to women. Therefore, the introduction of tractors, harvesters, insecticides, weedicides, hormone accelerators, high yielding variety seeds and mechanical cotton pickers has meant that tasks traditionally performed by women and on which many women depend for their livelihood have been appropriated.

Various micro studies have shown that technical change has eliminated many jobs traditionally performed by women and alternative job opportunities have not been created for women at the same rate as for men. Weeding in paddy producing areas is a female dominated task. When chemical spraying replaces weeding, the spraying is performed by men. Similarly, the introduction of rice mills has displayed hand pounding done by rural women. Rice mills utilise husking equipment with the consequence that women who use traditional husking mechanisms have lost their means of livelihood.

In some sub-sectors in the textile and garment industry, mechanisation has displaced women workers. For instance, the replacement of hand wheels by power winders has displaced a large chunk of the female workforce. A single worker using a power-operated winder is capable of winding four to five times more yarn than a woman worker, winding on a hand wheel. By replacing hand-operated wheels with power-winders, the employer not only benefits economically, but also saves space and time. Even in sectors where liberalisation has increased employment, women workers are getting paid less than men and, in most cases, much below the minimum wage. It is unjust that a worker spends many hours at difficult work and does not even earn enough to feed herself and her family. It is surprising, that even when opportunities have increased, women are earning a pittance. For the majority of women engaged in paid economic activity, the fact of being female means being paid less than men for their work. Gender-based wage disparities exist across all sectors and all occupations. One study[11] calculated the earnings differentials for the year 1989, 1991 and 1995 for manufacturing, plantations, tea and mines. Earning differentials are higher in the manufacturing and tea sectors and are lowest for plantation. Manufacturing sector appears to be the most discriminatory towards women.

There is enough evidence that women are paid less than men for the same work. Coupled with gender discrimination in wage differentials is inequality in access to superior positions and promotions. Women are often seen in the lower categories of the job hierarchy. Discrimination exists not only in terms of wages, but also in terms of access to employment. Often women are found concentrated in occupations where the wage rates, as well as working conditions are poor and substandard. Low levels of skill on entry, lack of access to on the job training, employment histories punctuated by time spent bearing and raising children, time off to care for family members and the assumption that men are the primary earners all contribute to the implicit assumption that women should be paid less then men.

Burden of Work on Women Workers

In the globalisation era women's participation in different production units has been increased but most of them are engaged in lower and middle category jobs though in the export sector their participation has to unionize and can be paid less. Actually the benefits of competitive markets are due to globalisation. The women workers spend more time in work compared to male workers. The following table shows the present situation of the burden of work.

Table-3 : Burden of female worker (% of male)

Country	*Female work time (% of male)*
India	117
Bangladesh	110
Nepal	105
Thailand	124
Malaysia	104

Source : Human Development Reports.

From Table 3 it can be observed that in all countries the burden of work on female worker is more compared to male counterparts. In Thailand this burden is the highest among five countries where the process of globalisation has started earlier compared to other countries. In Bangladesh it is also high. In garment industry the situation of women workers is serious. Apart from this the women workers work under very unhealthy and unhygienic conditions, but they get lower wages compared to men.

Economic Deprivation of Women Workers

The women workers are economically deprived in almost all less developed countries. In the era of globalisation this situation has gradually become worse. Informalisation of women workers leads to economic exploitation. Burden of unemployment and extreme poverty force the female workers to work at a very low wage. Even in the formal sector we can find male-female wage difference. Gender-based wage disparity exists across all sectors and in all occupations, despite labour laws which are made to ensure equity. In comparison with the economic activity rate the female workers earn less income compared to male workers which is shown in following table.

Table-4 : Deprivation of Women Regarding Income Share (1995)

Country	*Economic activity Rate (female as % of male)*	*Earned income Share (female as % of male)*
India	50	34
Pakistan	40	26
Bangladesh	76	30
Nepal	67	50
Sri Lanka	55	55
Maldives	79	55
Thailand	73	67
Malaysia	62	54
Bhutan	65	48

Source : ILO Report.

This table clearly shows that compared to the economic activity rate the female workers get lower wages than male workers. This situation is alarming in the Indian sub-continent. This is because of the fact that in this region the percentage of informal worker is high compared to East-Asian countries. Actually social structure of the Asian countries lead to such deprivation. In patriarchal society the women workers are supposed to be second-grade workers; so they are eligible for lower wages.

Health Hazards among Women Workers

Apart from all kinds of deprivation the women workers work in a very unhealthy environment. Working women all over Asia share the same experience. Even in the industrially developed countries the condition of working women living below poverty line is not better. In South Korea where 'economic miracle' has supposedly worked wonders, we see the same unhealthy miserable condition of the women workers. If we cast a glance at the women workers working in the garment factories, we can find that working under extremely high temperature and dealing with cotton fibres have resulted in 70 per cent of the women suffering from lung ailments. Besides, they have to work for a long time in a moist atmosphere due to which they suffer from diseases like arthritis and rheumatism. In many factories the workers have to face the ordeal of compulsory 'overtime'. As a result, the working women toiling hard under inhuman work-pressure, often suffer from psychological disarray.

Other Exploitation at Work

Apart from economic deprivation and health hazard the women workers often face sexual harassment in many Asian countries. Globalisation has opened up the scope for the women workers to enter in different industries but in many cases they are facing sexual harassment from their male colleagues or bosses.

Even the journey to and from the workplace is fraught with danger. Women workers run the risk of rape and harassment.

In Bangladesh the study revealed an alarming lack of awareness of safe sex practices and the likely spread of the HIV/AIDS disease. Sexually transmitted diseases (STD) are widespread. The number of infected people stood at 2.3 million at the end of 1996, according to official estimates.

In the last decade Thailand has made remarkable progress under globalised market economy. The prospering economy has suppressed the cries of thousands. Extreme poverty has forced energetic young girls to move to the big cities only to become sex-workers. In the developed capitalistic countries, namely, U.S.A., Philippines, Canada etc., we see that a portion of the new generation have joined as sex-workers and it is globalisation which has created an international market for the sex-workers.

Actually the benefits of competitive markets due to globalisation have been skewed towards the elite women of South Asia. Urban educated and affluent women are taking advantage of new opportunities of work created by the influx of foreign firms. Poor, uneducated rural and urban women' especially those who are engaged in informal sector do not reap the benefits of globalisation at all. We may conclude that in the era of globalisation the less developed countries are guided by the large capitalist countries which results in widespread disparity in all the sectors. It is also destroying cultural heritage of the less developed countries. Ultimately this policy is bringing the people in front of danger, especially for the women workers. The fact is that globalisation has not uplifted all women in the society and has further marginalized the vulnerable section.

References

1. Cecilia Ng Choon Sim : *Making Women's Voice Heard : Technological Change and Women's employment in Malaysia*

(published in Gender, Technology and Development, Vol. 3, no. 1).

2. Maria Mies-Patriarchy and *Accumulation on a World Scale*, Zed Books, London.

3. Nirmala Banerjee : Can markets alter gender relations (published in *Gender, Technology and Development*-Vol. 3, no. 1).

4. *Human development Report*-2000, OUP, 2004.

5. Agnihotri, Indu "Globalisation and the State", paper presented at *DAWN Asia-Pacific Workshop on Political Restructuring and Social Transformation*, 8-11 October, Thailand, 1999.

6. All Women's Action Society (AWAM) *Draft Report on Rape Research*, 2000.

7. Ghosh, Jayati "Globalisation and Economic Liberalisation", *ISIS Women in Action*, 1999.

8. Jamieson, Lynn, Lecture Series organised by the Gender Studies Unit, Universiti Malaya, 2000.

9. Maznah Mohamad, Cecilia Ng and Tan Beng Hui (forthcoming) "Globalisation, Industrialisation and Crisis : The Coming of Age of Malaysian Women Workers?" *United Nations Human Development Report* (1996–1999).

10. Women's Development Collective, *Women's Agenda for Change*, 1999.

WOMEN AND POLITICS

6

Quest for Identity : A Brief Sketch of the Palestinian Women's Movement

Aditi Bhaduri

In order to start talking about the identity of Palestinian women, it would be useful to first start with the concept of "identity". "Personal identity" is the identity of an individual and it means defining people as to who they are (who am I?). This will always be related to how others define them, and usually means defining an individual or a group as "different" from another or other individuals or groups.

Question of Identity

Identities are usually shaped by local and global history and politics, and most often appear as a manifestation of resistance or as a search for justice. "Identities are not primordial, they are not natural, permanent, or fixed though they may often seem to be so."

Historically speaking, national identities are relatively recent forms of identity. In Europe, it was the 19th century that saw the rise of nationalism and the division into the countries we now think of as units. In the Arab Middle East, nationalism arose in the context of 20th century European colonial control and was crucial, in struggles for independence.

Arabism first arose in the nineteenth century not as a direct reaction to Western rule, but as a critique of the state of the Ottoman Empire, whose reach had extended over most of the Arabic-speaking peoples since the early sixteenth century. The Ottomans professed Islam and their state evolved as a partnership in Islam, embracing all of the Ottoman Sultan's Muslim Subjects, whatever language they spoke.

Those who spoke Arabic had a sense of pride as God revealed the Qur'an in Arabic to an Arab prophet in the seventh century. Thus, Islam was an "Arab" gift to the world, appearing as it did in Arabia. Arab speakers were also proud of their history which spread Islam from the Pacific to the Atlantic Oceans and had created an Empire that stretched from the Oxus to the Pyrenees. But with the relative decline in Ottoman power, especially in the nineteenth century, the foundations of this symbiosis began to weaken. By the eve of World War I, Arabism did begin to take a more palpable form against the two challenges of Turkification and Zionism.

Turkification threatened the cultural status quo. As the Ottoman Empire stumbled, Ottoman authorities attempted to give the polyglot Empire more the character of a European nation-state by enforcing the use of Turkish at the expense of other languages, including Arabic. This policy is said to have may helped to rally the supporters of cultural Arabism to a political purpose.

Zionist settlement in Palestine threatened the political status quo. Ottoman authorities tolerated the influx of Jewish immigration in the belief that it would ultimately benefit the Empire, as it had in successive waves since the Spanish Inquisition. But not all of the sultan's subjects concurred, since this latest wave of immigrants saw the land on which they were settling not merely as a refuge but as a state in the making. As the pace of Zionist immigration and settlement increased, their immediate neighbors grew apprehensive about the looming possibility of dispossession. From the turn of the century, Ottoman policy toward Zionism became a matter of growing debate and criticism in the Arabic press.

State formation in the Palestinian case, thus, was first and foremost to do with Jewish immigrants entering the country with the specific aim of establishing a Jewish state. The "non-Jewish" inhabitants fought a defensive battle on 2 fronts against both the British and the Zionist movement and at the same time were involved in a process of identity transformation. Having been Ottoman subjects for hundreds of years Arabs in Palestine were now declared officially Palestinian.

The mandate regime culminated in their defeat and a physical expulsion in the destruction of their societal institutions which had been built during the thirty year period of the British rule. The very fact of dispersal and exile after 1948, their new status as "Arab refugees" militated against the development of a distinct national identity until such a time as they were able to reorganize themselves and appear as independent action on the political stage. This they were able to do in the aftermath of 1967. Their status as refugees, the Arab states attitude towards them as wards and as pawn at one and the same time and the prevailing perception of the international community all conspired to withhold from them the "permission to narrate" in the eloquent words of Edward Said.

In his book *Palestinian Identity : The Construction of Modern National Consciousness*, Rashid Khalidi has tried to show that Palestinian identity, at least among the educated elite, was well grounded by the end of the first decade of the mandate contrary to mainstream Zionist historiographers who tend to insist that Palestinian nationalism is a phenomenon of fairly recent origin and only arose as a specific response to Zionism.

Khalidi's main thrust is to refute claims that Palestinian identity emerged mainly as a response to Zionism. While conceding the importance of Zionism in the formation of Palestinian identity as the primary other faced by Palestinians for much of this century–he tries to show that elements of attachment to Palestine antedate the Palestinians encounter with Zionism. He goes on to point out that the argument that Zionism was the main factor in provoking the emergence of Palestinian national identity ignores one key fact : that a universal process was unfurling in the Middle East during this period involving an increased identification with the new states created by the post World War I partitions. As part of this process Lebanon, Syria, Iraq, Jordan all managed to develop their respective nation-state nationalism during this period "without the dubious benefit of a Zionist challenge".

However, Khalidi also warns of the tendency, common in most engaged in Palestinian writings to see an essential Palestinian identity going well back in time. Zionism, therefore, if not the only cause, was certainly the most crucial one in shaping the "Palestinian" identity.

In this context the voice of women in the Middle East is just beginning to be heard. It is true that through the centuries some women have played significant roles and can be found in the history of each nation. But the voice of the "ordinary" woman has been slower to appear.

As regarding Palestinian women's "voices" perhaps the truth is best voiced by Ghada Talhami. In the preface to the book *Images and Reality : Palestinian Women under Occupation and in the Diaspora* she talks of "the near-total silence in academia on the contributions of Palestinian women to the process of nation building". This indeed is a big injustice to the contribution of Palestinian women to their society.

Palestinian Society

However, it is imperative to first talk a bit about Palestinian society. Then, as well as now, Palestinian society was far from being homogenous. There were religious differences–12 per cent of mandated Palestine's Arab population was Christian, this number has now steadily declined to 8 per cent, largely due to the exodus of Christian Palestinians to the West, under Israel's increasingly harsh occupation. And as Christians, they have been more willingly accepted by the West than have Muslim Palestinians.

Next, the Palestinians were also divided along class lines. On one hand we have the rich, Westernised, often "absentee" landlord class, who have been much accused by historians of selling off their land to Jewish immigrants from Europe and thus playing a large role in creating the Palestinian problem. On the other hand we have the kuffiya clad poor peasant, with little or no education, steeped in his religious and social traditions, many of whom found themselves landless and jobless after they were evicted from the land they had tended to for generations by their new Jewish landlords. Somewhere in between were the educated middleclass and upper middleclass.

After the 1948 Arab-Jewish war came the actual political awakening and the formation of variously oriented parties-Fatah, the Democratic Front for the Liberation of Palestine, the Popular Front for the Liberation of Palestine, the Communist Party of Palestine were some of the main ones. Whatever their orientation, almost all of them were quite secular, their main patron being the USSR and other socialist and non-aligned countries, including Arab ones. It was with Israel's occupation of the West Bank and the Gaza Strip after the war of 1967 that religiously oriented parties like HAMAS, Islamic Jihad started appearing, being actively encouraged by Israel, as a counter-force to the PLO. After the Oslo process these religiously oriented parties started gaining power and Palestinian society started becoming more polarized along religious lines and definitely much more radicalized.

It is against such a social, political and historical background that this paper will attempt to sketch a brief profile of the Palestinian women's movement.

Women's Movement

Throughout its history, the Palestinian women's movement has always been influenced and linked to the Palestinian national liberation movement. Although this link, at times, has been a source of strength for the women's movement, it has also exposed the women's movement inherent weakness of the women's movement.

Initially, the national movement and the women's movement attracted upper-middle class, educated Palestinians. Since the beginning of the twentieth century, Palestinian women have been active in charitable work out of a belief that their task was to help the poor and the disadvantaged. The first women's organization was established in Akko in 1903. Aware of the constraints on them imposed by traditional Palestinian society, these women decided to help by giving assistance to men–the family head. Through the purchase of land and the creation of vocational schools for boys, this first women's organization was able to improve the conditions of Palestinian families, thereby also improving the lives of Palestinian women.

Soon other charitable societies were founded, primarily by middle-and upper-class Palestinian women. Although these were based in cities, their work was aimed at helping the rural poor, primarily farmers in small village communities. One of the most noteworthy of these groups was the Palestinian Women's Union, created in Jerusalem in 1921.

This union exemplified the women's movement's intrinsic link with the national movement and national issues. In the Women's Union, Palestinian women struggled, along with men, against the pressing issues facing the Palestinian people in the early 1920s : the practices of the Mandatory government and its Zionist immigration policy. Women protested with men against the Jewish immigrants to Palestine intruding on Palestinian land. The Palestinian Women's Union organized the first women's conference, held in October 1929, attended by an estimated 300 women. The conference established the basis for the women's movement agenda in protesting the British. During the conference, the women's movement was concerned with national issues facing the Palestinian people and not specifically women's issues.

In 1921 the "Arab Women's Union" was set up in Nablus, and in 1923 the "Child Care Society" in 1923. Hence, the women's movement began as an outlet for women to discuss and confront national issues. The national struggle was the women's movement's main priority. Because women participating in the women's movement were, in actuality, participating in the national struggle, these women were marginally allowed to enter the patriarchal, traditional realm controlled by men.

As a movement, it gave expression to a female, and not a female consciousness, based on 'women's awareness of their rights within the prevailing division of labor and dominate ideology'. Thus, the Palestinian women's movement, much like the women's movement in India, at its inception had no feminist agenda based on a feminist consciousness, i.e. women's awareness of their subordinate position within a cultural and power system and the articulation of a specifically female perspective on the social process.

Valentine Moghadam, author of *Gender and National Identity : Women and politics in Muslim Societies* notes three distinct phases in the participation in and the development of the women's movement in Palestine : 1920-1948; 1949-1967; 1967 to the present. Other historians argue that the periods of 1920-1948, 1949-1982, and 1987 to the present mark more clearly the development of the women's movement. Though distinguishing the Palestinian women's movement through the wars of Israel and political occupation, in a sense denies women their own history and voice, it is however, inevitable as the Palestinian national struggle still continues.

The period of 1920-1948 characterized the women's movement as one of charity and social support. All actions revolved around the daily survival, struggle and assistance to the hundreds of thousands of refugees. "They provided care for a sector of the population ... but they did not provide these women with the tools that might enable them to involve themselves actively in the operations of Palestinian society and effect social change."

Soumaya Farhat Nasser is of the opinion that during the British Mandate period in Palestine, Palestinian women were united in their acceptance of a supportive role in society. Palestinian men were struggling politically and militarily for independence, and their wives and mothers and daughters were expected to support these efforts. Political action on the part of women was strictly limited to peaceful demonstrations and actions.

During the 30s and 50s some educated women, from certain well known families at that time, started joining some political parties. In the big cities women contributed to the establishment of popular organizations that had a role in the famous 1936 strike, where they worked on health (first Aid)committee, boycott committee. None of these activities however had anything to do with women's issues or rights specifically. Women often adopted singing and chanting as means of resistance and intimidation of British soldiers widely in Palestinian society during the time of the 1936 Palestinian Revolution.

But a militant women's organization called "Zahrat Al-Okhowan" is also heard of at this time, though not much is known about them except for the fact that they fought against the British.

In the 1930s and 40s, early attempts were made to organize women into associations and societies, mostly initiated by bourgeois class educated women, who's main focus was on the right of education and work for women, with rare discussions about political participation. In this context names like May Ziyadah is heard of. A renowned writer, May was one of the first women artists who held meetings in her house (in the thirties) for artists and poets.

In 1948, with Israel's independence, called "Al-Nakba" or "The Catastrophe" by Palestinians, forced displacement of more than 800, 000 Palestinians to neighboring countries took place. The Palestinian woman became a refugee. Her critical mission was keeping the Palestinian National Identity intact. She had to heal the pains, re-unify the dispersed family, secure food on the table with her partner, and above all, keep the memory of Palestine alive. Here it might be mentioned that it is usually the task of all women in the diaspora–whether refugee or a migrant out of her own free will, to keep the memory of the "homeland" alive. Palestinians raised by refugee families, who never saw Palestine had a clear, if a trifle too "bounteous" image of it, just from the memories, tales, narrations, accounts of their mothers and grandmothers which were passed down from generation to generation. More women joined the work of charitable societies, eager to relieve the homelessness, poverty, and sickness tearing apart their society.

The period of Jordanian rule, 1948-67, saw further growth of Palestinian women's organizations. Since all political activity was strictly forbidden by the Jordanian government (whose goal was the suppression of Palestinian national identity), women took on the role of filling in the gaps in the social services offered by the state. And these were many! For the first time, women's organizations were required to register with the Ministry of Social Affairs. The Jordanian government's desire for social control was so fervent that a permit was required for each group meeting of the organization. A representative from the Ministry of Social Affairs would attend each meeting, taking notes for a report to the government. Later, under Israeli occupation, the same regulations were applied.

Mention must be made of people like Samiha Khalil and Maha Saca. Khalil, a mother of five who has little formal education, started her organization—the Society of In'ash El-Usra, Arabic for "revival of the people"—in 1952 with a secondhand sewing machine and eight students in a neighbor's garage in the West Bank city of Al-Bireh.

The society has grown into a multimillion-dollar nonprofit organization that employs 123 people full-time and provides part-time embroidery work for more than 5,000 women living in villages and refugee camps. Similarly, Palestinian women's societies, by providing work and social services, gave people the means to remain on the land during the occupation. "And this was significant because if Palestinians had left in 1967, we would be in a much weaker position now to negotiate with Israel for land," she said. "So these women's groups have had a profound political impact. But many people don't see it."

In'ash El-Usra has a folklore center and cultural museum. "A people without history and culture is a people without identity," Khalil said. "How can you build a nation without an identity?"

Maha Saca, an American Palestinian left her comfortable life in the USA to come and set up a museum in Bethlehem dedicated to preserving Palestinian tradition. So throughout the dispersal and occupation Palestinian women in the Palestinian territories as well as in the diaspora have been performing the very important task of maintaining and keeping up the Palestinian cultural identity and legacy. Apart from that, with their various charitable and self-employment schemes and projects Palestinian women also helped to a large extent to keep the Palestinian population in their territories and prevent migration.

This trend continued until the 1960's. The mid to late 1960's marked a turning point for women and their movement. The inception to the Palestinian Liberation Organization in the 60's and subsequently the General Union of Palestinian Women provided an outlet and format for formal organizations to discuss women's needs, as well as increase mobilization efforts. However, "the absence of a Palestinian state [continues to] intensify the significance of informal social or communal groups (as opposed to formal state structures) in the expansion of women's participation in social and political activities..."

The Palestinian Women's Union joined the Palestinian Liberation Organization upon its formation in 1964. This brought about fundamental changes in women's role in Palestinian society. For the first time in Palestinian history, women were not restricted to social and charity work. They could engage in military actions, struggling alongside men! Their military successes were noted by society, bringing Palestinian women recognition and respect previously reserved only for men.

The year 1967 marked the second great disaster in the history of the Palestinian people. When Israel won the war, Palestine fell under military occupation and more than half the Palestinian population lost their homes. Perhaps more than at any time in the past, women and women's organizations were needed to lend assistance. The younger generation of Palestinian women involved in this effort were invariably better educated than their predecessors. They were also highly politicized, having spent their entire lives under Israeli occupation. Joining one of the existing women's organizations was not a viable option for this new generation of women, since these organizations were conservative, their members (still) belonging to the middle-and upper-classes.

The new generation of highly politicized, younger women was rejected as too young and too radical. They sought to sweep away the old and bring in the new. Their principles included an end to charity work, which they felt perpetuated a relationship of dependency and maintained the (capitalist) class structure. In place of charitable acts, these women proposed helping women help themselves through education, vocational training, and economic independence.

This new generation also wanted to introduce democratic elements–such as elections and civic participation–into Palestinian society. For older women, some of them having spent thirty or forty years as members of the same women's committees, this was impossible. Such changes were rejected outright by them.

This call for Palestinian women to become politically active was perhaps one of the great turning points in the women's movement. Such a confrontation between old and new ideas about the role of women in Palestinian society resulted in the formation of the Palestinian Political Women's Committees, each of which was affiliated with a political party. These new political committees were highly visible, engaging in activities different from–yet complementary with–those of the charitable societies.

The activities and experiences of the first two generations of charitable women activists nevertheless paved the way for the more radical women's movement which developed in the early 1970's ... The third generation of women activists, aware of the limitation of the traditional charitable work, set up a separate political women's movement in Ramallah in the 1970's. The late 1970's saw the rise of popular women's committees and the drastic advancement of the women's movement. A new generation of women, many of whom had been politicized in the student movement at the Palestinian universities, founded grassroots women's committees that, in contrast to the charitable society network of women's organizations, sought to involve the majority of women in the West Bank who lived in villages–along with women in camps, the urban poor, and women workers as well as intellectuals and urban middle-class women–in a united women's movement.

A small number of women became fighters, like Fatima Barnawi, who threw a bomb in an Israeli cinema, or Leila Khaled, who carried out military operations as a member of the Popular Front for the Liberation of Palestine (PFLP), in the late 1960s. She created quite a storm not only in the Arab or Islamic world, but in the whole world in general as a female hijacker who blew up the TWA aircraft after evacuating people from it. Is she a Palestinian first, or a woman first? "I cannot differentiate," she says. "A woman and a Palestinian at the same time." She flamboyantly overcame the patriarchal restrictions of Arab society where women are traditionally subservient to their husbands, by taking an equal fighting role with men, by getting divorced and remarried, having children in her late 30s, and rejecting vanity by having her face reconstructed for her cause.

But even Khaled could not escape the clutches of the patriarchy that dominated and permeated every aspect of Palestinian society, even in the radical PFLP. There were difficulties with being both a woman and a fighter. "In the beginning, all women had to prove that we could be equal to men in armed struggle," says Khaled. "So we wanted to be like men-even in our appearance." The men in her organisation resented the attention she got, while women were frustrated that she never spoke about women, only about the revolution. She once said, "I represent Palestinians, not women."

The occupation started other effects upon Palestinian women. Ghada Talhami points out that Israeli tax laws, land confiscations, and political repression have led to out-migration of men, leaving many families headed by women. The difficult economic situation also has resulted in women joining the paid work force, but only as non-unionized workers. Consequently, they are exploited by their employers on Israeli farms and their Palestinian employers in the West Bank sewing factories.

Education became a great asset to middle-class women in becoming involved in the struggle while keeping a balance between tradition and political activism. An interesting fact is that Palestinians have the highest literacy levels in the Arab world, believing that education was all that was left for them to battle the occupation with. Five universities were founded in the occupied territories-quite an achievement in itself. This made higher education a possibility for women.

An interesting phenomenon was-and still is the fact that women from refugee camps are often more educated than ordinary Palestinian women. While women cadres were critical of women's position and the role in the movement,-their welfare work among ordinary women in literacy classes, vocational training in sewing, typing, hairdressing, education on nutrition, health and child-care-gives them the satisfaction of having a role in the movement. There is no denying that all these programs were essential to the quality of life of people even under occupation, and it was necessary to have these programs and projects to allow the movement to continue its struggle.

The growing realization of the significance of women's participation in the national struggle led to the formation of four women's committees in the late 1970s and early 1980s. The first of these was the Women's Work Committee set up in Ramallah in 1978 by a group of highly educated and ideologically and politically motivated women. It aimed at reaching large numbers of women to mobilize them to join the women's and national movements. It developed rapidly in many parts of the Occupied Territories, reaching a membership in the range of two thousand. However, growth also brought problems; there were debates on priorities and the emphasis given to different issues. A Working Women's Committee was then formed whose priority was to make working women aware of their threefold oppression-that originating in the traditional patriarchal nature of society; that to be found at the workplace; and that caused by Israeli occupation. Through their struggle at the workplace, in many organizations they won a paid holiday on 8 March, International Women's Day.

In 1982, two other committees, the Palestine Women's Committee and the Women's Committee for Social Work, were formed in the same way. While women in all these committees were active in the unionization of working women, generating social and political consciousness, supporting prisoners' families etc, the divisions which led to the establishment of the four different committees seemed to be a reflection of the ideological views of the factions in the larger movements itself. Moreover, as women's groups were part of the national liberation movement, their programmes and policies were linked to the movement's wider policies, which it might be argued are in the interest of Palestinian people in general. However, the policies were conspicuous for their segregation of the world of women from that of men.

The Golden Age for the Palestinian woman, is usually considered to begin in 1987 with the start of the first Uprising (*Intifada*). The uprising was a popular revolt against occupation. The Palestinian woman played a big role in it and her contributions are said to be tremendous. Boycotts became the favoured weapon. The Palestinian woman boycotted Israeli products, and found alternatives to them, much like our "Swadeshi" movement. The women snatched those detained by the Israeli army from them and freed them into the refugee camps. She broke stones and threw them–that unique weapon of the Intifada, which became a symbol of Palestinian resistance, and is still being used today by children and adults-both men and women. The Palestinian woman also focused on education, sourcing and facilitating education outside the schools when the schools were shutdown for days and months by the Israeli army. Cooperatives of all kinds were formed to provide a home alternative to working outside the home.

During the Intifada, the women's political committees were instrumental in mobilizing and organizing women for political action such as street demonstrations. As more and more Palestinian men were imprisoned by Israel, much of the responsibility for political action shifted to women. They broke the taboos of women being physically involved in the political arena. They were beaten, imprisoned, tortured, killed. The Palestinian home, which has been the place of seclusion and sanctity for women, became violated on a daily basis, by army searches and demolitions.

This brought the issues of female sexuality from the private domain to the public sphere. Female sexuality, which is so sacred to the honor of the Arab family and clan, was threatened by the Israeli soldiers, through sexual harassment in the home and the prisons. But this did not intimidate these women, neither did it prevent them from further participation in the struggle. On the contrary, it made them more determined to fight and this in turn accorded them a great deal of respect and regard from the male population who by now have come to depend on them for much more than participation in the political struggle.

Initially men were proud of this kind of participation by women, not least because it helped them to a large extent too–women kept the family and home going while the men were in prison, and often also helped hide men wanted by Israeli forces or freed those in custody by petitioning, by demonstrating and by fighting lawsuits. However, when women began to demand social change–human rights and equality for women in both the public and private sphere–the men balked : "This is a critical stage in our struggle for national liberation. We must focus all our energies on that. Once liberation comes, then we will work on social change."

The struggle demanded the unity of the sexes but there was no equality in this unity. Both inside and outside the movement, political awareness eclipsed social consciousness; the patriarchy that dominated and in fact still dominates the social system, shaped the political structure of the movement. Consequently the role of women in the movement was generally seen as the support of the fidayin, the freedom fighters. In order not to disrupt power relations between men and women, the movement played safe by encouraging women to serve the struggle in their socially acceptable role-as mothers preparing their sons to fight and as wives producing fighters for the 'cause'. Palestinian women who were members of political parties felt the greatest pressure to go along with this decision. Committed to the ideology and regulations of their party's platform, many women felt unable to struggle on so many fronts simultaneously. Reluctant yet resigned, these women compromised and set aside their interests for the greater good of the national struggle.

Women were caught in a trap where they had to find a balance between challenging their subordinate position and political exigencies which demanded upholding the same cultural values in the interests of national integrity which restrained women from participating in the movement. The subordinate position of Palestinian women in the movement was further shaped by the movement's class structure. The military, political/ diplomatic and administrative wings of the movement evolved into complex organizational modules. A new breed of educated Palestinians that constituted the aspiring middle-class, active in the movement, along with members of old prestigious families, formed the hierarchy. Their leadership was patriarchal in nature which, to a certain extent, favoured women's participation; especially, of women from the same social groups who themselves had attained higher educational qualifications. The decisions to set priorities for, and policies regarding, participation of women remained in the hands of male members of the movement. The participation of women even in the most radical faction, the PFLP (Popular Front for the Liberation of Palestine) was subject to male domination, as already seen in the case of Leila Khaled. It mainly involved working on women's projects, or domestic support for the revolutionaries (producing children, arranging social activities and so on). Inasmuch as the leadership set its political goals for women in correspondence with the social system, women's participation remains contingent upon their social position. This situation seems to have changed over the years, in the sense that, whereas in the past the structural mechanism was set to organize women separately and impose strict control on men-women relations, now women have more freedom of movement.

However, independent Palestinian women were of a different mindset, believing that national and social liberation should be fought for simultaneously. Over time, these women created independent women's centers such as the Women's Affairs Center in Nablus, the Women's Studies Center and the Women's Legal Aid Society in Jerusalem, and the Women's Studies Unit at Birzeit University.

In the crucial and heady years of the late 1980s and early 1990s, Palestinian women–having played a critical role in both the Intifada and in preparations for a peace process with Israel–expected to be involved in the negotiating process. But this was not to be. Once official negotiations began, it was remarkable how, almost without exception, only men were nominated for inclusion.

In 1993, the ground-breaking Oslo Accords were signed and Palestinians began to believe that at last they would be able to function as a normal society. Many Palestinians are of the opinion that Oslo was facilitated by and for wealthy Palestinians in the Diaspora, who wanted a home for their capital, and in return, they agreed to a flawed "peace" and autonomy. Women received the lowest wages and many small businesses started closing down, making way for the new Palestinian wealth mass production with cheaper prices. The Palestinian Authority with its increasingly authoritative and unaccountable rule began to reflect the patriarchal trends that had always characterized Palestinian society. Laws were framed which did not always benefit Palestinian women.

The Palestinian women's movement began to split over agendas and approaches to the women struggle. There was a split over social issues and issues of the national struggles. Part of the movement believed that peace was being achieved and therefore social issues could be dealt with now. The other part believed that the Israeli occupation still existed, and the national liberation movement and women's movement should go together. There is also said to be a horizontal split over approach. People like Hanan Ashrawi, the Palestinian legislator and academician, have been accused of focusing too much on research and maintaining and normalising relations with Israeli women, receiving in turn a lot of funds from the West and Israel, while ignoring grassroots Palestinian women and organizations. It is a fact that she or others like her, for e.g. Palestinian journalist Kawther Salam, who lives in Hebron and defies many Palestinian traditions and maintains links with Israeli peace groups are not popular amongst most Palestinians while they are greatly admired by the Western world and many other foreign countries. On the other hand, organizations dealing with grassroots levels, like UPWC (Union of Palestinian Women Committees) in Gaza became quite popular. It is a self-funded organization that is encouraging and empowering women, mostly housewives with children, and other working women to become self-sufficient. Rather than service women, the organization tries to focus on training women to service themselves and their communities.

Nevertheless, women were able to achieve some rights and gender equalities during the ensuing years between Oslo and the second Intifadh (Uprising) that erupted in October 2000. In 1992, the Women's Affairs Technical Committee (WATC) was established at the beginning of negotiations between Israel and the PLO in 1992. The WATC is a coalition of women's political activists affiliated with the six main political parties in the country, as well as independent professional women working in Universities. The Palestinian Women's Health Coalition and Al-Haq, a human rights organisation affiliated with the International Commission of Jurists joined the WATC in 1996. In the years between 1995 and 1996 the achievements of the group were significant:

Women were no longer required to obtain the permission from their male relatives in order to apply for travel documents.

Women could keep their maiden names after marrying.

Women were no longer required to take along a chaperone while taking driving lessons.

Women could open bank accounts in their children's names, which was a right only given to men by some local banks.

Widows could have passports issued for their children without obtaining the permission of their in-laws.

29 women were appointed to positions on local councils and municipalities as a result of WATC advocacy work.

Women became eligible to have three months maternity leave and one hour a day for nursing according to the new Civil Administration Law.

The number of female general directors in government ministries was increased.

A large range of modifications to draft legislation (civil status law and election law) had been achieved.

However, in spite of these achievements, On the other hand :

Abortion is illegal in the Palestinian Territories administered by the Palestinian Authority.

In personal law, women are guided by the provisions of their religions–Islam and Christianity–the only two religions practiced in the Palestinian Territories.

Palestinian women married to foreign men cannot pass on their citizenship to their children.

Foreign men married to Palestinian women do not qualify for obtaining Palestinian citizenship.

Honor killings are prevalent in Palestinian society and do not qualify as a crime under the existing criminal law in the territories administered by the Palestinian Territorries.

It is also important to talk about a radicalization and "Islamisation" of Palestinian society that started taking place during the first Intifada and intensified during the rule of the Palestinian Authroity. In 1987, a new movement emerged on the national political scene by the name of 'Hamas' the Islamic Resistance. According to the ideology of this movement were constructed as complementary to men, not a new phenomenon in Palestinian society. Women have no place in actual violent actions or resistance, but are rather seen as healers and care givers in the back seats. Along with this women are to don all the other symbols required to identify a 'Muslim Woman'; like the veil, piety. etc. Starting from 1988 and also because of the fundamentalists pressure, secular nationalist women defied for the first time the way they were constructed by the national movement, and in the middle of the uprising claimed their rights in freedom of movement, freedom of expression, freedom from harassments for being dressed differently... etc. Women were very successful and since then their 'feminist' identity was clearer.

Soon after the establishment of the Palestinian authority, the second Intifada broke out in the West Bank. It is beyond the scope of this paper to look into the reasons for the failure of negotiations and out-break of the second Intifada and unprecedented level of violence, and the reoccupation of Palestinian territories by Israeli forces. We shall limit ourselves only to the effect the new uprising has had on women.

Women in this uprising are facing three major challenges: occupation, social discrimination, and class struggle and increased polarization and radicalism. Hannan Ashrawi in an interview with this author pointed out that the new Intifada, as opposed to the older one was militarized, reflecting the patriarchal tendency in Palestinian society since the rule of the Palestinian Authority began. And since this Intifada is much more militarized, women play a very insignificant role in it, again as opposed to the former Intifada. Nevertheless, the Palestinian woman continues to use those weapons available to her. Since the beginning of the current Intifada, in spite of her marginalized role, she continues to participate in demonstrations of every kind. She is the widow, whose husband has been killed or the wife, whose husband is in prison or who has lost his job inside Israel. So she has become once again the bread-earner, working on embroidery, taking up odd-jobs, opening a beauty parlour in her house or looking after the poultry farm that her husband used to. She is the mother whose son is in prison or has been killed, or in more rare and sordid cases, has blown himself up trying to kill the enemy, so she glorifies him and holds him up as an example to her other children. She is the sustainer and the wound healer. Above all, the Palestinian woman uses her body as the ultimate weapon–by producing children, who would grow up to be Palestinians and demographically would soon outnumber the Jew.

In this *Intifada* Palestinian women found yet another way to use their body as a form of resistance. Reflecting the patriarchal tendency and the militarization of the new Intifada is the new phenomenon of female suicide bombers that appeared last year in the West Bank.

And this brings another point to light that it is women in Palestine who have usually focused on non-violent struggle. As we have earlier seen during the Arab boycott of 1936 and in the previous Intifada she played a significant role, employing totally non-violent ways. Since the beginning of the current *Intifada* she participated in demonstrations of all kinds. Here the example of Huwaida Arraf is interesting. A 28 year Palestinian, born and brought up in the USA, she returned to the West Bank city of Nablus, in 2001, where together with her Jewish husband Adam Shapiro, has launched an International Solidarity Movement (ISM) which involves non-violent civil disobedience against Israeli occupation. The ISM has specially been able to attract foreigners–mostly from America and Europe who find it easier to travel to the Palestinian territories. Huwaida and Adam impart training to foreigners and Palestinians in non-violent actions of resistance and participate in acts like disobeying curfews imposed by Israeli forces, taking children to school which have been ordered closed, helping and accompanying foreign journalists to especially affected places, crossing checkpoints, disobeying closure etc.

Women are also leading organizations that are not necessarily focusing on women issues. An organization like Addameer in Ramallah, is largely operated by women. It works for rights of political prisoners and at present is involved in more than 1600 cases of political prisoners. Many of the women working there were themselves once political prisoners, and many continue to have their partners or family members in Israeli jails.

However, in contemporary political activism only the forms of control have changed; the constraints in themselves have not disappeared. Physical control and segregation of sexes are replaced by verbal ridicule. Female activists who interact with men are looked upon with contempt and termed 'loose women'. Islah Jad, senior academician at the West Bank University of Bir Zeit is of the opinion that the concept of 'woman' is under continuous critique by many grass roots women in reaction to the more generic concept of 'equality' in its liberal sense, new women's organizations emerged 'representing' new women's elite mainly from the middle class, claiming equality for 'all' women and of course representing themselves as the 'representative' of all women, there are lots of conflicts going on between the old national elite mainly developed in the confinement of the grass roots movements, and women in the new structure of the 'civil society' mainly in NGOs beside women in the Islamic movements.

Women often encounter intimidation from male members when they try to raise women's issues, since these are not considered 'political' and are regarded as trivial. Thus most women either find it difficult to continue their political involvement, or content themselves with the secondary roles available to them. This obviously reflects the attitude of the majority of male members who consider the women's role as associated with home and domestic affairs. It proves that non-participation of women in the movement is mainly due to social constraints. While the political participation of women is impeded as shown above, at the same time political oppression itself and the question of national liberation provide no impetus to any radical transformation of their social position. On the contrary they re-impose socio-cultural traditions, and therefore an autonomous women's movement which is likely to challenge social control is discouraged. Although such a challenge is expected to lead to the increasing participation of women in the movement, it is certainly not acceptable to the majority of male members. Therefore either the leadership of the movement does not consider it, or it has secondary status as the women's role itself.

Nevertheless, it must be emphasized that there can be no doubt of the political awareness existing among Palestinian women. Whether living in the diaspora or confronting soldiers and settlers in the Occupied Territories, Palestinian women are conscious of the dialectical nature of their struggle-in other words, both the political struggle for national liberation and the need to bring social change within the society in order to extend their contribution in the national struggle.

As Reem Alnuweiri, Palestinian Delegate and speaker at the Conference "Towards Our Liberation" last year in November said :.. when we are speaking about the struggle of the Palestinian women, we are speaking about the history of the Palestinian people's struggle. We cannot speak about one without the other. Half the struggle, half the suffering, half the pain, half the achievements.

The situation the Palestinian woman finds herself today in and the challenges facing her under the dual yokes of foreign occupation and a highly patriarchal society is perhaps best summed up by the following lines spoken by Palestinian feminist and Director of the Women's Center for Legal Aid and Counseling Maha Abu-Dayyeh Shamas in an address before the U.N. Security Council in May 2002 :

"The Palestinian women's movement has succeeded in making inroads in addressing cultural values and attitudes particular to the Arab world that handicap the healthy development of girls and women. We Palestinian women were in the process of engaging ourselves in legislative development at the local as well as the international levels... We were witnessing the development of a budding but vibrant young feminist movement, an essential sector for democratic development within the Palestinian society. However, the last so-called Israeli re-occupation of Palestinian-controlled areas has manifested itself in the systematic destruction of all that we have been able to achieve in the last ten years."

References

Professor Lila Abu-Lughod : Thinking About Identity in Spotlight on The Muslim Middle East-Issues of Identity, Edited by Hazel Sara Greenberg and Liz Mahony.

Kramer Martin : *Arab Nationalism : Mistaken Identity*, Published in Daedalus, Summer 1993.

Mandel Nelville J., *The Arabs and Zionism before World War*. Berkeley and Los Angeles : University of California Press, 1976.

Images and Reality : Palestinian Women under Occupation and in the Diaspora. Ed. Suha Sabbagh and Ghada Talhami. Institute for Arab Women's Studies, 1990.

Moghadam Valentine : *Gender and National Identity : Women and Politics in Muslim Societies, 2000*

Farhat Naser Sumaya : *Palestinian Women and Girls*, paper presented at Between the Lines : German, Israeli and Palestinian Women in Dialogue, Jerusaelm, 2000.

Farhat Naser Sumaya : *Palestinian Women and Girls*, paper presented at Between the Lines : German, Israeli and Palestinian Women in Dialogue, Jerusaelm, 2000.

Krodel Beth : *Interview* in The Detroit Free Press, May 27, 1998.

Warnock Kitty : *Land Before Honor : Palestinian Women in the Occupied Territories*, New York, USA : Monthly Review Press. 1990.

Mayer Tamar (ed). Women and the Israeli Occupation : *The Politics of Change*, London, UK : Routledge Press. 1994.

Farhat Naser Sumaya : *Palestinian Women and Girls*, paper presented at Between the Lines : German, Israeli and Palestinian Women in Dialogue, Jerusaelm, 2000.

Augustin Ebba (ed). *Palestinian Women : Identity and Experience*. London, UK : Zed Books Ltd., 1993.

Giacaman Rita and Johnson Penny : *Palestinian Women : Building Barricades and Breaking Barriers*, 2001

Viner Katharine : , Interview with Leila Khaled, *The Guardian*, 26 January 2001.

Images and Reality : Palestinian Women under Occupation and in the Diaspora, Ed. By Suha Sabbagh and Ghada Talhami. Institute for Arab Women's Studies, 1990.

Saida Nusseibeh : *Palestinian Cultural Identity and the Role of the Palestinian Women–from a Palestinian Perspective* : Speech in Amman, June 2001.

Farhat Naser Sumaya : *Palestinian Women and Girls*, paper presented at Between the Lines : German, Israeli and Palestinian Women in Dialogue, Jerusalem, 2000.

Jad Islah : *Email to author, Ramallah*, 17 December 2001.

Alnuweiri Reem : *Speech at Conference Towards Our Liberation*, November 2001.

Abu Dayyeh Maha : *Address to the UN Security Council*, May 2002.

7

Between Secular Teaching and Islamic Preaching : Confused Identity of Soviet Central Asian Women

Nandini Bhattacharya

Central Asia was a part of Soviet Union and its socialist secularism for about seventy years. During this time, attempts were made from the government authority to impart secular, atheistic and scientific education throughout the USSR in order to remove unscientific and irrational influences of religion from public minds. These attempts were stronger in Central Asia, because, Islam, the religion of the majority in this region, was not just a religion, rather it controlled the way of life, education and had became part and parcel of the popular culture since the medieval times. Again, Islam as a tool of orthodox culture, used to put a number of restrictions on its women–and Central Asian society was no exception. The position of women under the Islamic rites was quite non-progressive and dependent on their male counterparts. This gender hierarchy, definitely, used to dwarf the identity of woman and her individual or collective position in society. When the Soviet rule ensued with a host of revolutionary ideals, it gave exposure to and brought many new dimensions to the women of this conservative society. In fact, the Soviet authorities claimed that scientific socialism and egalitarianism brought a phase of freedom and self-assertion to the women folk of Central Asia. At the same time, secular teaching under the banner of scientific socialism tried to impart atheistic education which challenged the centuries old position of Islam. And this uneasy tension between the Islamic ideals and Soviet ethos was reflected in the general psychology of Central Asian people. Women's identity was also largely affected by these two conflicting ethos, working against each other. Though women benefited from the introduction of secular scientific education, they could not, however, embrace the atheistic ideology as an alternative to Islam.

This remained a perpetual problem of the Soviet regime in Central Asia. Women's identity and position suffered because of this prevailing dichotomy in the ideological sphere.

History of the Process

In the initial phase of Soviet rule, there was more stress on eradicating superstitions and malpractices attached to Islamic beliefs. In fact, many of the Islamic practices were criticized and banned as unscientific and contrary to the socialist ideal. In the initial Soviet writings references are made of such practices as Paranza, Kalym, Polygamy, marriages of adolescent girls, and so on which used to affect the general position of women in society. That the attitude towards women in general, was very derogatory, is revealed by certain popular expressions used for women. For example, women were called, "long hair and short brain", or "*ozhia, zaif*" (useless, weak). There were popular proverbs which declared, "a son is a wealth, a daughter–a burden". These expressions implied the distinct hierarchical position of men and women in pre-Soviet Central Asian Society. Often unwanted daughters were given peculiar names, like Doyduk (we have enough), Besdir (sufficient) Ogul gerek (son wanted) and so on which indicated the humiliation and mental torture that the women used to undergo in the family.

This derogatory attitude towards women in general was referred to as 'feudal-Bay practices' or 'feudal survivals' by the Soviet authorities. In fact, according to Shariyat law women (girls) were fit for marriage at the age of nine and men (boys) at twelve. Though polygamy was a regular feature, it was limited to the wealthier section, because of another malpractice of 'bride price' (*Kalym*). Families with sufficient cattle and wealth at their disposal could think of marrying more than one girl to their son. The Soviet system, in its initial days tried to stop this malpractice which they thought would not give due justice to the position of women in society. The task was not so easy, as it was found as late as 1956, that in a collective farm of Kirghizia, eighteen men were found who had practiced polygamy. Another very obvious consequence of the abolition of *Kalym* apprehended was the increase in the number of divorces. It was surmised, as no stake of returning properties remained involved, the girls would take advantage of the Soviet courts and opt for divorce in large numbers. Cases of divorce really bean to occur. But, interestingly, men giving divorce to their wives were much more in number, than the other way round. So it was true that the girls' families did not have the obligation to return the amount of property given in *Kalym*–yet demand of divorce increased on part of the native males. This implied that ban on *Kalym* had little to do with increasing divorces. Increase in the number of divorce implied the change in the general attitude. Moreover, in pre-Soviet stage the presence of polygamy might have been another reason for less divorces. Anyway, compared to white Russia, or the other European parts of the USSR, the rate of divorce in this region remained relatively less throughout the Soviet period, as family bonds remained stronger.

The nature of marriages also began to undergo changes. Earlier, marriages generally meant negotiation between the two families. Men and women were not free to choose their life partners–but had to depend on their parental decision on this issue. As a result of Soviet influence, (many parents have come to believe that their children should be free to find their partners, but this liberalism was limited mainly to sons; daughters on the whole were not given full freedom in this respect; but at least they can usually accept or reject the matches arranged for them.) However, seeking the consent of the bride was not new with the Muslim society, as this provision was there in traditional Islamic laws. But, the pressure of the medieval feudal society had turned all these provisions into useless formalities. The Soviet system at least reopened the chances for the girls to use their will or consent in such a major decisions of life. Another result of this openness was occurrences of some mixed marriages between Central Asian and Russians or other Europeans residing in the provinces. But in most cases, the Central Asian women were not allowed to such alliances–rather, Central Asian men marrying Russian women became more marked in number.

Remarkable changes came in the practice of certain customs and costumes of traditional Islamic society, with the introduction of Soviet rule. Of these changes, the campaign against the use of *parandzha* (*pardah* or veil) was directly related to the changing social position of women. The Soviet authorities organized regular meetings to convince women to throw off this extra–cloak which posed some practical hindrances to work and was also objectionable by notion. B. Baybulatov mentioned that in Oshoblast of Kirghizia in an anti-*parandzha* meeting on 8th March, 1928, 110 women took vows to do away with *parandzha*. But, it was not a very smooth journey for women to emancipate themselves under the aegies of the socialist rule. There had been strong coercive forces working side by side against this 'move from above'. The anti-*parandzha* movement was at times faced with grave consequences, so much so, that men tried to murder their women who did not succumb to the reactionary pressure in favour of *parandzha*. An Uzbek woman named Tagirova who was strongly vocal in the anti-*parandzha* campaign, was murdered by her husband's initiative. There was another similar garment, popular among Turkmen women, named Yashmak–this was an ancient Persian custom of covering women's faces, so that their impure breath could not destroy the purity of the fire. This custom, in fact, was pre-Islamic in this region and equally derogatory to the image of women. The removal of *parandzha* and Yashmak were taken as wrong influences of westernization by the indigenous conservative society. Thus, the movement took a wrong turn to be misunderstood as a cultural encroachment. The Soviet authorities, in the late 50s, therefore, tried to give a new perspective–positive and practical, to remove the uncomfortable habit of *parandzha*. It is found that the Tajik daily 'Kommunist Tajikstana' highlighted the voice of a *Kolkhoznika* (a woman worker of a collective firm) in favour of removing *parandzha* and the reasons she furnished against the veil was not offensive towards indigenous tradition, but rather showed a simple realization of practical discomfiture for a working woman in her pedrformance. The Soviet system through its Kolkhoz models wanted to bring the women folk out of the domestic sphere and make them an active part of the mainstream workforce. Discriminatory and uncomfortable dress habits posed a hindrance to such developments. Thus, the anti-*parandzha* movement was not confined to fight against a symbol, instead it acquired a larger dimension which indirectly linked the whole issue with the new economic perspective of the region as well.

As a precondition to the introduction of women in the work-force, the Soviet authorities felt the need to educate women of this region along with their male counterparts. There had been a drastic change in the sphere of general education in the entire Soviet Union. For, through education, the authorities tried to impart the new ideology, values, ethos and scientific knowledge to re-build the material world with a revolutionary perspective. Different branches of education was bestowed with various responsibilities to realize the communist goal. The impact of this multi-dimensional education Programme had been uneven and complex in the multi-culture zone of Central Asia. Especially, the women's benefit from the Soviet secular and scientific education remained extremely inadequate and lopsided during the early decades of the regime because of many complex reasons. Soviet education had a number of missions, firstly, to remove illiteracy and attain the basic minimum education for all, secondly, practical and vocational education leading to job opportunities, thirdly, education used as a tool to promote atheistic feelings and most importantly, different branches of scientific knowledge used for eradication of all sorts of superstitions and malpractices. Especially, in the sphere of medicine and health, the scientific knowledge and practical use of that knowledge was stressed in the backward zones like Central Asia. Now, all these general educational move had its specific implications and consequences among the Central Asian women of different categories, i.e. rural, urban, old, young, working and housewife.

Most Soviet propaganda literature depicted the achievements of women in glorious terms. One such work by an Uzbek author, R. Tuzmuhamedov claimed, that having absolutely equal rights with men, the women of Central Asia are confident of their future. What better proof of this is there than the extent to which the Soviet East participates in state administration.

There is a high percentage of women in the Supreme Soviets of the Union republics : in Uzbekistan 30.8 per cent (141 women), in Kirghizia 35.4 per cent (120), in Tajikistan 33 per cent (104), in Turkmenia 35.1 per cent (100). Their percentage among the deputies to the local Soviets is still higher : in Uzbezistan 44.7 per cent (37030 women), in Kirghizia 43.6 per cent (10412), in Tajikistan 43.9 (8974) and in Turkmenia 42 per cent (7768).

He further continued with the achievements of the Uzbek women in educational and occupational grounds. Today almost a million women or 45 per cent of the total labour force are employed in the Uzbek national economy, 650, 000 of them work at collective forms. An estimated 176, 000 women have a higher and secondary specialized education, including 26, 000 engineers and technicians. Uzbek women plan an especially important role in the field of education and health protection. Nearly 2000 women are university and college instructors and 7000 are scientific workers. While, before the Revolution only an occasional Uzbek woman had a secondary education, today about 130, 000 girls study at schools and institutions of higher learning.

Just forty years ago Uzbek women were restricted to the *ichkari,* the inner part of the house, set aside for women and children; they were permitted to leave the house only with a *paranjah*, a thick horse hair net covering their faces. Today 22 of them are deputies of the Supreme Soviet of the republic. About 37, 000 are deputies of local Soviets, more than 2000 chairmen, vice-chairmen, secretaries or members of their executive committees and about 20 women are ministers or deputy ministers.

Source of Problems

The above picture, however, gave a partial representation of the women's position in Central Asia as could be realized from other documents like Soviet news daily and research papers. Neither in education, nor in occupation, was the emancipation of women complete. The process was much more complex, enduring and tenuous. The old tradition had deep-rooted and strong instruments of control which prevented the process of women's advancement in its full swing. Islamic belief and prejudices which fostered a patriarchal way of life in the medieval times, had much which prevented and restricted the growth of communist model in women's affairs.

It is true that there had been attempts to remove illiteracy and schools of primary and secondary levels were established in numbers in all parts of the USSR, Central Asia was no exception. In fact, women were encouraged to enter schools for education from the very onset of the Soviet rule. But, women's participation in literacy programmes remained markedly low compared to their male counterparts. The awareness to remove ignorance, however, might have developed through the decades of Bolshevik rule, which is why, the enrolment of girls in the primary education was, however, at par with the boys by the 70s. The marked drop appearing in female percentage in secondary education or middle school indicated the still prevailing discriminatory attitude towards women's need for education. In higher education, there was a sharp drop of both male and female participation. But the pattern of ratio, i. e. male : female did not change. The table below would indicate the level of education in each republic of Central Asia with a distinct male : female ratio per thousand.

	Primary Education		*Secondary Education*		*Higher Education*	
	1959	*1970*	*1959*	*1970*	*1959*	*1970*
Uzbek	192 (m)	272 (m)	392 (m)	476 (m)	16 (m)	39 (m)
	182 (f)	283 (f)	251 (f)	365 (f)	4 (f)	13 (f)
Kazakh	229 (m)	294 (m)	369 (m)	469 (m)	20 (m)	44 (m)
	215 (f)	289 (f)	207 (f)	347 (f)	5 (f)	20 (f)
Tajik	223 (m)	293 (m)	370 (m)	452 (m)	13 (m)	35 (m)
	198 (f)	311 (f)	229 (f)	321 (f)	2 (f)	7 (f)
Turkmen	185 (m)	277 (m)	427 (m)	486 (m)	20 (m)	42 (m)
	165 (f)	281 (f)	302 (f)	382 (f)	3 (f)	10 (f)
Kirghiz	189 (m)	282 (m)	403 (m)	469 (m)	17 (m)	41 (m)
	186 (f)	285 (f)	228 (f)	349 (f)	4 (f)	15 (f)

The above table shows how consistently, the women's participation in secondary and higher education remained lower compared to their male counterparts. Interestingly, the ratio of female enrolment in primary education remained higher than male during the 70s. This was a remarkable take off for the Central Asian republics. But the picture in the secondary level showed lack of sustenance in tempo. Moreover, there was another common feature of middle school drop-out's which could not be ignored as the data included enrolments of both complete and incomplete secondary education. The drop-out syndrome of women was so common and alarming that it used to be flashed in the republican newspapers, and also became an issue of concern for academic journals.

The Tajik daily Kommunist Tajikistana recorded as late as 1960/62 the problem of girl students dropping out with concern. 'Of girls entering the first grade in Tajik schools, only 14 per cent complete the 10th grade. Most of those who give up school are from the native population'. Two years later, the same newspaper flashed a more depressing picture, 'Speaking about the shortcomings in the educational system in Tajikistan at the 15th Congress of the Komsomol of Tajikistan, G. Bobosadykova said that in the Gissar Rayon out of 2000 girls entering the first grade of their secondary school, only six completed the course.10 Similarly, the Turkmen newspaper iterated the same complain, "Of every 100 Turkmen girls entering the first grade, only 15-20 finish middle school, and of every 100 admitted to the 8th grade, 30-35 finish school. Thus, there is a shortage of women among the Turkmen intelligentsia; for example, of the 14, 000 teachers in the republic only 1300 are women".

Probably, the feudal-bay mind set prevented the women's education programme after a certain point because education was rapidly enabling women to develop their independent opinions regarding marriage partners and such other vital decisions of life. Central Asia Review highlighted an individual case, where a girl named Bilbil Yalkabova, who was too keen to continue higher study in the Mary Pedagogical Institute and marry a man of her choice, was killed by her father's men the day after she passed the entrance examination for the said institute. This extreme event indicated how difficult the struggle was for a women to come out of the traditional framework, in spite of assistance and encouragement made by the government.

Thus, the Soviet programme of educating women, especially beyond the primary level remained a disappointing experience. That Tuzmuhamedov's narrative was just a half-story of the complex scenario became obvious from further research. The next important target of education was to create job opportunities and give rise to a conscious work force imbibed in Communist ideal. It is true that women in noticeable number began to join outdoor jobs, which was unthinkable prior to the Soviet regime. Yet, there were a number of constraints which hindered women's participation in the productive economy.

This was partly due to anchorage to past prejudices and partly due to excessive and elaborate family responsibilities. The real situation was, somehow, far from Tuzmuhamedov's account. In fact, his data on women's achievements in working place seems like a fairly tale if compared with the other side of the story. It is undoubtedly true, that the Soviet government could induce some women to come out of the traditional family network to devote time to the productive sphere of Soviet economy. Authorities also tried to encourage this attitude among the people of the region in general. For this, a new image of a worthy woman was created favouring revolutionary ideal. But the authorities, at the same time, were cautious enough to see that the new woman should fit into the traditional units of families. The popular Uzbek daily Pravda Vostoka mentioned a wedding where it praised the bride for she was "a beauty, who this year has picked nine tons of cotton. Everybody would be eager to marry one like her. But this luck has befallen but one man." The further detail about the wedding added that as the ceremony was taking place in winter, it did not divert people from their work in the Kolkhoz. Thus, encouragement to work was highly stressed equally for men and women. And eligibility of both men and women in the Bolshevik ideal began to be measured on the sole criterion of productivity and contribution to the national wealth.

However, in spite of the official encouragement and furnished data by propaganda literature, the general standard of women's participation in the work force remained quite dissatisfactory. In fact, later, minute research proved that lack of women's participation had hampered the growth of both industry and agriculture in this region compared to other parts of the USSR. More interestingly, it was found that even if women came to work, they came with lesser skill and therefore, their labour could not be utilized in its full scope. As Ajay Patnaik analysed, "Women constituted about half the able-bodied population on the Uzbek collective farms, but constituted less than 3 per cent of the mechanized agricultural workers. As many as 99 per cent of the manual workers on the state farms were women. In the industrial and service spheres, the same sex disproportion in skill terms existed. A. Patnaik also gave the percentage of working women in each republics : Uzbeks 34 per cent, Tajiks 31 per cent, Kirghiz 41 per cent and Turkmen 33 per cent.

Susan Bridger's finding draws attention to skilled-unskilled differences among working women of Central Asia. She found that in a good number of cases where women even after graduating from rural vocational-technical colleges, could cope with the terms of neither the duties of machine operators nor leave for other jobs to town–they preferred to stay in the villages and work as manual labourers–in spite of being over qualified for these jobs.

Thus problems regarding women's occupation remained a chronic feature of Soviet Central Asia mainly because of the traditional attitude. The role of family as a restrictive force continued to hinder the development of women, in spite of the revolutionary regime.

Impact of Religion

Another perspective of education, which seemed most relevant in the context of Muslim society, was atheistic propaganda and its impact. Here the attitude of women appeared most varied, paradoxical, confused yet understandable from the psycho-social perspective. Atheistic propaganda was a universal programme of the Soviet regime, directed against all religious beliefs. Though the Soviet constitution gave her citizens the ideological right either to follow or not to follow any religion, there was a constant and conscious attempt to reduce the influences of religion, especially unscientific, superstitious practices allied to popular religious perceptions. But atheistic propaganda in various forms became a serious experimentation on the largest non–Slavic population of the USSR, who followed Islam. The impact of atheistic propaganda in Central Asia was varied and complex, and it was even more complex and peculiar with the Central Asian women. This was partly because of the strong old ties and customs prevailing in family and society, it was also partly because of lack of education and exposure for which dependence and faith in religion remained strong.

There was a common perception, that with the spread of revolutionary ideal and scientific knowledge, religiosity would naturally wither away. Therefore, official position towards religion was that of an obsolete ideology, only followed by the uneducated and old people. But, by the 70s, there matured a young generation who were born in the post-revolutionary phase, when these young people, both men and women, began to embrace Islam strongly, it created an alarm among the authorities. Consequently, the atheistic activities came under minute scrutiny. In the process, many interesting information about the religious attachments of Central Asian women were also revealed.

The official survey on atheism basically divided the society into three groups, believer, non-believer and indifferent. Or, at times a sub-group titled 'mildly believer' appeared which included a floating number, whose religious behaviour was usually restricted to participation in occasional rituals and festive ceremonies allied to Islam.

However, in general Soviet studies, majority of data on beliefs were not gender-specific, therefore the exact position and number of women divided in these three/four categories could not be made. Yet, it was secured from some articles of 70s and 80s, that the Soviet scholars seemed perplexed by the higher percentage of women's allegiance to Islam, compared to their male counterparts. M.A. Tolmacheva, in her article titled, "The Muslim Women in Soviet Central Asia" stated, "The phenomenon which appeared as a paradox to many Soviet sociologists in the allegiance of markedly higher percentages of women, than men to Islam in the face of the generally discriminatory, anti-feminist spirit of Islamic law and the conservative social customs it supports". Reasons were sought for this over religiosity amongst women. In a survey under Tolmacheva amongst Turkmen women, it was found that education had a direct correlation with spreading atheism amongst women. According to her findings, "Those with higher and junior-college education provided the bulk of atheists and non-believers (up to 100 per cent); those with elementary education or less-the bulk of believers". Another reason for women's over-religiosity pointed out by scholars was the lack of participation in the productive economy outside home. In fact, Tolmacheva quoted an extremely bold and practical statement by a worker woman of Ashkabad : "I have six children, and if I don't work Allah will not feed them". This kind of practical realization was possible in cases of those who had to struggle for their survival in the outside world. Interestingly, here too, the concern of the woman was the well being of her family. She did not seem to get into any ideological debate on religion vs. atheism.

Again, S. Dadabaeva, the director of the Scientific Atheism Department of the Philosophy Faculty of the Tajik SSR, Academy of Sciences, who made serious efforts to make the atheistic propaganda useful for the women of Central Asia, also wrote that women usually became victims of the preaching of mullahs and ishans because, not all of them took part in 'social production'. Interestingly, she tried to locate the reasons for the non-participation of women outside home, in the lack of necessary support systems, such as kindergartens and crèches, rather than inherent conservatism of the society. She also highlighted the fact that in residential areas, the educational work was lax and that too contributed to the attachment to tradition and in conformity to tradition–attachment to Islamic belief and practices.

However, some aspects of women's religiosity or attachments to religious customs and practices remained inexplicable in terms of education or occupational attachments. In fact, atheistic education became almost a complete failure so far as observation of religions rituals and festivals were concerned. From different researches it appeared that those who were, otherwise, reluctant to observe everyday practices under Islam, eagerly participated and enjoyed the ceremonies, festivals and important family rituals, like marriage, circumcision, religious burial, fasting of *uruza* or *Ramadan* and so on. However, participation in this kind of religious festivals was not gender specific. Rather, it was found that the young generation, who were otherwise quite indifferent about religion, seemed equally interested in observing such practices. It is revealed from different Soviet research that the number of believers markedly increased during the month of *uruza*. However, the intensity of observance varied from person to person. From Tolmacheva's research it was revealed that in an Ashkabad factory, the ritual prayer was observed by a small minority of believers at the prescribed rate of five times daily (none or 1.3 per cent). No prayer at all was offered by 67 to 85 per cent; of those who do pray, the majority perform *namaz* 1 to 2 times. The fast during Ramadan was observed by 1.2 to 16.9 per cent.

But, Tolmacheva also observed that, "Once it comes to the celebration at the conclusion of the fast, the nature of statistics changes and the figures begin to include non-believers as well. While Ramadan is mostly observed by the older people, the feast at the end of the month is observed by many young women (and men), believers and unbelievers alike, and the Feast of Sacrifice (Kurban-Bayram) is celebrated by all. The fast of Ramadan used to be observed widely, yet unevenly and irregularly.

However, this intensity of general religiosity alarmed the Soviet authority during the 70s and 80s, because, the younger generation took up these religious festivals and rituals as part of their national tradition and gave a stronger dimension to the survival of Islam in its changed atmosphere. In fact, once Islamic rites and rituals began to be taken with a spirit of national identity, it threatened the alternative secular identity preached so long by the Soviet regime. To prevent this development, the strategy taken was to monitor the family atmosphere of the children so that any kind of illusory identity could not be introduced in their innocent minds. Here, special attention was given to the mothers as the primary mentor of the children at home. Dadabaeva also admitted the fact that, many women in Tajikistan, Uzbekistan etc. were housewives, and therefore, played a greater role in the upbringing of their children than their European

(Russian) counterparts and 'there are indeed more believers among the men'. Atheistic propaganda among women, therefore, received a new acceleration at this stage. 'Special Universities had been set up in Kirghizia's Osh oblast, catering mainly for housewives, with lectures on child education, running the household and health. The Komsoml's girls brigade was supposedly very effective in this new method of propaganda which was directed to be 'individual work with believers' instead of confining into impersonal formal lectures. The new intensity of atheistic propaganda was found at its height in Tajikistan in 1980, when within six months of time, there were 4000 lectures held on atheism aided by practical-scientific conferences, question answer evenings and film lectures.

Anyway, regarding observance of religion and manifestation of religious attachments, women often differed from their male counterparts. For example, in day to day prayer women could seldom visit the mosques, even the annual pilgrimage to Meccah (Hajj) hardly included any women. This was because of the restrictive nature of the traditional society and obviously had nothing to do with Soviet atheistic preaching. Women's religiosity used to find expression in some other spheres which were totally denounced as unscientific activities by the authorities. In fact, imparting scientific knowledge was supposedly the most important responsibility of Soviet education. But to their utter disappointment, the authorities realized that belief in super-natural powers inexplicable in terms of science kept containing in various forms, in spite of providing good facilities in health and medicine.

Soviet regime was strongly opposed to all sorts of cult worshipping which composed an important part of popular Islam and denounced them as unscientific superstitions. Writing as early as 1960, O.A. Sukhareva described in details about these religious practices outside the official stand of

Islam. Her list included the cult of saints, visit to the holy *mazar* or holy shrines or mausoleums of saints, which was very popular, the influence of the sufi saints or Ishans also served as an important feature of popular religious activities. Along with these, there were deification of many saints, that included some women saints as well, such as, Bibi-Seshambe, Bibi-Mushkilikushayi, Ambarona etc. Belief in magic, witchcraft, evil eye and charms were widespread. Sukjareva lamented that, "Survivals of ancient cults existed under the cover of Islams and acquired a Muslim aspect by the inclusion in exorcisms and appeals to the spirits of the name of Allah". This tradition, though firmly opposed and banned by the Soviet authorities kept continuing. There are references of these localized practices of Islam, as popularity of Ishans as effective faith healers, dispensers of amulets and talismans, venerating the holy shrines of Shah-i-Zindeh in Uzbekistan, Tomb of Sultan Vais Baba in Turkmenistan and so on, as late as 1989. All these places were visited by women of different ages and backgrounds in order to rid themselves of various types of sufferings. At times of distress or to seek peace in general, women found the teachings of Islam or their interpretations in local forms quite comforting. In fact, the use of amulets and magic designs were most popular among women.

The amulets, which were actually certain types of wood pieces, supposedly containing magic power and were largely bought by Central Asian women. The reasons for such dependence on unscientific powers were usually related to fertility, childbearing and illness of the children. Overstress on motherhood as a feature of popular culture can probably explain the local cult of female spirits denoting the spheres of fertility, ancestral tradition of venerating mother and health spirit etc remaining so strong in practice.

Conclusion : One very interesting feature of believers in Central Asia was their lack of knowledge about the real meaning of rites or ceremonies. Actually, the use of Arabic scripts for any holy word gave it a magical appearance, as most people could not read this script. So women were also mostly oblivious of the actual words written on amulets and their meanings. Rather they preferred blindly to believe in the magic power of those unknown symbols. In spite of rigorous propaganda against these unscientific activities and state arrangements to protect health and hygene through modern medicines-the dependence of women on these unscientific and inexplicable supernatural powers continued. Tolmacheva admitted, "And finally, each child's illness, especially in rural families, tend to perpetuate women's belief in evil spirits and the evil eye and promote their spiritual dependence on amulets, saints, pilgrimages, prayer and sacrifice (This continues to be a widespread phenomenon even where medical assistance is really available". Women's dependence on these magic powers can be explained in terms of the well being of their children and attainment of motherhood–which together implied their close ties with their families. S. Dadabaeva, after long analysis accepted that, religion meant a complex social phenomenon, with traditions, rites and festivals formed over centuries, that in the past permeated people's mode of life and psychology which along with the new method of education gave rise to "split" personalities with knowledge ensconced on the one side and conviction on the other. But Dadabaeva, being an active cadre did not take a defeatist attitude. Rather she suggested that forms of atheistic work which would influence a person's emotional world should be stressed. That women took religion as an emotional anchorage was understood in the last lap of Soviet rule.

Interestingly, because of the traditional character of Islam, it did not or could not inspire much ideological or nationalist aspirations among women. Cultural impact of Islam on men and women had two distinctly different directions. Tolmacheva observed, "while the nationalist component feeding Islamic sentiment seems to come primarily from men, the women's contribution to maintenance of the ritual arises mostly from the home and child bearing. Even during the period of religious revivalism leading to nationalist movements here, seldom references of women's participation in those movements were found. In spite of women's continued faith in the religion, they never showed any mass character of violence against the atheist regime, or participated in any extremist or militant incitements inspired by Islamic fundamentalism.

Finally, Perestroika and the removal of Soviet regime from this territory created a tremendous chaos and indecisiveness in all spheres of life. As an alternative ideology to socialism, Islamic revival became strong. Most of the Soviet restrictions on Islamic institutions and observance were removed. The number of mosques multiplied, prayers increased, most of the banned religious societies were legalized, traditionalist fervour was consciously revived in all spheres of life. This widespread 'go-back' psychology, never the less, had little imposition on the Central Asian women. Even the most severely fundamentalist political groups thriving in power, or after coming to power, did not issue any universal dress code for women. Re-introduction of *parandza*, which was widely apprehended by the outside world, did not take place. Revival of Islamic tradition, however, did not include suppression of women and restriction in their movements. Absence of reimposition on women is a strong indicator of a distinct respectful position of power in indigenous Islamic society, accepted by their own male counterparts. And this was to a large extent, the result of Soviet experience.

Soviet Central Asian women could and did absorb some of the secular scientific influences, yet could not do away with all the tenets of Islam. Religious attachment of the region was too deep rooted to be removed only by scientific arguments and legal restrictions. Women kept on clinging to the irrational faiths, mainly for emotional support.

Thus, very interestingly, these dual forces of atheism and Islam which stood juxtaposed against each other, gave birth to a very confused identity for the majority of the Central Asian women. Actually, both Soviet secularism as well as Islamic belief and practices were two exclusivist ideologies. Embracing either of them imposed a number of restrictions on the observance of the other. This created a consistent problem to the spontaneous development of women's identity. Interestingly, women themselves, unconsciously though, partially absorbed both the ideologies and were partly benefited by them. But the clause of rejecting one to embrace another created the sole trouble and confused the position of women in this complex socio-cultural context.

References

Central Asia Review, *People of Central Asia : Social Customs*, 1959, p. 214.

R. Tuzmuhamedov, *How the National Question was Solved in Soviet Central Asia*, 1974.

(A Reply to Falsifiers) Progress Publishers, Moscow, 1973.

Shirin Akiner, *Islamic Peoples of the Soviet Union*, Kegan Paul International, London, Boston, Melbourne and Henley, 1976.

Kommunist Tajikistana, 7. 8. 60.

Kommunist Tajikistana, 26. 1. 62.

Turkmenskaya Iskra, 18. 8. 60.

Pravda Vostoka, 1. 1. 58.

Ajay Patnaik, *Central Asia, between Modernity and Tradition*, Konark Publishers Pvt. Ltd., 1996, p. 137.

Susan Bridger, *Women in the Soviet Countryside*, Cambridge, 1987.

M. A. Tolmacheva, "The Muslim women in Soviet Central Asia", *Central Asian Survey*, 1993, 12 (4).

S. Dadabaeva, Sama Soboi ne Otmoret, Kommunist Tajikistana, 31st October, 1980.

M. A. Tolmacheva, *op.cit.*, pp. 540-545. Alexander Bennigsen, Islam in Retrospect, Central Asian Survey, 1987, pp. 93-97.

B. Ryspaev, Sovetskaya Krigizia, 16. 9. 1980.

O. A. Sukhareva, Islam V. Uzbeskistane, Tashkent, 1960.

Maria Eva Subtelny, The Cult of Holy Places : Religious Practices Among Soviet Muslims, Middle East Journal, Vol. 43, No. 4, Autumn, 1989.

As part of Soviet Education policy, one uniform script was introduced for all languages. Cyrillic script had, therefore, replaced the Arabic scripts of the Central Asian languages. That is why whether educated or uneducated Arabic script remained mostly alien to the indigenous people.

M. Haghayeghi, Islam and Politics in Central Asia, St. Martins Press, New York, 1995.

8

Between "Homeland" and Home : Russian Women in Uzbekistan

Anita Sengupta

Most discourses on gender and nation are interwoven and never more so than at times when nationhood is being reconstructed. It is not surprising therefore, that, the process of reconfiguration of new states in the post Soviet space has a gender dimension and women form a significant social group in the process of the redefinition of the states. Much of the literature that focuses on this ongoing process of redefinition examines the reconsolidation of control mechanisms over women in the course of the reconstruction of the nation and the reinvention of their role as repositories of tradition. The focus of this literature, however, is only on the titular nationalities. Women who constitute national minorities in the post Soviet states are confronted with an entirely different set of dilemmas while redefining their identities in the course of this transition. This article is an attempt at examining the unique position of ethnic Russian women in the non Russian regions of the former Soviet Union in general and Uzbekistan in particular and the various questions confronting them as they redefine themselves as a "new" ethnic minority in a nationalizing state.

Caught between their Central Asian "home" and Russian "homeland" and faced with an increasing sense of isolation and alienation in regions where they have been born and where they have lived all their lives, Russian women today constitute an unique group of persons faced with difficult choices. Most of them have not been physically dislocated from regions that they had considered as "home" and now also recognize that actual threats to their life and security is very nearly non-existent. Yet there is a sense of unease about the fact that their "ethnic homeland" has over the recent past become more and more distant and their economic and social position in the new states more fragile. This has been prompted not so much by external factors as by the necessity of an internal reconstruction of ones views about one's place in life beyond the borders of the ethnic homeland. Refused dual citizenship in states like Uzbekistan they are also faced with having to readjust to new situations where legislation has forced them to rethink their cultural linkages and linguistic abilities. All of this leads to a pervading sense of dislocation and insecurity that today characterizes their position as they search for their own political space and identity.

This article examines the complexities in the narratives of displacement among Russian women in Uzbekistan and reflects on how in its turn this affects their sense of belonging and identity. This examination would necessarily have to be made in the backdrop of the present search for identity and territorial identification among the Central Asian peoples themselves that today presents all other minorities with difficult choices. However, it also needs to be kept in mind that while the current projection of "Uzbekness" is problematic it is equally true that cultural assimilation of the Russian population within the states has also traditionally been low to the extent that few are familiar even with the local languages.

Homelands and Identity

Central Asia is my homeland because it is here that I was born, was moulded as a specialist and achieved recognition. But Russia also is my homeland because from childhood my soul has been infused with Russian culture.

The making of political identity has inevitably been accompanied by a search for territorial spaces as the legitimate homeland of communities. This sense of spatial identity and the search for homelands gained momentum in the wake of post imperial attempts at assigning clearly demarcated spaces to groups defined as "nationalities" and the subsequent acceptance of identities as place bound. The assertion behind this emphasis is the claim that every community essentially belongs to its "homeland". This sense of exclusiveness was enhanced by the naming of the entities after the majority national communities, Kazakhstan, Uzbekistan and so forth literally meaning "land of the Kazakhs, land of the Uzbeks".

Homelands have been variously defined. In one of the most comprehensive definitions, Michael P Conzen, defines homelands as geographical cultural regions with special characteristics (of long ancestry, once exclusively occupied and now or once politically independent) result only from self consciously separate "peoples" whose sense of peoplehood and control of territory sustains the fact of, or ambitions for political and cultural independence.

It is significant to keep in mind that homelands have been variously conceptualized and are most frequently characterized in the language of nostalgia and longing, of a search for self or origin. Homelands are also conceptualized as places of geographical and ethnic origin and as a space of social, economic and political security. In situations of displacement, homelands are often imagined as the place where ones' ancestors were born. A major problem that remains unresolved is that of determining whether homelands are time specific. In many cases it has been noted that homelands have been identified with residence and as the place where a person was born rather than as the place where ones ancestors were born. Concepts of the homeland therefore change over generations and with time. It is now generally accepted that "homeland" is a political category. A state becomes a "homeland" when a claim is made that the people belong to the state and that their interests must be protected by the state. Brubaker notes :

"The concept of homeland.... denotes a dynamic political stance or a family of related yet competing stances—not a static condition—not a "thing". Common to homeland stances are the axiom of shared nationhood across the boundaries of state and citizenship and the idea that this shared nationhood makes the state responsible, in some sense not only for its own citizens but also for ethnic co-nationals who live in other states and possesses other citizenship... But there is a great variation among particular homeland stances, great variation in understandings of just what the asserted responsibility for ethnic co-nationals entail."

Conceptions of homelands and how these affect the sense of nation, community and identity is significant for an understanding of the relationship between territoriality and identity. An understanding of the concept of homelands has become particularly significant for the Central Asian region in the wake of the emergence of the sovereign states as they offer new insights into changing notions of sovereignty and territoriality. The legalization of political boundaries, however, has complicated this search as most demands for homelands do not correspond to present demarcations. And in any case, most concepts of homeland overlap with that of others leading to potential conflict situations. Narratives of displacement become significant here and in most cases the reassertion of identity is based on ideas of a mythical space to which the community claims special rights.

The determination of previously determined space brings to the forefront the significance of identification of homelands and the claim that the current boundaries of the state correspond to these ancient homelands. Along with this, the construction of a "post-Soviet" identity becomes imperative for the legitimization of the new states. For Uzbek nationalists today, for instance, it is deemed crucial to have a political community to belong to and to define that community in terms of language, religion and history. Yet, this requirement also inevitably results in a dilemma for minority groups whose own claims of a homeland are then challenged and cultural identities questioned. A closer look at this shaping of a "post-Soviet future", through the negotiation of the politics of transition by the state and the question of how the new state legitimizes its emergence as a new entity and deals with the problems of transition to a new state form, becomes crucial here. Such examinations clearly demonstrate that there is recognition of the fluidity of cultural identity within the boundaries of the state, which predicates the nationalist imperatives and constitutes the dilemma of a transitional polity.

The Russian Dilemma

"It is hard to go back... It is not even back really."

... She trembled a little as she spoke. "But they are making it hard for us. If you want a job you have to apply in Turkoman. The first question they ask is : Do you speak Turkoman? But I have never learnt this language..." She said this with wondering regret... overnight she was a foreigner in her birthplace.

I asked "But where will you go?"

"I don't know. I have relatives in Moscow, but its impossible to find work there... Its too hard a place... harder than here"...

This poignant description is from Colin Thubron's *The Lost Heart of Asia*, where in the course of a conversation to a half Russian, half Armenian lady, married till recently to a Turkoman, the author portrays the sense of insecurity that is today evident among ethnic Russian women in the Central Asian region. Her ambivalent, "... in a way", in response to the author's query of whether she belonged to the region is interpreted by the author to be reflective of the fact that she did not, in fact, belong anywhere, neither to Russia nor to the Central Asian region. This passage, where the author records her predicament, is representative of the position of groups of ethnic Russian women who now feel displaced from places that had till recently been "home".

One of the most dramatic transformations in recent years has been the change in status of some 25 million ethnic Russians, now resident in the various independent states of the CIS, from a majority group into minorities with disputed identities and uncertain futures. The designation of non-Russians as minorities in the former Soviet Union, has been reversed through an abrupt change of fortunes where Russians are today the new "minorities" in the post Soviet states. Ethnic Russians are now a people in quest of an identity as suddenly many of them find themselves to be deemed as "foreigners" in what they had once considered their "homeland". As reconfigurations create "new" minorities and construct new definitions of majority identity notions of "homeland" have been transformed among Russian women in the Central Asian region.

Russian migration to the Central Asian region is not a recent event. The first wave of Russians to have settled in Turkestan consisted of former soldiers, colonial functionaries, traders and priests who arrived in the second half of the 19th century. The second wave consisted of peasants who were settled in the newly acquired lands. Further migration took place during the period of the Revolution and the post

Revolution decade and consisted of soldiers and new functionaries as well as a section of the Russian peasantry. The fourth wave of Russian migration began in the years of the Second World War due to the evacuation of industrial units and consisted of workers. The fifth and final wave of Russian migration to Central Asia began around the end of the 1960's and early 1970's and was stimulated by the government. Consisting of the technical intelligentsia and workers, this migration also led to a significant rise in the number of Russian functionaries in the Republics' administrative and industrial structures. Many women were part of the waves of migration, including workers, engineers and technicians. Russian women also came to Central Asia with soldier or officer husbands. With the dissolution of the Soviet Union, the dilemma of how and where to live in the future came to the forefront in a big way for many of these women. Responses to the situation has differed widely, ranging from recent migrants who wish to repatriate to Russia and those who were born here and still consider this as home. The dilemma of Russian women married to Uzbek, Kyrgyz, Kazak or Turkmen spouses is a particularly difficult one, as their acceptance within the Central Asian families, has in a number of instances, been reduced in the aftermath of disintegration of the Soviet Union.

There are different ways of conceiving what it means to be a Russian in Uzbekistan today. Russians in Uzbekistan may be understood as being persons of Russian ethnic origin, most of whom speak Russian as their native language who nonetheless belong to the Uzbek nation, understood as a political territorial or civic nation as the nation of and for all its citizens regardless of language and ethnicity, not as the nation of and for ethnic Uzbeks. Were this the prevailing self-understanding of Russians in Uzbekistan there would be no Russian "national minority". There would be persons of Russian ethnic origin and persons speaking Russian as a native language but they would not claim to be members of the Russian nation or nationality. However, unfortunately, this is hardly the dominant notion, particularly in the face of the policies of the "nationalizing" state.

The question of "national minorities" thus has to be essentially examined against that of the state which designates them as the minority. Brubaker refers to these states as "nationalizing" states to emphasize that what is being referred to, is once again, a dynamic political stance.

Characteristic of this stance or set of stances is the tendency to see the state as an "unrealized" nation-state, as a state destined to be a nation-state, the state of and for a particular nation, but not yet in fact a nation-state (at least not to a sufficient degree); and the concomitant disposition to remedy this perceived defect, to make the state what it is properly and legitimately destined to be by promoting the language, culture, demographic position, economic flourishing or political hegemony of the nominally state bearing nation.

The problem in Uzbekistan, as in all the other states, is the creation of a "national identity". Yet, to a very large extent there remains even today a sense of uneasiness about this new found "nationalism" and "national identity". Amidst this uncertainty is a persistent effort to stress on the "Uzbekness" of the nation, particularly in the official political rhetoric "... a feature distinctive of Uzbekistan is its original ethnic structure. Although representatives of more than 100 nations and ethnic groups live on the territory of the Republic, the majority of the inhabitants are Uzbeks". There is also an attempt to point out that the "Uzbek Republic is the homeland of all Uzbeks." Since the territory of Uzbekistan is virtually the only domain of Uzbek national statehood, the Republic is called upon to become a cultural and spiritual centre for all Uzbeks irrespective of their domicile. Citizenship in the Republic is open to all Uzbeks who themselves or whose predecessors had to emigrate from Uzbekistan during the tragic circumstances of the past."

Scholars like Kadir Alimov have pointed out "there can be little doubt that all the individual Muslim inhabitants of the territory now known as Uzbekistan have a strong attachment to their homeland and its Islamic culture". The propaganda of the "titular ethno-nationalists" is based on the fact that there exists an ancient Uzbek nation to which the indigenous population of Uzbekistan belong and that Uzbeks live on the territory of their nation state. Elements of this history, which seek to emphasize a long suppressed and dormant Uzbek identity, have the potential to aggravate relations with the numerous ethnic minorities residing in Uzbekistan. In common with all new states, Uzbekistan is faced with a difficult conundrum : it must simultaneously promote and implement a rediscovered history to the satisfaction of the people, while restraining those elements from pursuing an overzealous application of Uzbek ethnic identity.

While the need for preservation of national culture is clearly stated, statements with regard to ethnic rights are much more generally worded. "Uzbekistan is a state which ensures the rights and freedoms of all citizens irrespective of their ethnic origin, religious beliefs, social status or political conviction," or "the protection of the interests and rights of ethnic minorities by creating guarantees for the preservation and development of their cultures, language, national customs and traditions and participation in the activities of the government as well as public life". These generalizing statements serve the purpose of ignoring the existence of any ethnic problem.

The ethnic identity of Russians and their attitudes to ethnic relations have changed significantly with the collapse of the Soviet Union. According to Leokadia Drobizheva three factors played a role in this (1) the shock of losing their status as the ruling nation (2) the political struggle in which leading groups want to rely on ethnic patriotism (3) the sharp rise in ethnic competition in the social and working spheres. Whereas the Russians lost their ruling status in 1988-89 and were drawn into the political struggle in the last few years ethnic competition had begun to be felt even earlier. The abrupt end of Russian dominance means that they are now having to think hard about their Russian identity, something they always took for granted. The questions that seem to be uppermost in their minds today are-can they be full citizens of Russia and of another Republic simultaneously? And where exactly do Russia's borders end?

Russian ethnic attitudes in Central Asia today are "complex and tense" for here there have been no great shift in political or economic position with Soviet era leaders having changed stance to retain power. However, the fact remains that 36 per cent of the workers in heavy industry are Russians. Russian education standards are higher than Uzbeks, a significant proportion of Russians, 48 per cent are professionals and there is no competition in management. By 1970 Muslims accounted for only 51.15 per cent of all industrial workers in Uzbekistan, 44.3 per cent in Tajikistan, 31.2 per cent in Kyrgyzstan, 31.1 per cent in Turkmenistan, and 24.1 per cent in Kazakhstan. In Uzbekistan, Uzbeks accounted for 36.25 per cent of the overall industrial labour force, and even less in many essential fields : 18.35 per cent in machine building, 20 per cent in chemical and petrochemical industries and 22.45 per cent in oil refining. 1973 data shows a slight improvement : 39.95 per cent in the total labour force, 20.7 per cent in machine building, 29.5 per cent in oil refining, 26.4 per cent in chemicals and petrochemicals. What is more serious is that no significant progress had been achieved since 1967, in spite of educational advancement.

Results of representative cross-cultural investigations carried out in 1970-71, 1980-81, 1988 and 1991 showed that while previously a majority of Russians had been satisfied with their work and viewed their life optimistically now a majority do not think so. Also a larger percentage now consider working in ethnically mixed groups difficult. About 70 per cent now oppose mixed marriages, twice as much as ten years ago. By the end of 1991, 80-90 per cent of Russians in Tashkent felt that ethnic attitudes had deteriorated, and 70-80 per cent expected further problems. Also Russians feared the rise of Islam and were terrified by the events of Ferghana, Namangan and Osh.

There is also rising ethnic consciousness among Russians whose cultural adaptation has never been very high. That assimilation of ethnic Russians is weak was reflected in a study conducted in January-February 1992 which recorded the responses of children of old Russian inhabitants and Uzbeks in Tashkent. The author has used the responses of the children to show that children followed ethnic characteristics in their choice. This has been interpreted as a sign of the cultural distance between the two groups. On the other hand despite the presence of large Slavic and other minorities in the state, Uzbeks found it difficult to name even a few social traditions of another ethnic group. A majority of Russians in Uzbekistan feel that there should be two state languages in Uzbekistan, not just Uzbek.

The massive effort at politicization of space that has resulted due to the emergence of "nationalizing" states in the Central Asian Republic has meant that a number of changes are now underway in the states. One of the most significant is the proclamation of new language laws in the states, establishing the legal hegemony of local languages over Russian. This has meant that the socio-professional status of the Russian population is seen as being threatened in the newly independent states. It is significant to keep in mind that the integration of the Russian population within the Central Asian societies was low. In particular, most of the Russian population never felt the need to learn the local languages. This today means that in the face of introduction of new language laws, the possibility of discrimination is higher. Here, the most commonly heard complaint is that the possibility of finding jobs and prospects of promotion has been significantly reduced in the aftermath of independence of the Republics. Also there are doubts about the future of children particularly since the ability to acquire the Central Asian languages has now become very important as the use of Russian for all official purposes is likely to be reduced.

This is clearly evident from what Alla Chervova notes:

> The number of Russian schools will be reduced, Russian will no longer be used in business correspondence and so the demand for Russian language teachers will fall. Russian will gradually lose its present social status, particularly the female teachers will have to go for less meaningful jobs.

While the out migration of Russian population from the Central Asian Republics to the RSFSR had begun by the end of the 1980's, there is also the understanding among the Russian population that Russians in the Central Asian Republics are different from the Russians living in Russia. This is because their domestic lifestyle has assimilated much of what is characteristic of the Central Asian way of life. In fact on migrating to Russia they are identified as "Kyrgyz Russians" or "Uzbek Russians". Life in Russia is difficult and more often than not job prospects are low. Moreover, for most of the migrating Russians, Moscow and Russia were alien regions and their sense of displacement is magnified by the fact that integration into Russian society in Russia is proving to be difficult.

In general the impression is that of not wanting to go anywhere but to continue living in Uzbekistan, since life in Russia is said to be even more difficult. This has led to a tragedy that is reflected in these words of Natasha, a school teacher in Samarkand.

> It is not a question of returning to Russia. I have never lived there. I was born and brought up in Samarkand and my parents have lived here most of their lives and are committed to it. I love this place and my whole life is here. I don't look forward to going to Russia. I hardly know it, I hate Moscow... Increasingly we are being looked upon as foreigners and I do not think it will be long before we hear shouts of "Russians go home".

A Search for Homelands

> I myself grew up in an Uzbek mohallah and the question of where to live has simply not arisen until now. The point is not the state language—to a certain extent it is possible to learn Uzbek, even at my age, the point is different—a question of one's homeland. It would be strange to suddenly find oneself an emigrant, it is something entirely unexpected. Yes, this is our home, we have many people dear to us here, one has passed one's whole life here. But life is just not going to be the same here as it was before.... we have many friends, people of many nationalities. And they have passed a good citizenship law. But I see my future as lying in Russia. Not because someone is making me leave... I am not certain that my opinions will count when decisions regarding my fate are being made. I know that in Russia it would not be easy for me either because there too there are strong vestiges of the old regime. But I believe that nevertheless, I need to be in my homeland, although in my heart I will always retain a great love for Uzbekistan.

A sizeable proportion of the Russian women living in the cities of Uzbekistan today were born in Central Asia. They have memories of their fathers or grandfathers who had fought and sacrificed here during the Revolution and also for most of them their parents or grandparents are buried here. Yet, while recognizing that having been born here, this is their "homeland", most of them also point to the fact that having been infused since childhood with Russian culture, Russia is also "homeland". In fact many point out that this cultural difference is so significant that the sense of Central Asia being "homeland" is significantly reduced. The ambiguity and uncertainty that pervades is evident from responses to a study that sought to interpret the recent changes in the lives of Central Asian women.

That this sense of duality is being felt by the younger groups of Russian women also and among those who were born in the region is evident from the reply of a young student at the Tashkent Institute of communications, while answering the same question

Uzbekistan is my homeland, it is difficult for me to imagine that I could be able to live elsewhere. My home, friends and relatives are all here. But neither is Russia an alien country... I have always found that Russians in Central Asia differ from Russians in Russia itself. My elder sister and her husband left four years ago for the Orenburg region. They are very depressed... I do not want to go anywhere, The main problem for me is the language, even though at the daily level, I do not have any problems with it. But if it came to using Uzbek for my professional work, it would be very difficult for me. Life in Uzbekistan differs from life in Russia and is dictated by another way of doing things, another way of thinking.

The last decade has shown that in diaglossic societies, like the Central Asian one, abrupt changes in language usage is improbable. While this largely negates the most significant difficultly identified by the Russian women in the Central Asian region, yet, the sense of displacement that has now become pervasive means that most echo the desire to repatriate to Russia. In a process of what is termed as "hidden migration" many of the younger generation are migrating to Russia with the hope of the older members of the families following subsequently. There are other instances of "hidden migration" where Russian women, born and brought up in the Central Asian states, are marrying men settled in Russia in order to migrate. A search for "homeland" thus continues to be one of the fallouts of the politicization of space that accompanies the process of nationalization of states.

There is also a sense of unease about the future of children. Galina Pugachenkova, clearly states "... for my children and grandchildren there is no future here." Vallentina Artemova, similarly notes

> I have no specific ideas about my future. I would like to leave but my husband and his parents do not want this. The children are growing up, one needs to think about them. But here I have an apartment and interesting work. I love the climate here and the people are also warm. Here things are peaceful. In Russia even though it is my homeland, no one will look out for us and we would have to start everything afresh.

Conclusions

The reconfiguration of political authority along national lines has once again focused attention on the compelling political need to identify ethnic "homelands". Conceived as "nation-states", there is a distinct project in all newly independent states of the former Soviet Union to promote the language, culture, demographic position, economic development and political hegemony of the ethnic group after which the state is named. This programme of "nationalization" of political space has meant that large numbers of people are now left outside their own national territory or do not have one at all and are faced with the dilemma of having to redefine their identities vis a vis the regions that they inhabit or emigrate to regions they consider "home". This article has attempted to examine the dilemmas that ethnic Russian women are now faced with while attempting to reconcile their identities as new minorities in a nationalizing state.

References

G. Duveen and B. Lloyd "The Significance of Social Identity", *British Journal of Social Psychology*, 1986.

Suzanne Skevington and Deborah Baker : *The Social Identity of Women*, Sage, London, etc 1989.

Islam A Karimov, *Uzbekistan—The Road of Independence and Progress*, New Delhi, 1993.

Leokadia Drobizhyeva, "Russian Ethnic Attitudes in Changing Political Situations" *Economic and Political Weekly*, Special Number, December 18, 1995.

Galina Pugachenkova, in Marfua Tokhtakhodjaeva and Elmira Turgumbekova, *The Daughters of Amazons : Voices from Central Asia* (translated from Russian by Sufian Aslam), Lahore : Shirkat Gah. Women's Resource Centre, 1996.

Report of a speech delivered by Michael P. Conzen at American Ethnic Geography Specialty Group by Susan Hardwick, "A. E. G. S. G. Distinguished Scholar Award : Michael P. Conzen", *The American Ethnic Geographer*, Vol. 7, No. 2, Autumn 1999.

Roger Brubaker, "National Minorities, Nationalizing States and External National Homelands in the New Europe", *Daedalus*, Vol. 124, No. 2, Spring 1993.

Colin Thubron, *The Lost Heart of Asia*, London : Penguin, 1994.

Brubaker, "National Minorities, Nationalizing States and External National Homelands". 1994

Islam A Karimov, *Uzbekistan—The Road of Independence and Progress*, New Delhi, 1993.

Kadir Z. Alimov, "The Rediscovery of Uzbek History and its Foreign Policy Implications", in Fredrick Starr (ed) *The Legacy of History in Russia and the New States of Eurasia*, New York : M.E. Sharpe, 1994.

Karimov, *Uzbekistan—The Road of Independence*, 1994.

Michael Rywkin "Cadre Competition in Uzbekistan, Ethnic Aspects," *Central Asian Survey*, Vol-5, No 3\4, 1986

A. Selebyerstova, "Deti Russkikh Starozhelov v Uzbekistane" *Vostok*, No. 2, 1994.

Reuel Hanks, "The Islamic factor in Nationalism and Nation Building in Uzbekistan-Causative Agent or Inhibitor?", *Nationalities Papers*, Vol. 22 (2), 1994.

Alla Chervova, in Marfua Tokhtakhodjaeva and Elmira Turgumbekova, *The Daughters of Amazons : Voices from Central Asia*, 1995.

Trevour Fishlock, *Out of Red Darkness, Reports from the Collapsing Soviet Empire*, London : John Murray, 1992.

Elena Topornina in Marfua Tokhtakhodjaeva and Elmira Turgumbekova, *The Daughters of Amazons : Voices from Central Asia*, 1995.

Marfua Tokhtakhodjaeva and Elmira Turgumbekova, *The Daughters of Amazons : Voices from Central Asia*, 1995.

Olga Egunova, in Marfua Tokhtakhodjaeva and Elmira Turgumbekova, *The Daughters of Amazons : Voices from Central Asia*, 1995

Galina Pugachenkova in Marfua Tokhtakhodjaeva and Elmira Turgumbekova, *The Daughters of Amazons : Voices from Central Asia*, 1995.

Vallentina Artemova, in Marfua Tokhtakhodjaeva and Elmira Turgumbekova, *The Daughters of Amazons : Voices from Central Asia*, 1995

WOMEN AND SEXUALITY

9

Women's' (Non) Identity : the Case of the Bauls' *Sadhansanginis*

Rajasri Basu

The intellectual debate and controversy as to whether identity which has a cultural pre-eminence should replace class–which has a predominantly economic component, or, citizenship–which is primarily a political concept will not be dealt with in my paper. Instead, I would start my discussion accepting 'identity' as a popular and acceptable notion with the help of which we could explain the various nuances of society.

It has been the experience of social science in general, and political science, in particular, to remain under the tradition of Enlightenment political philosophy. Anglo-Saxon political philosophy with its individualistic overtone not only foregrounded a particular set of ethical values but also interpreted them in a specific way. That specific component is the individual sans community. This individualistic overtone of Anglo-Saxon philosophy has been challenged in several ways. The communitarian challenge showed the relevance of culture to identify formation was more explicitly registered. The recognition also came that culture related self-esteem matters to people as much as the fulfillment of material needs. Equally significant was the recognition that the self of identity and self worth of persons derives from cultures that they not only know well but can and may call their own. Thus if the communitarian standpoint questioned a political order constructed purely from the vantage point of individual well-being the importance of cultural particularity raised doubts about the desirability of a unicultural polity. Instead it enjoined us to design a community with multi-cultural ethos. Thus deciphering the proper linkage between identity and cultural community is essential in understanding a multi-cultural society. Thus, one of the ways of understanding the multi-cultural Indian society happens to be studying 'identities' at several strata, finding out the linkage between identity and the cultural community in which it is formed.

Coming to the question as to why identity has acquired a significant meaning with respect to its specific gendered component, it may be said that gender is an indispensable concept in the analysis of political-cultural movements, of transition and of social change. Self-identity of a woman in a particular community is essentially tied up with the character of the community. This self-identity in most cases is fashioned by the community itself through the permeation of each group's values, specific cultures, life-style, dress code etc.

In this context I have selected the identity of women in the *baul* community who are known to the commoners as a minstrel group with a particular dress. But baul is essentially a philosophy a particular life-style having a strict meditational path; it is not and should not be equated with music. They are mostly found in the Murshidabad, Birbhum, Nadia, Bardhaman and Bankura districts of West Bengal on the Indian side; and Rajshahi, Kushtia districts on the Bangladesh side. Before delving into identity of the female members of the *baul* community let us have a brief discussion about what is identity. Philosophically speaking, the most intriguing and disturbing question that churns philosophers for generations, is perhaps 'who am I'. This 'pointing to oneself' lands us to the notion of identity.

Amelie Rorty has pointed to four clusters of notions, namely class differentiation, individual differentiation, individual reidentification and individual identification for understanding personal identity. Class differentiation implies identity of a person as a member of a particular class which again is different and distinct from other classes. Individual differentiation implies distinction of an individual from others in terms of attributes and qualities of others. By individual reindentification is meant the criteria of reidentifying the same individual in different contexts, under different descriptions at different times. Finally, individual identification denotes the characteristics that identify a person as essentially the person is, such that if these characteristics were changed (s)he would be a significantly different person, though (s)he might still be differentiated and reidentified as the same.

It should be remembered, however, as Montefiore says that there is, despite initial appearances, a fundamental structural interrelationship between what one might call the outline concepts of individuation and reidentification on the one hand, and those of essential identification, on the other. Besides, changes over time have an important bearing on the 'identity' of an individual. This is also true with respect to what Amelie Rorty calls essential identity. She may have been thinking primarily of the individually personal characteristics that may be held to 'identify a person as *essentially* the person she is', but for the great majority of people, of course, their relations to certain other people, their job or their role in society and so on—may also count, as among the strands entering into their essential identity, and in such cases changes to others or changes in the nature or status of the relevant group, may well constitute changes in the essential identities of whoever is to be counted as remaining among that group's members. Thus, identification and reidentification, identity, difference and time, and essential identity are themes which are all intertwined, by one's primary concern with the identities of historically given social groups or with those of the individual human beings who may make up their membership. With this theoretical perspective, let us turn to the identity of 'female bauls'.

II

At the outset, it should be made clear, that to me, female *baul* is a misnomer. There can only be *sadhansanginis* or females helping the *bauls* in their path of meditation. Before dwelling on this theme further, let us have a description about the *baul* way of life.

The *bauls* to the mainstream society has an enigmatic appeal by their colourful dresses and spiritual songs on the one hand, and fascinating and secretive life-style on the other. The middle-class Bengalis have a romantic image of a Baul clad in a saffron robe singing and dancing mad songs of ecstasy with *ektara* in his hand. The high-pitched tone of *baul* songs attracts many.

Etymologically, the Bengali word Baul is derived from the Sanskrit word *byakulah (byakulah>batul >baul)* which means an eager or restless person showing signs of insanity. In *Shreekrishnabijaykabya* written by Maladhar Basu during the last quarter of 15th century, we first come across the term *baul* in Bengali literature. However, a different version regarding the origin of the word baul is given by S. M. Lutfar Rahman, a Professor of Bengali literature in the Dhaka University. According to him, the word *baul* had its origin from the word *bajil (bajil>bajul>baul)* as used in *Charyapadas.* Whatever the origin of the word baul may be, it mainly denotes an insane person during the middle ages. Now, however, it typifies a group of people whose vocabulary, dress code, life-style etc. are completely different from the rest of the society. Songs and music are essential parts of their life-style which are, in fact, the vehicles of expressing their spiritualism.

Bauls consider Shri Chaitanyadev as their first guru but they do not belong to the sect of Vaishnavism which was founded by him. However, many *bauls* consider themselves to be 'Vaishnav-Baul'. Again, the *sadhansanginis* of *bauls* are also called *Boshtumis* (Vaishnavis > Boshtumis). But still they form a completely different sect who do not accept temples or mosques, Hindu deities or Allah, performing religious practices like offerings to God or performing *Rojas* and the ritual. They consider the human body as the highest temple of God. Their goal is to get the unrealizable eternal pleasure. They try to find out how eternal pleasure, infinite happiness and unlimited light reside in limited, narrow human body. They consider the human body as the location of God. That is why the *baul* way of meditation is always a conjugal meditation—sexual intercourse and the bodily pleasure are vehicles of achieving the highest level of *baul* spiritualism. Women therefore to the *Bauls* is not just a female body of sexual pleasure but the source of real Truth, highest form of Love and the absolute form of Life.

The *baul* way of spiritualism is not written down in a book, or in other words, they do not have a religious scripture or idols. It is transmitted across generations from *Gurus* to his disciples. Persons belonging to any religion can become a Baul. Thus Hindus as well as Muslims can become, and in fact, have become disciples of baul; but once they become followers of *baul* way of life, they sacrifice all of their earlier religious beliefs and become only a *baul*.

The very basis of *baul* way of meditation, the way of achieving the *baul* form of truth and the methodology for securing that Truth are distinctly and remarkably different from the mainstream way of life. Sexual life without procreation is normally not considered to be an acceptable practice in the mainstream society. On the contrary, this is exactly what is practiced in the *baul* way of life. The four types of excreta (as considered in the mainstream society) namely, stool, urine, menstrual blood and sperm are considered to be sacred things *(charichandrabheda)* in the *baul* society. All these have made the *baul* way of life unacceptable to the mainstream society which again has given rise to a deliberative secretive nature of the *Bauls*, which they cautiously cultivate and properly guard. That is why, the *Bauls* live in what is called *ankharas* (although there are few who remain in homes and are called *Grhi Bauls*) and remain 'marginal' in all senses of the term even when they live territorially within the area of the mainstream society or even when they participate in different festivals.

The above description of the *baul* life will help us to understand the role of a woman in a Baul's life, but only to an extent. In true philosophy, women, as mentioned earlier, are not just objects of sexual love, but are vehicles of attaining highest form of spiritualism. But this very expression creates a problem for the identity of the women in the *baul* community both from a theoretical and from a practical standpoint.

Speaking theoretically, the singularly important question that comes to one's mind is that if the women are the stooges or the helping media of the *Baul* for achieving their spiritual truth, are they also included in the purview of achievement of Truth or do they remain outside that purview? The *baul* meditational path reveals that *Bauls* are only entitled to attain that truth, not their women associates. They are, therefore, *sadhansanginis* but not *sadhikas*. They help the *Bauls* in cleansing their bodies by massaging oil, putting on soaps, oiling and combing the long hair and making the *jatas*; they do all the household duties like taking care of the kitchen through cooking, washing of utensils, they are the singing and *yogic* partners of the *Baul* and, of course most importantly, they are the sexual partners of the Bauls. Thus they can only *help* the *Bauls* but cannot *become Bauls*.

Although true *baul* path of meditation does not allow association of a Baul with more than one woman, sometimes the women associates themselves choose and pick up a second woman for his *baul* or what they call their *gosain*, *guru* or *kshyapa,* as a post-menopausal woman is of no use to a Baul's meditating path. Thus even though the women help the *Baul* in every possible means or more precisely speaking, *without a woman*, a *baul* cannot attain his spiritual truth, women are not the sharers of that truth. Thus, they, I believe, do not have any identity of their own other than being partners of *Baul.*

If we look now at a Baul *sadhansanginis*' realistic identity, the picture is grimmer. The true *baul* path of meditation, as described earlier, is seldom to be seen in real life. What happens in reality is behind the facade of a 'true' *baul* life there exists free sex, desertion of long time women associates for others etc. on the one hand, and the exploitation, loneliness, poverty and deprivation of the woman, on the other.

The association of a man and a woman in the *baul* way of life is not based upon any law, mutual accountability or mutual responsibility. The custom of *mala-chandan* (somewhat akin to formal marriage) is not a sacrosanct custom and can be broken at any point of time, whenever there is disliking of the one toward the other. This is obviously done more by the *gosains* toward their women associates rather than the other way round. This has naturally led to the creation of *Shyamadasis* and *Kalyanis,* who after desertion of their *gosains* in old age had to lead a lonely, impoverished and hapless life.

III

With this description of a Baul *Sadhansanginis'* life, we may now return to the question of identity. Class wise they no doubt have a definite identity as members of a *Baul* community as distinct from the mainstream society. But coming to their essential identity it seems to me that they are nothing but shadows of objects, where not only the archlight is entirely on the object, but at the same time the shadow has no identity of its own.

Since the *baul* philosophy prohibits procreation, females of this community come mostly from the mainstream society. Widows and women deserted by their husbands of rural Bengal mostly become *sadhansangini*s out of sheer poverty in most cases; although some women accept this role out of eagerness to enjoy a life where sex plays a predominantly prominent role. They search a *gosain* and clung on to them as their source of identity only to be left out in old age. Meditation, attainment of spiritual goal may have an attraction for these women associates of *bauls* but it is to be remembered that attainment of that goal, is reserved only for *bauls*.

The path of meditation or the period of meditation that is required for a man to become a *baul* consists of four stages where concentration, respiratory control through *yogic* exercises is taught. These are, as mentioned earlier, to be taught through a *guru* and not through reading of books. In the first two stages, namely, *sthula* and *prabarta*, there is no need of a woman and here the *guru* gives certain advices to his disciple regarding *charichandrabheda* and teaches him the respiratory *yogic* exercises so that the mind could search the Truth, the Love and the Light with single minded devotion. The third stage namely the *sadhaka* requires the companionship of a woman. However, women, who are considered essential in the *sadhana* of the *baul* do not require any formal training. If the first two stages may be called the stages of theoretical knowledge, the third stage may be called the stage of practical knowledge. The last and the fourth stage—the *siddha*—signifies the attainment of the highest Truth where again the dissociation with the woman is required and which is seldom achieved.

With the essential necessity of a woman in a *Baul* way of life, it could have been easily transformed into a *matriarchy,* but what has come to exist is not only a *gosainarchy* but an over-deterministic male society where the females have no identity other than providing bodily, sexual pleasures to their *gosains.* That is why, the oft quoted, soliloquized words of Hamlet, written as early as in 1603—"To be or not to be, that is the question"—resonate most powerfully in the context of the *Bauls' Sadhansanginis* whose only task is to help the *Bauls* to achieve their spiritual goal, through voluntarily providing all sorts of sexual pleasure. The stories of Pinjiradashi of Nadia, Kamalinidashi of Birbhum, Sulakshmanadashi of Murshidabad substantiate my thesis that the bauls' *sadhansanginis* are only *sanginis,* they can never be *sadhikas*; or in other words they have no identity of their own. All these signify a non-identity of the *sadhansanginis*; they do not have any *essential* identity.

IV

In conclusion, I would like to touch the issue of individual reidentification and the issue of essential identity getting transformed over a period of time in the context of the women associates of the *baul.* Conceptually, these two notions of identity have been differentiated by Amelie Rorty but as has been stated earlier, these two are intertwined in individual cases of identity and, perhaps more so in the context of those who have no essential identity.

For the last two or three decades, a change could perhaps be noticed in the female members of the *baul* community. The instances of Sumitradashi, Krishnadashi, Gayatridashi and Kalyanibala may be cited here. All of them had been *sadhansanginis* of their *gosains* at one point of their life. It was Subal Das for Sumitra, Nabakumar Das for Krishna, but due to various reasons they had been deserted by their *gosains* and now with the help of *baul* songs they are trying to assert themselves without any help from the male members of their community. They have developed the identity of 'female singers of *baul* songs'.

It is true that *baul*-ism does not consider *baul* songs as a main part of its philosophy. Songs are essential but only as a medium of expressing their ideas about life. Conjugal meditation is the basic premise of *baul* philosophy. That is why, although *Baul* and *baul* songs seem to be inseparable to urban eyes, establishment of a singer identity is not important to a *Baul*. The *baul* identity is more important to them.

The woman—Sumitra, Krishna, Gayatri, Kalyani and others—by their sheer singing ability and skill have been able to develop essentially a female singer identity. They know it very well that it is not possible for them to establish their identity as Bauls although they had a stronger personality, a superior singing ability and a greater capacity for independent thinking vis-à-vis their *gosains*. Had they been woman of some earlier period, they may not be able to assert their 'singer' identity in this fashion. There was some sort of mental confusion amongst these women till the 80s of the 20th century. They were torn by two opposing feelings–whether to remain as an associate of a *baul* or whether to establish an identity of her own through singing.

But a new way of thinking began to develop since the time when Sumitra, Kalyani, Gayatri and others started a new journey of their life–with songs and without a gosain. They do not follow the path of Meera Mohanta or Nirmala Goswami who after the death of their respective gosains Narottam Das and Haripada Goswami, have set up their own akharas where they have (or controlled) younger Bauls and their women associates as their disciples. On the contrary Sumitra, Krishna and others have successfully treaded the path shown by Nanibala Dasi, Radharani Dasi or Phulomala Dasi. These women could dominate the Baul festivals with their superb singing ability but could not come out of the influence of their gosains or perhaps, more importantly could not see themselves only as 'singers', which Sumitra, Krishna and others successfully could.

Thus there has been a distinct and perceptible change in the essential identity of *sadhansanginis* of Bauls who have re-identified themselves as female singers of baul songs.

Acknowledgement

All those Bauls' *sadhanasanginis*, conversation with whom provokes me to write the paper.

References

Alan Montifiore, 'Identity and Integrity', in R. Bhargava, A.K. Bagchi and R. Sudarshan (eds.) *Multiculturalism, Liberalism and Democracy,* Oxford University Press, Oxford, 1999.

Amelie Rorty, *The Identities of Persons,* University of California Press, California, 1976.

Leena Chaki, *Bauler Charandashee* (Bengali) Pustak Bipani, Calcutta, 2001.

Sanat Kumar Mitra, 'Baul/Fakir/Sufi' in Mitra (ed.) *Baul Lalan Rabindranath* (Bengali) Folklore Research Institute, Calcutta, 1995.

Shaktinath Jha, 'Gupto Dehasadhana Ebong Tar Samajtattwa' in Sudhir Chakraborty (ed.) (Bengali) *Banglar Baul Fakir,* Pustak Bipani, Calcutta, 1999.

Sudhir Chakraborty in Chakraborty (ed.) (Bengali) *Banglar Baul Fakir,* Pustak Bipani, Calcutta, 1999.

10

Con (fused) Identity of a flying Woman

Swati Ghosh

Would you call her a street walker or an escort women? Or a *flying prostitute* as she calls herself?

Whatever be the name, the number of such women is alarmingly on the increase in recent times. They are to be seen everywhere in the metropolis, at every hour and place. Most of them are not permanent dwellers of the city like the brothel prostitutes, they keep plying from the rural home to the urban workplace, between the position of a housewife and a whore, within the zone of social sanction and illegality. The belongingness of a *flying woman* to this gray and blurred area, shapes her *being*, her *identity*. She inhabits a volatile domain defined by quick flights from one position to another rather than remaining loyal to specified identities and familiar roles assigned either to a prostitute woman or a housewife. This is what makes her position as a woman phenomenal and projects her as a subject of unique interest.

This paper intends to examine the contradictory positions of a flying prostitute woman, to explore the dimensions of multiple identities that constitute her and to elucidate the aspects of identities that are directly in conflict with and over-determine each other. The paper is organized as follows: the first section while describing the position of the flying prostitute focuses on the fusion of social roles within which she has to reside, the second section elaborates upon the instability that constitutes her and brings forth the con (fused) position emerging from the multiple identities that she cohabits simultaneously, the last section attempts to explain the contradictions at the level of the economic, the cultural and the political and presents a Marxist feminist analysis of the vulnerable identity of a flying woman.

Fusion of Roles : A flying Woman is a Housewife and a Whore in One Self

The flying woman is a housewife who undertakes part-time prostitution under economic compulsion. The flying woman, is also a (sex) worker who has a family to tend and a house to keep. She is a housewife, stepping out of the household to earn a living, a breadwinner for the family, a working woman. A working woman selling sexual service for money, a whore. She keeps plying between two contradictory poles, between the home and the street, from one woman-position to another. For her it is a tight rope walking along the trajectory connecting the two socially extreme sites of homemaking and prostitution.

The flying woman has been pushed out from the domain of an ideal family set-up into the large arena where whoring is the easiest way to keep afloat. Again, she does not belong to the brothel. She is rather an independent streetwalker whose career is marked off with queuing up in the lines of the red light zone. Yet, she is no rival to the prostitute. She stands in line waiting for customers in the tropical mid day sun when the line girls doze off after a busy night and a lousy morning. She is available at weird, arcane places away from the shades of red light zone where line girls would not prefer to visit. She operates in-between spaces left out by the brothel girls and at a price that they would hate to accept.

For the flying woman, her work-shifts are followed by home-shifts. As a housewife, situated within bonds of marriage and family, she performs the household chores of cleaning, cooking and looking after the children. This daily running of the household is managed single-handedly, with little or no help from her spouse. Within the family she is supposed to perform sexual activity with a single male partner: her husband. Thus childcare and housework constitute the reproductive role of the housewife, the natural behavior as anticipated from the women of the family.

Taking part in productive activity begins as soon as the flying woman takes to the streets for a living. When her male partner, the usual bread earner of the family is dumped by the market as inefficient or when the male member is incapable of earning enough, the woman of the home steps out to feed the family. With no specialisaion whatsoever, for any kind of work apart from home-making, she has to make the most of her body and sexuality available to her at hand. She becomes a working woman, being paid for the work she performs in exchange of money. A working woman with a difference. Her work performed out of love for one male individual within the family.

In course of her work she operates as a 'public woman' providing pleasure to male clients. In this role of a pleasure-giver, she possesses the 'dangerous sexuality of the non-mother' and draws clients for the service she provides. She represents the element of *recreation* for male customers who buy her service. While within the family her sexuality is related to *procreation*. As per the family code of conduct the role of a wife and mother is prioritized and therefore child-birth and child rearing are the major assignments designated for her. For the woman of home, pleasure seeking/giving attitude is far away from the code of family norms.

For a flying woman, there are no separate compartments to dwell. She has to fly through the narrow alleys of rigorous domestic norms inhibiting sexual pleasure and land up in the socially forbidden arena of providing sexual pleasure, with ease and, ceaselessly. As for her, a part of the social standing is sacrosanct and moral while another part is equally profane and immoral. Within domesticity, her housewife image is primary, she remains unrecognized as a worker and the nature of work is not disclosed. As a prostitute her non-reproductive role is more important; she is into productive activity as a working woman with career in sex and also a wife and mother as if by default.

Again, she does not occupy a space that may be termed 'in-between'. Unlike a woman in mid-way position, possessing some of the characteristics of both the extreme positions of a whore and a housewife. Rather, she shuttles between a prostitute at work and a housewife at home. While she is neither an all time prostitute nor a total house-wife, she is both at one and the same time. The space she occupies is hazy and undefined.

Thus for a flying woman the mother and the non-mother roles, the productive and the non-productive activities, the moral and the immoral images fuses into one and acquires a unique feature in her context.

Confused Identities

At the level of meaning the flying woman dwells in a space that is equally *moral* and *immoral,* she plays the dual role of *productive* and *reproductive* and she is associated with *procreation* in one domain and *pleasure* in another. She is the *mother* and the *non-mother* at the same time. In the role of the housewife she is expected to be *affective* and *caring* while at work she has to be *lustful* and *licentious*. She performs a very *private* act in *public* place, such that the public-private binary is redundant for her. In fact, all the binaries mentioned above lose their usual connotations with respect to her.

At the level of the politics, she has to yield to the power processes that dominate her in different ways. The state excludes her from the domain of civil society as lesser-citizens. She is spatially and morally quarantined and does not possess freedom to move or reside anywhere. In the eyes of law her worker status is illegal and she is invisible to administration that knows but pays no heed to her existence. Therefore she has to function in an undetectable space and remain non-acknowledged as a worker. The law-keepers thus take advantage of this dubious situation and try to extract money from her for practicing immoral act in public space. She has to face harassment and fine for practicing what is ***non-work.***

For other women workers one role does not negate the other, for a housewife the role of the bread-earner is highlighted positively, if not with sympathy at least with silence. For a flying prostitute the earning potentials are not only not recognized within the family and community, the question of morality stoops large. The family tries to maintain secrecy for its desperation of living through immoral acts the community wants to discipline the element of immortality that it wants to disown. For the flying woman *non-recognition* marks her working status. Patriarchal family norms oppresses her by excluding her from the decision making process in spite of being an earner.

At the level of the economic, the labour process she is engaged in is somewhat confusing. It is not a proper employment at all, employment not enumerated in any sort of information collecting systems. Among other marginal group of workers, she belongs to a group of prostitutes with primarily sexual identity that fetches a living. She has no employer and therefore is not a wageworker by any means. She is a self-employed individual engaged in a kind of 'work' without a place of work. The work involves monetary transaction with clients for exchange of a service provided by her. Her body is the site of work and the client who buys a piecemeal ownership over the body dictates the nature of service she provides.

The flying woman has to live the multiple identities that constitute her. She is the manifestation of conceptually opposing positions that negate each other. This creates conflicts within her and she succumbs more and more to the social forces that forge her entity. She lives with the conflict all by herself, being isolated from other workers, woman workers or even other marginal groups based on distinct identities of their own. Identity formation based on class, caste, gender or other markers and a solidarity emerging from the cross cuttings of such attributes are not shared by a flying woman. The sexual and non-sexual traits directly in clash with each other are unique to her and construct a vulnerability which others can resist to some extent. In spite of certain commonalities with other workers, the flying woman belongs to a space that is blurred and undefined with overlapped and fragmented identities. She remains confined within the contradictions and conflicts that exclusively shape her self.

Vulnerability Explored

In this section, we try to locate the uniqueness of the flying woman and the aspects of commonality she shares with others and in the process attempts to offer an analysis of her vulnerable entity. Her gendered identity of a woman overlaps with that of the class identity as a worker, her identity as a mother clashes with that of the non-mother, her identity as a minority group of sexual worker stands in contrast to her familial identity of a citizen. Again all these identities are partial and fractured, constituting each other and being constituted by them.

To describe the susceptibility of the flying woman, let us explore the nature and cause of her belongingness to various positions and examine the social forces that shape her being.

Home and work are the two domains that constitute a flying woman. Yet, her vulnerability is deeper than other women workers. This is due to the specific nature of her work, which is different from any other form of labour. Marxist-feminist analysis of her position depicts that she is the victim of economic exploitation and political domination simultaneously at work and at home respectively. This overlaping of two dimensions holds for both the domains that she plies. The two processes are not very distinct and invisible to a large extent.

At Work

At work the flying woman operates as an independent worker. She is a self employed woman selling sexual service for money. She is the trader, the worker and commodity (or service) all in one. As a worker she produces a service to be consumed by the logic of the market from the site of her body. As a trader she exchanges her own use-value in every transaction with a client. In spite of being able to name her price in the market and provide the service, she is refrained from being able to act with autonomy and agency. She has to deliver 'pleasure' in compliance to the desire of another. The subjugation of her labor to capital is rather invisible in her case. There is no capitalist class visible for appropriation of surplus value. The complexity is further intricate with her class position and subjection to power within the trade network.

The implication of the body as the site of work is a significant marker of difference for her. She delivers the service in exchange of money. The amount of money paid is collected and used by her. Though production of pleasure is in no way comparable to the production of a commodity or a service in capitalistic framework, the nature of exploitation is somewhat similar. The product is intangible and inseparable from the site of production-the body, and immediacy of consumption follows. The nature of work is such that the 'sexual' component of the work performed cannot be wished away.

Sex work is in no way a 'pleasure' for the flying woman. It is a market contract for which she is paid in cash. She produces a determinate form of pleasure in a limited period of time according to the desire shaped by purchasing power of the client.

Unlike any other labour form, prostitution involves the female body to be used as an object for producing sexual ximulations, not for herself, but for her client. Since, one of the partners is forced to act in compliance with the desire of the other, withholding oneself, the act is coercive. This coercion is less physically abusive, than a violation of selfhood of the woman partner. This pain and coercion results from the domination of the client over the female self with the compulsory obligation on her part to satisfy the temporary master over her body. The oppression resulting from the relations of power in a livelihood where body and sexuality are instrumental cannot be traced in any other work.

Marxist class analysis distinguishes necessary from surplus labour, defining necessary labour as that required by the producer for her own consumption and surplus as the amount performed beyond what is necessary. As a self-employed worker, the flying woman produces and appropriates both necessary and surplus labour. It meets the subsistence for her and that of her family. The amount of necessary labour provides reproduction of her labour power and surplus labour power provides for that of her family. The surplus labour she performs is received and distributed by her towards her family who did not produce it. This appropriation and receipt of surplus labour is economic exploitation to which the flying woman is subject. Without a capitalist class, the moments of generation and appropriation of surplus value are not distinct and the woman becomes instrumental to the process of exploitation.

At Home

At home, within domesticity, the flying woman is the housewife. She performs the task transforming raw-materials into processed meals, clean rooms and washed clothes. She produces use-value. Her work helps to reproduce the labour power sold outside the household and future labour power of children to be sold later. This use value is consumed by her and by other members of her family. Thus she performs necessary labour for her own and surplus labour for the consumption of others. This is not exchanged for money since market does not enter directly into the household economy. The class process remains feudal to a large extent so far her reproductive role is concerned.

At home, she is the housewife who is forced to take up a job primarily to meet the economic crisis that arises when the husband does not earn enough or does not earn at all. The latter case might emerge even if the husband deserts his wife and family or the wife is a widow. The wife having to take up the productive (to earn as labour) and reproductive (to reproduce labour power) role, leaves the husband with options of either taking up productive or reproductive, both or none of the roles. We discuss all the options open to the husband assuming that the wife has to perform both the roles.

1. The husband works and earns and also helps his wife with housework that is participating both, in productive and reproductive work. This is rather unlikely and rare in a social milieu where the wife has to supplement family earning by whoring.

2. The husband works and earns but does not take part in cooking or cleaning looking after the children to reproduce labour power. This is likely

and common and also shared by other women workers who do not have to eke out a living through their bodies.

3. The husband does not work. It could be he is either unemployed due to retrenchment or prefers to live off his wife's earning. The productive role being absent he eagerly takes part in a reproductive role in carrying out the household duties and helps his wife. This is not unlikely, but rather uncommon.

4. The husband does not participate in either productive or reproductive role and leaves both for the wife to perform. Even if the wife is not a widow or deserted by her husband, this is highly likely and not at all uncommon. In all the four cases, the husband enjoys the earnings of his wife, which could be partial or total. If the husband works himself they share their income among themselves. If the husband does not work he enjoys the fruits of labour of his wife without contributing anything on his part. That is the husband enjoys the surplus labour performed by his wife, partially (cases land 2) or totally (cases 3 and 4).

That is, exploitative relationship prevails within the household between the husband and the wife, totally or with variations in extent. The non-monetary exchange and absence of market marks the relation to be non-capitalistic class process regarding the productive role of the husband.

In the above instances, an obvious relation of power exists within the household, which again may be categorized as being partial or total with respect to participation in reproductive work. The relation is relatively egalitarian when the husband takes part in household chores (cases 1 and 3) and is oppressing on the wife if he does not (cases 2 and 4). Thus within this limits of work and household duties, we find case 1 is least exploitative and dominant in contrast to case 4 which is totally exploitative and oppressive for the wife. Instances 3 and 4 represent variation in degrees, with 3 being more exploitative and less oppressive while 4 is less exploitative and more oppressive respectively. The relation for power within the household is feudal.

Economic exploitation of appropriating surplus labour along with social oppression of domination converges at the site of prostitution practiced by a flying woman. In addition to the economic class process, the cultural (meaning) and political (power) processes shape the entity of a flying woman. She has to bear the brunt both as a homemaker and as a whore.

Thus a flying woman is pushed into situations of contradictions and conflicts over which she has not much of a control. In spite of her earning potentials she remains excluded, exploited and oppressed. The multiple identities fragmented and overlapping at different levels rather, leaves her vulnerable and confused.

References

Arnold David, "Sexually Transmitted diseases in Nineteenth and Twentieth Century India", *Genitourin Medicine*, 69, 1993.

Austin Sydney Bryn, "AIDS and Africa : United States Media and Racist Fantasy", *Cultural Critique* Winter 0882-4371, 1989-1990.

Bandopadhyay Sandip, "Swadhinatar Andolone Barbonitara", *Bratya Jibaner Barnamala*, Kolkata, 1999.

Banerjee Sudeshna, "Embodying Space and classifying Bodies : The Transforming 'inner domain' in Colonial Calcutta", in Space and Power in History : Images, Ideologies,Ranjan Chakrabarti *Myths and Moralities*, Chakrabarti, Kolkata. 2001.

Banerjee Sumanta, *The Parlour and the Streets : Elite and Popular Culture in Nineteenth Century Calcutta*, Kolkata, 1989.

Banerjee Sumanta, 'Women's Popular Culture in Nineteenth Century Bengal' in Kumkum Sangari and Sudesh Vaid (eds.) *Recasting Women : Essays in Indian Colonial History*, Delhi, 1989.

Banerjee Sumanta, *Dangerous Outcasts : The Prostitute in Nineteenth Century Bengal*, Kolkata, 1998.

Bell Shannon, *Reading, Writing and Rewriting the Prostitute Body*, Indiana University Press, 1994.

Butler Judith, *The Psychic Life of Power : Theories in Subjection*, California, 1997.

Castillo A. Debra et al, 'Border Lives : Prostitute Women in Tijuana', *Signs* : Journal of Women in Culture and Society, Vol. 22, No. 2, Winter 1997.

Chakrabarty Dipesh, *Rethinking Working Class History : Bengal 1890-1940*, New Jersey, 1990.

Chakrabarti Uma, 'Whatever Happened to the Vedic Dasi?', in Kumkum Sangari and Sudesh Vaid (eds.) *Recasting Women : Essays in Indian Colonial History*, Delhi, 1990.

Chatterjee Indrani, *Slaves and Gender in Colonial India*, Oxford, 1999.

Chatterjee Partha, 'The Nationalist Resolution of the Women's Question' in Kumkum Sangari and Sudesh Vaid (eds.) *Recasting Women : Essays in Indian Colonial Hisotory*, Delhi, 1990.

Chatterjee Partha, *The Nation and its Fragments : Colonial and Post-colonial Histories*, Princeton University Press, 1993.

Chatterjee Partha, 'Talking about our Modernity in Two Languages', *A Possible India : Essays in Political Criticism*, India, 1997.

Chatterjee Patha and Gyan Pandey (eds.), *Subaltern Studies* Vol. VII. Oxford University Press, Delhi, 1993.

Chatterjee Ratnabali, *The Queen's Daughters : Prostitutes as an Outcast Group in Colonial India*, Bergen, 1992.

Dasi Binodini, *Amar Katha O Anyanya Rachana*, Subarnarekha, Kolkata, 1987.

Durbar Mahila Samanwaya Committee, *We Demand Worker's Rights*, Kolkata, 1998.

Foucault Michel, *Discipline and Punish*, trans. Alan Sheridan, New York, 1979.

Foucault Michel, Power/Knowledge, ed. Colin Gordon, trans, New York, 1980.

Foucault Michel, *The History of Sexuality. An Introduction*, Vol. I, Robert Hurley, New York, 1980.

Guha Ranajit, 'Chandra's Death' in Ranajit Guha (ed.) *Subaltern Studies V*, Delhi, 1987.

Ghosh S. K., *The World of Prostitutes* Vol. II. New Delhi, 1996.

Irigaray Luce, '*This Sex Which is not one*' trns. Catherine Porter, Ithaca: 1985.

Joardar Bishwanath, *Prostitution in Nineteenth and Silence? The Sexual Economies of Modern India,* Delhi, 1985.

John Mary, 'Globalization, Sexuality and the Visual Field : Issues and Non-issues for Cultural Critique', Mary John and Janaki Nair (eds.), *A Question of Silence? The sexual economies of Modern India,* Kali for Women, Delhi, 1996.

Mahila Samanwaya Committee, *A Report on West Bengal State Conference, Kolkata,* 1996.

Mahila Samanwaya Committee, *The Fallen Learn to Rise : The Social Impact of STD-HIV Intervention Program*, Kolkata, 1997.

Mani Lata, "Contentious Traditions : The Debate on Sati in Colonial India' in Kumkum Sangari and Sudesh Vaid (eds.) *Recasting Women : Essays in Indian Colonial History,* Delhi, 1989.

Millet Kate, *The Prostitution Papers : A Candid Dialogue*, 1971.

Nari Janaki, *Women and Law in Colonial India : A Social History*, Delhi, 1996.

National Commission for Women, *Societal Violence on Women and Children in Prostitution, A Report,* Government of India, New Delhi, 1995-96.

Niranjana Tejaswini, "Left to the Imagination : Indian Nationalism and Female Sexuality in Trinidad' in Mary John and Janaki Nair (eds.), *A Question of Silence? The sexual economies of Modern India,* Delhi, 1996.

O'Hanlon Rosalind 'Issues of Widowhood : Gender and Resistance in Colonial Western India', in Douglas Heynes and Gyan Prakash (eds.) *Contesting Power : Resistance and Everyday Social Relations in South Asia,* Delhi, 1991.

Oldenburg Veena Talwar, *The Making of Colonial Lucknow*, New-Jersey, 1984.

Oldenburg Veena Talwar, 'Lifestyle as Resistance : The case of the Courtesans in Lacknow' *Feminist Studies,* Vol. 2, 1990.

Pateman Carol, *The Sexual Contract,* Cambridge, 1988.

Ram Kalpana, 'Uneven Modernities and Ambivalent Sexualities : Women's Constructions of Puberty in Coastal Kanyakumari, Tamilnadu', Mary John and Janaki Nair (eds.), *A Question of Silence? The sexual economies of Modern India,* Delhi, 1996.

Sanlaap, "Theme paper of the Seminar *"Yet Another Right*", and "*The End of a Beginning*", Kolkata, 1998.

Sangari Kumkum and Sudesh Vaid (eds.) *Recasting Women : Essays in Indian Colonial History*, Delhi.

Sharge Lauric, 'Comment on Overall's "What's Wrong with Prostitution? Evaluating Sex Work", *Signs : Journal of Women in Culture and Society*, Winter, Vol. 19, No, 2, 1994.

Singh Richa, 'Masculine Identity, Workers and HIV/AIDS', *Economic and Political Weekly*, Vol. XXXVI, No, 22, 2001.

Singh Sujata, *Five Years Stint at Sonagachi : 1992-1997*, All India Institute of Hygiene and Public Health, Kolkata, 1997.

Spivak Chakravorty Gayatri, 'Woman in Difference : Mahasweta Devi's *"Douloti the Bountiful"*, Outside in the Teaching Machine, Routlege, New York, 1993.

Sunder Rajan Rajeswari, 'The Prostitution Question(s) : (Female) Agency, Sexuality and Work', Research in Progress Papers, *History and Society*, Third series No. V, Center for Contemporary Studies, Nehru Memorial Museum and Library, New Delhi, 1996.

Sunder Rajan Rajeswari, *Signposts : Gender Issues in Post-Independence India*, Delhi, 1999.

Thaaru Susic, 'Citizenship and its Discontents' in Mary John and Janaki Nair (eds.) *A Question of Silence? The sexual economies of Modern India*, Delhi, 1996.

Veen van der Marjolein, '*Beyond Slavery and Capitalism : Producing Class Difference in the Sex Industry.*

Walkowitz Judith R, *Prostitution and Victorian Society*, Cambridge University Press, 1980.

World Bank, *Confronting AIDS : Public Priorities in a Global Epidemic*, Policy Research Report, New Delhi 1997.

Zatz D. Noah, 'Sex Work/Sex act : Law, Labour and Desire in Constructions of Prostitution', *Signs : Journal of Women in Culture and Society*, Vol. 22, No. 2, Winter 1997.

11

Identity–Women–Advertisement: Politics of Viewing

Sarbani Guha Ghosal

History of human civilization revolves around the idea of developing an identity. Identity can be treated as a device for building up a composite portrait from a large number of different elements related to one's personality–visual, mental and cerebral. Looks and culture are intertwined in reality and are in a process of continuous transformation drawing influence from history, society and power relations. The mosaic of modern culture is shaped predominantly by different vision oriented aspects. Our contemporary culture, is essentially, a culture of the eye and thus looks have become the buzzword of the day. In the words of Contance Classen, "We are constantly bombarded, seduced and shaped by the visual models and representations ... The rule of sight carries with it a powerful aura of rationality and objectivity, even though many of its contemporary manifestations such as advertising images, seem designed to manipulate the emotions more than to exercise reason. The photographic nature of much of the twentieth century representation helps to maintain the aura of objectivity by appearing to provide the viewer with direct access to reality, rather than only mediating reality. The visualist regime of modernity, in fact, prides itself on its transparency, everything can be seen, everything can be known, nothing is withheld from our inquisitive and acquisitive eyes."

Modernity, thus has upgraded vision in relation to all other senses. It is the most privileged sense of today with the unprecedented proliferation of the electronic media and the opening up of the sky. One must remember here that vision is never innocent. Contrarily the act of looking is very much a political phenomenon as it clearly involves a relationship of super-ordination and subordination always. Whenever we view something, as viewers we invariably develop a relationship with the viewed and vice-versa. The viewer-viewed relationship, like all other kind of social relationships definitely involves elements of power. Thus, initially though a biological task, looking is very much constructed by different social forces with definite social, political and cultural implications.

It is especially in this context the present paper seeks to delve with the issue of identity of women vis-à-vis the advertisements and its socio-political implications. But before proceeding in this direction the author proposes to take into account briefly the issue of body and power relationship.

The perception of body is very much a product of culture. Culture trains our perception and experience. It is in this adjunct that Mary Douglas has brilliantly observed, "the social body constrains the way the physical body is perceived. The physical experience of the body, always modified by the social categories through which it is known, sustains a particular view of society." Thus the female body, as we live in our daily life is not a simple issue and it is much more conditioned by the social culture, the social outlook. Large number of images, customs, behaviour, rules, practices and everyday talk about how a female body should look and act in the context of a particular culture sets up certain standards which everyone is responsible for maintaining. It is exactly for this Simone de Beauvoir said, "it is not the body object described by the biologists that actually exists, but the body as lived in by the subject." We have to remember here that women's repression in the social context actually emanates from their 'female body'. The repression helps the construction of female image and at the same time this female image again helps to repress the women unceasingly. Everyday we come across thousands of instances where women are being victimised just because of their biological difference all over the world. Though forms of such subjugation have multiple faces, but male and female of their own community as well as the outsiders contribute to the subjugation of female body.

In other words, it can be said that at every moment of our existence we constantly feel the prevalence of gender. By and large in every society people as male and as female are expected to make some exclusive role performance. The expected role performance of the female places them in a secondary position in the social structure and in the minds of the men and women alike. Seldom women are viewed as persons on their own rights neither do they view themselves, obviously because of their cultural socialization, as autonomous beings. Now why are women being rendered subordinate, what are the instruments of subordination, how is the male authority being exercised-all these questions embroil us at the same time. But our concern for the time being is only with one particular device, which is considered as a fundamental one in developing and perpetuating male domination in any kind of modern patriarchal social arrangement.

This is nothing but the advertisements, and more precisely the audio-visual advertisements which can be considered as the latest ground of 'male-gaze'. On this point we must note that 'male-gaze' of course, is not exercised only by the male viewers. This gaze is something which in a patriarchal ideological order is internalized by the female viewers also. Thus, male gaze undoubtedly becomes an arena of power where the male standpoint is the dominant one and the female position is always subordinate.

The History of Advertisement

The concept of audio-visual advertisements in India received prominence since 1991. Before that its circulation was largely restricted to the cinema houses and telecast through Doordarshan. The inauguration of Star TV in 1991 and the subsequent launch of Zee and Sony networks along with several other satellite channels all of a sudden led to an advertisement boom in the electronic media. The marketing experts find a very convenient medium to sell their products with a deeper effect. In all these representations women are being featured in a number of ways and the targets of these are also women in most of the cases. In the words of Uma Chakravarti, "Given the importance of advertisements in shaping TV viewing and manipulation of our ways of thinking and buying-it is important to try and examine the unstated and stated assumptions of the advertisements. Among the most striking feature in this segment of programming is the shift that has occurred in portraying women, whereas earlier women were almost invariably used instrumentally to sell goods, many of which they did not use, now women are being targeted directly by the market. Further, they are being targeted not merely as consumers of goods but as desires and active buyers of goods". In other words, this entire gamut of events, no doubt has become a very interesting field of social science analysis.

The gender ideology embedded in the umpteen number of advertisements focus on some glaring aspects. At the very onset it seems that contentwise most of the ad-spots are almost cloning each other with minor packaging differences only. In a large and diverse country like India the sudden spurt of audio-visual media has a tremendous impact in shaping social values as they inform, educate and entertain at the same time though there is virtually no mirroring between advertising and social milieu on which it interacts. In the opinion of Laurent Gallissot, "Theoretically speaking, advertising and culture are related to each other. Advertising as a symbolic form of the capitalist economic system governs the principles of social exchange in which the reciprocal limits of the world of objects and of subjects are elaborated... Modern advertising is defined as a mode of discourse that is a particular way of using resources for expression. It gives objects their meanings and shows target audience their use. It creates a certain intelligibility of the cultural categories, that it, at the same time, visualizes and ritualizes."

Representations of women in advertisements carry both a message as well as a set of instructions on how to make sense of it. The structure, format of any advertisement and its mode of presentation communicate instructions about how to interpret the meaning of a particular advertisement. It is precisely in this context in this arena of audiovisual advertisements we can easily spot some major archetype casts of women as well.

Women, the World of Advertisement and Her Identity

The major bulk of representation presents women as docile home-makers whose world revolves round the well being of her husband, kids and in-laws. In this category of presentation whenever she does anything for her ownself, like taking any particular food or drinks or cooks something, or dresses up in a particular way or takes any medicine even, that is always for the sake of others and not for her own self in any way. Examples can be drawn from the Horlicks or Moov / Amrutanjan or series of edible oil like Sundrop, Saffolla etc and many other spots. In the Horlicks campaign the lady offers that health drink to her husband, kids, father-in-law to keep them healthy but when she herself drinks the same the audio says that only in order to keep the entire household she is taking it and it does going not have any reference to her own health. Similarly, in the painkiller ointment, the theme is that the wife is tired due to regular waist / back aches and fails to cater to the demands of the family members properly. Suddenly the father-in-law shouts to all and directs the daughter-in-law to take some medicine. The lady uses a particular pain balm and at the next moment starts to perform all the household chores with gaiety and dance. The visual ends with a snap of the happy and smiling family members. The underlying message of this ad-spot is that a daughter-in-law has to use a pain balm to do her duties properly and to make all happy and the relief of her own pain is a secondary purpose only. But why did she not take it earlier? Why did she have to wait for the order of her father-in-law? No doubt it is obviously to ensure the patriarchal family structure only. The nod from the patriarch and instant relief of the *bahu* perhaps provides greater sanctity to the product.

Similarly, seldom do we find a wife taking any food cooked by herself with all the family members or the guests together and also none of them even bother to offer any share to her. According to Uma Chakravarti, "The adaptation of local specificities is very evident in the incorporation of the parents-in-law into the family advertisements; ... kitchen goods in particular often play on the mother-in-law vs. daughter-in-law relationship often seeking to subvert, through its images, the power of the mother-in-law, the crucial alliance that leads to success in between the clever daughter-in-law and the gender friendly maker of goods; no woman's movement is necessary in India to counter the power of the mother-in-law as the young wife has now been emancipated by the market! The market provides ingenious ways by which a *bahu* can be free as well as please the *saas* and others while making sure that the market keeps the sexual division of labour, and ideologies that go with it intact". Examples in this regard can be drawn from the MDH masala, Everest masala or Ayush herbal spots.

There is another kind of representation parallel to this where sexual objectification of the women with the product is made directly. The much circulated AC apple juice spot displays this form in a crude way, whereas the spot on Ericson mobile does it in a subtle manner. In the Ericson spot a beautiful woman is speaking into her palm-sized cell phone and a middle-aged man assumes from her talks that she is asking for a dinner and when he approaches her, she removes her palm and orders a black coffee assuming him the waiter. The ad clearly disseminates an idea of equating a lucrative product with a successful and beautiful woman. Though this is not visually much disturbing apparently, but the spirit of it is extremely awful. Contrarily, in the AC apple juice spot the effect of the juice on the man is like disrobing of a sultry woman. In this spot the woman's body is being commodified openly. Similar is the case of the bikini-clad woman on the sea beach in the 7 Up ad commercial. Here the woman's body is being displayed like a cold drink bottle to generate a kind of titillating attraction towards the product. In the analysis of this kind of representation we can very well borrow the words of Laura Mulvey who in her analysis of the mainstream films has said long back that, "men are confirmed in their masculinity as powerful agents and women become the passive objects of men's scopophilic pleasure".

A large range of advertisement propagates the idea of beauty imperatives to which the women's body must adhere to. Innumerable ads of the beauty products like soaps, shampoos, skin nourishers can be put in this category. For the feminists all over the world, female beauty as presented in advertising and the popular media has been dangerously alienated from the real women and beauty is still a term of suspect. It is for this the feminists and health experts in different parts have started strong campaigns against the projected pattern of female beauty pervading the culture through numerous ads. In a multi-ethnic country like India this beauty imperative particularly has dangerous repercussions.

The beauty ideal promoted by the advertisements usurps female identity in an extremely derogatory way. In the words of V. Geetha, the beauty ideal "enables women to delight intensely in their becoming object status with pleasure. The question of their desires their subjectivity, is thus resolved within the terms of pleasure and power contained in the male gaze. Thus, in some instances, women even claim that they can best realize themselves through an active and defiant cultivation of their bodily good looks". It is precisely in this context we find a number of women who cannot live up with the sponsored ideals of beauty become victim with a sense of inadequacy and constant anxiety that they would have to face male disapproval and indifference.

The constructed beauty ideals in a very subtle way threaten and compel the women to believe that subscription to these ideals are essential to prove their worth as persons. Advertisement forces women to believe that expansion of avenues for achieving success and parity in relation to men can be attained by improving (!) their (women's) physical attributes according to the directions of the consumer goods industry. Use of particular talcum/ fairness cream / shampoo/ hair oil/ lipstick can put a woman "on the top of the world" (one lipstick audio). Thus, for bringing social change regarding the position of women, political movement or legal reforms or economic policy making is not essential at all. Only individuated commodity consumption is sufficient for ensuring the same. Wendy Steiner's profound inference in this regard appears as true when she says, "beauty is certainly a magnet for cultural anxieties of our day : the readjustment of gender roles that has been in the works since the Enlightenment, the commodification of the body in consumer culture, the genetic and evolutionary discoveries changing our understanding of human nature".

The next acrimonious category regarding the representation of women in advertisement centres around the concept of working women. This is an extremely immoral category burdening women from both inside and outside. The image of a successful woman as propagated in the ad-spots is completely divorced from the actual political and economic forces operating at the level of family and workplace. Television ads present women competing with men and at the same time submitting and reaffirming to the traditional roles. Think of the lady police officer in the Parachute Uttam hair oil, who in spite of her busy work schedule attends the temple with mother-in-law and kid and takes care of her long traditional hair with dark vermilion mark. Similarly woman executive of the MP Jewellers ad My World My Kingdom-from boardroom to kitchen, the quality tester lady in the Pilsbury wheat spot or the lady doctor of the Dettol floor cleaner spot-all belong to this category. In all these advertisements pre-existing norms of gender inequality is being compounded with imposing additional burden to the working girls only.

Another interesting feature can also be noted in case of the representation of career women. Most of these girls are conferred with married status serving the husband, kid and in-laws. Single woman and spinster are almost debarred in these projections. Child-caring is a must for the working ad-women. This is perhaps to reinforce the fact that "motherhood confers upon her (Indian woman) a purpose and identity that nothing else in her culture can". In other words, the concept of modern woman in advertisements hinges on the idea of a career woman but without making minimum compromise on what is expected traditionally from her. This naturally puts double burden on her. The innumerable ads on modern home appliances however spreads an idea that a modern woman does not find heavy the responsibilities of work place and home. The ad-spots on washing machine, microwave and other high-tech gadgets thereby legitimize this 'double-burden' on women. This super-woman image, who juggles the home and office fronts with same ease while maintaining her exquisite manicured looks, in turn, develops a kind of myth in reality leads to unrealistic expectations from husbands and families and to a lowered self-esteem in the real-life stressed out working housewife.

The preferential treatment received by the boy child in relation to the girls in the society also is revealed and legitimized through the electronic advertisements. For instance, in case of health drinks / foods and other products like Horlicks, Nestle Growing Up milk, Cerelac or Eureka Forbes water purifier or Dettol Suraksha and many other much circulated ad spots, all kind of care and affection is bestowed towards a child who happens to be a male in almost all cases. The underlying message perhaps is that the boys require this care and protection more than the girls. It also emphasises the unethical and unscientific craving for the boy child among the Indian masses. In the advertisement of the Life Insurance Corporation of India and some other nationalized banks also the savings habit and insurance habit of the people is attempted to encourage for a secured career of the boy-child and for managing the marriage expenses of the girl child. At the same time, in case of the beauty items, like soaps, talcum, hair oil etc, the projected child is necessarily a girl one.

Thus it can be observed that the idea of the so-called 'new-woman' in the advertisements is not bereft from the traditional customary enslavement of the woman. The ideological beliefs and assumptions underlying these clearly reinforce the stereotypical definitions of Indian womanhood. It is not unjust to say for the ad-media the body of the Indian woman is the locale of 'perceived modernity' and 'patriarchal morality' at the same time. Just remember the commercial advertisement on Wheel detergent bar, where the man scolds the wife for not getting a promotion for his shabby clothes. Actually for securing the approval of the majority, upper caste and upper class Hindu patriarchal morality is always presented as only good, powerful and normal. Overt reference of this category can be drawn from Bajaj motorcycle, Bharati telecom, Reliance India mobile or even Alpienliebe toffee spots. In all the spots a strong and deliberate endeavour is made to represent the Indian society and culture as a homogeneous one negating its inherent pluralism and thereby serving the interests of the ruling group of the society.

Further to this, constant airing of numerous ideals of ad-women, most of which have their origin in the capitalist extravaganza promotes a kind of 'de-territorialized' image of women. The television ads virtually becomes the melting pot of indigenous and global and thereby contribute actively in the construction of the multinational sponsor preferred 'modern' woman' Keeping an eye on this situation Uma Chakravarti quite aptly has made an extremely sarcastic comment that, "if one goes by the advertisements of today the debate on the existence of two Indias has now been decisively resolved, as there is only one India as far as the private channels go–a vibrant, rich and glossy urban India. Undeveloped, rural India has disappeared and in its place we often have a transformed ethnicized 'countryside' where the only structures are *havelies* set against a desert backdrop and the people are beautiful women in diaphanous clothing or men in Digjam or Siyaram suitings". Thus Lara Dutta or Malaika Arora or Lisa Ray become the representative of the millions of rural working women. Representation of real and local identities are loosing its ground very fast in this way. Forces of globalization in this way are aggravating the in egalitarian system of multiple hierarchies prevalent in the country. No wonder that the life style (whose!) magazine Femina, which is the main sponsor of annual beauty pageant contests talks of 'woman of substance' referring to the scantily clothed manicured women bodies in a society which provides little or no avenues for the socio-psychological development of majority of its women folk. Moreover, the sponsored ideal clearly construct women in terms of 'binary'. Sexuality and featured weakness (like cracked toes, dry/oily skin, sticky/ dandruff fed hair, smell of sweat and above all dark complexion) both become a site of viewing where male and female audience subscribe to similar kind of liking and disliking within the same ideological realism. This can be considered as an essential dimension of the politics of viewing.

Another form of advertisement broadly promotes the concept of marginalization where a particular group is thrown out from the centre occasionally on the basis of the possession of certain durable goods. For instance, in the HP gas commercial and BPL/Videocon washing machine spot the lady in focus takes command over her maid by possessing these goods. Another form of marginalization is done on the basis of one's looks and appearance. Remember the ad of krack cream where the girl is being ridiculed for her cracked toes and after using that particular cream only her status elevates. The spot on Clearasil also projects a group of girls teasing one of their friends for pimpled skin and then use of Clearasil comes as a rescue.

There is another level of representation which intends to impart the idea of 'barbie' culture to the girl child from a very early stage and thereby socialize her to remain as a subordinate throughout her life. The example of Clinic Protein Plus Shampoo and Pears soap spots can be shown in this regard. In these visuals the little girls are being prompted to gain acclamation from others by improving on their bodily looks following the norms of sponsor-preferred imperatives, like glossy hair or soft and unblemished skin that have adequate commodity back up. On the other hand advertisements of Ujala Supreme or Vaseline Skin Care preaches the girl child to feel glorified by winning male approval. On the Ujala spot in a children's skit a little girl is deprived from queen-ship by the king, played by another little boy, for her lesser white clothes. The maid of the same skit whose mother has used Ujala, for her brighter clothes is nominated as the queen by the king. The visual ends on large claps of the audience for the later girl and a proud smile of her mother. Similarly, in the Vaseline Skin Care a little girl of hardly five / six years of age is ridiculed by a boy of the same age for her dry skins in course of their plays. The mother of the girl is embarrassed and then the boy's mother comes to her rescue by offering a body care lotion with which the girl gains a position to retaliate to the boy with catcalls. All these clearly prove that women's sense of self, even that of the girl child continues to be influenced by the old and paired ideals. It seems that female sense of identity is only meaningful when they gain male applause for their physical attributes.

Thus putting together all these ad-spots it is evident that female body is a focal point of commercial buying and selling by exploitation of her sexual identity, familial and social roles and most importantly by manipulating her own self awareness and expectations. The advertising industries have successfully created a perfect image which no woman could ever achieve in reality. On the one hand, this provides the opportunity to men to judge women by this unnatural image and on the other hand the women are also pressuring themselves to approximate as far as possible to the dispersed visual presentations. But these exercises have severe consequences making the position of women more vulnerable in the society. The socially powerless position of the women as well as the extremely proficient campaign machinery of the ad agencies in reality do not allow to pose any opposition to the cultivated ideas. The politics behind the commercial way of seeing, which is essentially 'the male gaze' lies on the fact that ultimately it establishes itself as a way of seeing that appears as quite natural to human eye. The woman in this process, gradually succumbs to her pre-given and limited role. Even a woman feels empowered and free by subscribing to this 'male-gaze' and by transforming herself into an object. It is for this in the campaign of jewelers like A. Sirkar displays their products as 'no-compromise' goods featuring an apparently rebel actress with an assertion that "I never compromise on anything in my life so I choose this particular brand of jewelery". Unfortunately in each and every spot of that 'no-compromise' range of product this actress conforms to traditional male gaze by showing either the cleavage of her breasts or underarms or by appearing without any blouse and thereby allows to project herself as an object and her body as synonymous to the saleable ornaments merely.

Unfortunately we are yet to note any remarkable representation where the women is not being violated. The dangers of such uncountable pejorative representation of women in electronic media lies on the fact that all these tele-women have extensive power over the subconscious of the entire nation which ultimately is bound to cripple our consciousness.

To conclude, we can very well agree with Prof. Ipshita Chandra who in her well researched article has categorically mentioned that "these micro narratives, intensely packed with imperatives that form a part of their generic repertoire, are positioned to disrupt and supercede any other narrative ... The meaning of words like rights, equality, freedom or even empowerment seem to be sliding out of our control and even beyond our comprehension". Television ads with their preoccupation with the 'perfect' visual image are instrumental in nurturing the sense of self and others among the women folk. Moreover, the relatively shorter length of the ads depicting the 'problem' related to one's looks and appearance and their solutions have given birth to a kind of unnatural and impossible expectations among women which are bound to belie. This could have serious psycho-physical problems along with socio-political implications. The electronic advertisements have become important device to hold up the vitality of patriarchy in multiple ways. The infinite ad-spots approve the representation of women as mere objects. Thus, it can be said advent of modernity instead of providing equality, liberty and natural justice to women have made their unproportional position normal and acceptable. To put it simply advertisements have become parts of social organizations that perpetuate inequity through patriarchal control over women and thereby quite forcefully contribute to the process of what Simone de Beauvoir called 'becoming women'. This is no doubt an explicit political exercise.

References

Constance Classen, *The Color of Angels : Cosmology, Gender and Aesthetic Imagination*, London, 1998.

Mary Douglas, Natural Symbols, quoted in Terri Pitts, *Female Body Through Society : A Dialogue,* Barry and Rockliff, London, 1970.

Simone de Beauvoir, *The Second Sex*, , London, 1997.

Uma Chakravarti, 'Dreams Unlimited' in Tanisha Abraham (ed) *Women and the Politics of Violence,* New Delhi, 2002.

Laurent Gallissot, 'The Cultural Significance of Advertising : A General Framework for the Cultural Analysis of Advertising Industry in Europe' in *International Sociology*, Vol : 9, No : 1, 1994.

Laura Mulvey, 'Visual Pleasure and Narrative Cinema' (1975) quoted in Wendy Steiner, *The Trouble with Beauty*, London, 2000.

V. Geetha, *Gender*, Stree, Calcutta, 2002, p. 111.

Sudhir Kakar, 'Feminine Identity in India' in Rehana Ghadially (ed), *Women in Indian Society*, New Delhi, 1988.

Ipshita Chandra, 'Displaying the Modern Woman : Feminism in the Labyrinths of Media Culture' on *Social Scientist*, Vol. 28, Nos. 3-4, March–April 2000.

12

Religion, Sex and Issues of Identity: Women in Thailand

Lipi Ghosh

Thailand is one of our closest Southeast Asian neighbours. Its society is not very well known to us although it is known to be very close to Hindu and Buddhist cultures. Thai society is endorsed by many traditional and cultural phenomena. A researcher's eye is focused to a number of social and cultural provisions, which leaves remarkable impacts on the status of women in the society. One important mean to understand women's identity in Thai society is to look into the sphere of religion and sexuality. Interestingly in Thai society women are not allowed to take to monkhood but they can take to prostitution as an occupation. This paper takes into account the factors which motivate women's identity in the two above noted spheres. This paper looks into social and cultural ambiance permitting women's participation in sex trade and sex industry and at the same time attempts to analyse how and why women's participation in the domain of religion is restricted.

Religion, Women and Sex Sector : Tradition to Modernity

Thailand is one of those countries, which are admittedly important centers for the practice of the 'oldest occupation' in the world, i. e prostitution. This Southeast Asian country has been given the byname-*Prostitute's Paradise.* A considerable number of women are engaged in this occupation, of which a large number of female child prostitutes has been reckoned as one of the greatest social evils. In fact, history of the evolution of harlotry in Thailand is an interesting subject. The contemporary situation in Thailand reveals that the hard laws of economies rule the sex as an industry. The sex industry is characterised as the darkest underside of Asia's economic boom. But an in depth study of the history behind its growth reveals that in past while economy had a very limited role to play, religion and rituals paved the way for the development of the occupation.

While tracing the history of prostitution in Thailand, it is to be observed that religion had a definite role to play behind it. Religion in fact in any feudal and post feudal order is concerned primarily with man's inner personal adjustment to other-worldly ideal order. Patrimonial society is characterised by a monopoly enjoyed by moral and intellectual elite to sanction legitimate order and change. This is justified on grounds that social orders must be moral and inexpedient. Only morality imbued political elitists have constant right, responsibility and ability to both judge and execute that mandate. Thus any problem in the social order are typically viewed as individual failings. The moral / religious foundation of any social order were highly encouraged. Therefore, judged from this viewpoint, patriarchy definitely takes religion as a medium to fulfill their wishes. If they wish they may mould it on a platform of merit and morality but in contrary too, it may be moulded to justify some immoral functions.

In Thailand, a patrimonial political order ideally is a moral order. According to Thai philosophy, moral laws govern state and state is created primarily to uphold these moral laws. Thus when we view the Thai social system as a morality based patrimonial one; we proceed to discuss the system of prostitution with particular focus on their institutions of social system. In patrimonial Thai society as the relationship between religious values and society is an important phenomenon but at the sametime the relationship between diffused religious values and society is also very remarkable dimension. This notion of 'diffused' religious value analysis is one of the most controversial fields in contemporary sociology, fraught with logical and empirical pitfalls. This seems especially relevant in the Thai case because of the very nature of religious paradox or logical contradictions within the religious system itself.

What is this diffused religious values? To take an example, Thais are genuine, honest and sincere Buddhists, but at the same time they are unwilling to commit themselves exclusively to Buddhist rituals and doctrines. According to many observers it may be more proper to speak of Thais not exclusively as Buddhists but as followers of a religious system, which is eclectic, an amalgam of many different religious traditions. In other words it accommodates diverse religious elements within it and this may be called as 'diffused' religious values.

Hinduism and its Resplendent Influence

That being the character of Thai society and the character of the country's religion, it influences directly the process of social change. It provides flexibility to adopt foreign elements in to the social framework. In Thailand, therefore one must treat the evolution of prostitution as an institution having a Hindu religious sanction in society. How? From ancient times in the royal Thai court and aristocratic surroundings, the relationship between man and woman has remained similar to that of a master and a slave. Among all the thoughts and ideas of Hindu religion which influenced the Thai kings, the most notable was that of man's supremacy in society, highlighted by Brahmanical philosophy. Woman was regarded as a symbol of entertainment for men in the royal court. The Indian influence in Southeast Asia dates back to time immemorial. The Indian immigration to the Indo Chinese peninsula had begun before the Christian era and continued well in the succeeding period. The 'Suvarnabhumi' as it was called was well known to the Indians. They introduced Buddhism and Brahmanism into this peninsula. The early day's migrants came with a rich Indian culture, which they spread throughout this region through intermingling.

It is undeniable that Indian culture had the most dominant external influence in Southeast Asia, particularly in the form of Hindu and Buddhist religious-cultural system. The Two kingdoms, Sukhodaya (Popularly known as Sukhothai) and Ayudhya (or Ayuthia) confronted each other in Siam in the second half of the fourteenth century. In their administrative systems, although Theravada Buddhism was an important force, there was strong influence of Hinduism in society. Remarkable point is that throughout the period, the Brahmanical cult however lent their luster to royalty as early as an uncertain date before 1250 A.D. There were several Thai kings who patronised Hinduism.

Without going into factual details of the patronisation of Indian culture, it is our task to see how such Hinduism dominated Siam society defined the position of women in society and how there was gradual evolution of harlotry? The degenerated position of women in Ayuthia period may be due to the direct influence of Hinduism on the then Siam society. The Ayuthian civil law had a connection with *Dharmasastra* and the major portion of it dealt with Brahmanical religious observances, such as rites, purification and penance. Its authority is derived from Manu and its sanction from Brahmanical belief. Inscription xxxviii in which king Ramaraja of Ayudhya promulgates a law in the vassal kingdom of Sukhodaya in 1397 is a document of importance for the study of legal history of Siam. It is the only known legislative text engraved on stone emanating from any of the Southeast Asian kingdoms. The Indian tradition held that the universe is governed by an immutable natural law, the *Dharma* which was miraculously revealed to sage Manu and in turn revealed by him to other sages who made it known to mankind through abridged version called *Dharmasastra*. Professor Lingat has shown that Ayudhya was the only Southeast Asian kingdom to develop a code of civil law. Based on Hindu *Dharmashastra*, but all the Brahmanical matter removed and relying for its authority on a Buddhist adoption of the legend of Manu, it was intended as a guide for Buddhist kings in the administration of justice. In this context, it is important to note that textual comparisons of the ancient Siamese laws show that those were derived from the Manuic laws of India. In other words in the ancient times the monarchs of the Siamese nation governed their people with laws which were originally derived from the *Dharmasastra* of Manu, which was the then prevailing law among the inhabitants of India and the neighbouring countries.

To understand Thai women's identity in the sex sector, it is first necessary to understand the degraded position of female folk in the society. A concrete example of the derogated position of women is proved from the fact that one major characteristic of ancient Siam was the slave system and this slave system takes us direct to the question of prostitution. Many Thai kings had their slave wives, but apart from a few cases of slave wives, the general plight of the slave women was deplorable. There are many evidences, which speak about the practice of selling women for slavery in Thai society, particularly from the Ayuthia era. The most common form of prostitution during the Ayuthia period involved 'stationed' women. Those women were essentially slaves. Under Thai laws during most of the period, a slave was viewed both as an object and person. Although the slaves had a few rights, they were obliged to serve their owners. As objects, their owners could sell the slaves. In the case of female slaves, the price varied according to the degree of their beauty and character of the woman. The value beginning at 1,00, 000 cowries rose gradually to 1, 20, 000 cowries at the age of twenty one, remained there until the age of thirty and gradually decreased until it was only 75, 000 at the age of ninety-one. Women were commonly purchased to serve in the houses of slave owners-the forerunner of Thai brothel. In these houses there was a manager who supervised the female slaves, ensuring that they served their clients with good manner.

An analysis of the ancient customary law of the country also proves beyond doubt how socio-legal environment of the period, under influence of Hindu Manuic laws also served as a factor behind the growth of derogated position of women in the sex sector of this Asian country. A Royal Decree, issued on March 27, 1868, while banning the practice of selling women referred to the prevalent ancient laws : 'In accordance with customary laws of the land, if any husband, father, master of a slave, executes a sale-deed for his wife, daughter or slave, his legal right to this is admitted. They can perform this without the permission of the sold beings'. In another section of the same Decree, it was stated 'According to native law, no wife or daughter has the right to issue a sale-deed in the name of a husband or parents, as she is subservient to them. ' Such kind of legal system goes to prove that in Thailand, from the very early times, women's rights and their social status had been kept at a very low level.

Another important feature of Thai system was that women's status in society was tied up with the question of land distribution. In ancient Siam one prevalent system was Sakdina system. A law proclaimed in 1455 known as *Phra Aiyakan Tamnang Nai Thaharn Lae Phonlaruan* defined social rank as an indication of a person's status and authority in the social order and his responsibility towards society and the administration system. As the sole owner of all land, the monarch allocated it to his subjects according to their ranks. There was no private ownership *per se*. Sakdina derived from the Hindu concept of *Shakti*, which means power in terms of resource or energy. Literally, Sakdina means 'the control over rice field'. The actual operation of Sakdina had two dimensions. Sakdina was a unit of land (*rai* or about 0.16 hector) It was a numerically hierarchical system of dignity marks which substantiated the ranking of population through land allocation. For example those holding Sakdina of 400 up to 100, 000 rai were appointed directly by the king and formed the small ruling stratum. Monks were allocated from 400 up to 2400 *rai* and novices between 200 and 300 *rai*. Serfs (*Phrai*) were allocated 25 rai for an adult married male in service to the king and lords, 20 *rai* to one who supervised war slaves and refugee families and 10-15 *rai* for a common serf. That being the Sakdina system, the question of law, sexuality and gender under this Sakdina system emerged as an important phenomena. With such less protected personal rights, women were exposed to various forms of sexual violence, which might have included forced and indentured polygamy and prostitution. The typical example about less protection of women can be well understood when we read the Royal Decree of May 27, 1868 :

> *According to current domestic law, the measure of an abductor's guilt would be determined on the basis of the size of the landed property held by him. If a daughter was kidnapped, then at the very outset it was ascertained if her father had the Sakdina right or land measuring up to 480 rai. If he had then she belonged to the aristocracy. Next it was determined if the abductor's family had similar Sakdina rights. If the family had the rights, then the abduction was not considered as an offence and the abductor was not found guilty. But in the*

> *absence of Sakdina rights, the father of the daughter could claim compensation from the kidnapper because in the eye of law, the offender was guilty of a serious crime.* It is nothing but an instance of clear humiliation of women in society.

Another important example of social humiliation of women can be proved from the fact of marital relation. The marital relation in society in other ways and the sanction of Buddhism also led to social degradation of women. The question of polygamy is to be mentioned in this context. In traditional Siam the prestige of a man was measured by the number of wives and women who served him. A man was traditionally permitted to obtain wives in various ways. One could be selected by his parents, one chosen by himself, another taken by showing pity to a woman in distress, perhaps another was granted by the king as a reward for services rendered, plus a few slave or servant wives. Members of the ruling Sakdina (feudal-bureaucratic) elite could afford to practise polygamy to this degree. According to a law of 1361A. D., wives were divided into three categories : the principal wife *(mia klang muang)*, the secondary wife *(mia klang nok)* and the slave wife *(mia klang thasi)* This ranking of wives determined the worth of a woman in a number of ways. The lower the rank of the wife, the less consequential her seduction was thought to be.

Polygamy was also prevalent in ancient royal culture of Siam. The kings of Thailand traditionally abounded in wives, concubines and children and the practice continued until 1910 when the last polygamous king Chulalongkorn died. Social scientists sometimes refer to the excessive polygamy practised by the rulers. It has been said that King Chulalongkorn had 84 wives and 362 children. We have *The Chronicle* which is an almost complete record of the number of wives and children acquired by the kings of the House of Chakri. As per this chronicle king Chulalongkorn (1868-1910) had 32 sons and

44 daughters by 36 wives, king Mongkut (1851-1868) had 39 sons and 43 daughters by 35 wives.

The social dimension of such an institution of polygamy was important. Relation with more than one woman became a permanent feature of Thai society. It was women's duty to provide entertainment to rich and influential men. It became a permanent feature, which later helped in the growth of the practice and trade of harlotry. In later period when King Mongkut tried to reform the system of polygamy, his elite class counselor and a group of officials loyal to the court expressed utter confidence in Siamese tradition and wrote a text in defence of Polygamy. One of those men was Chaophraya Thiphakorawong (K*ham Bunnag),* the author of the *Defense of Polygamy*. The man was a member of the power-elite, an official loyal to the king and an intimate associate of king Mongkut. In his official capacities Thiphakorawong became acquainted with western envoys, travelers and missionaries, who came to Siam in increasing numbers during and after the 1855 treaties. Some westerners perceived Thiphakorawong as modern and progressive because of the minister's curiosity about the west and his ability to debate without xenophobic defensiveness. These qualities have been amply documented by nineteenth century European sources. However, Thiphakorawong was a person of contradictory visions. Therefore, on one hand he was critical of Siamese belief, particularly Buddhist beliefs, but, on the other hand, he defended lower status for women in Thai society by upholding polygamy. His book named Kitchanukit *(A Book Explaining Many Things)* has a section on polygamy, where he discussed several questions, such as causes behind polygamy, the question of its acceptance, Siamese Buddhist marriage customs, Buddha's teaching about polygamy etc. The overall picture presents women as passive and submissive but at the same time as jealously possessive, ambitious and ruthless, even capable of murdering their own husbands in pursuit of ambition. More thought is given to the sexual convenience of the husband and since he is the active partner, polygamy reduces misconduct or demerit because it prevents the husband from forcing a wife against her will. The image of the jealously possessive and ruthless woman explains why a woman can not have many husbands, for she would kill those she preferred not to love. While polygamy follows from the first image, an equitable polyandry is omitted by the second. The overall justification shown by Thiphakorawong for polygamy is that it contributes to social harmony by reducing antagonism and conflict between the sexes. Thus, the psychological undercurrents presented in the text justified the practice of polygamy. Such ideas dominated Siamese social life until its real modernisation started in very recent time.

Such being the social system under influence of Hinduism, keeping relation with more than one woman or extra-marital relation was a common feature in ancient Siam and so such kind of environment was congenial or extended the proper pathway for the growth and development of prostitution and concubinage. Therefore, it may be termed as the 'cultural environment' behind the evolution of prostitution.

Buddhism, Society and Sex

While influence of Hinduism speaks of its influence, the crucial question is what role Buddhism played to define women's status and position and how sexual society and the very question of prostitution have been treated by Buddhist philosophy. Theravada Buddhism has been a powerful influence in Thailand for about seven hundred years.

It is interesting at this juncture to discuss the question of Buddhism and sex in society. The third precept, which directly deals with acceptable sexual conduct, says one should refrain from violating others' wives and daughters. To put it in another way social critics and Buddhist scholars are of the opinion that there is a golden rule in Buddhist teachings which applies to all sexual relationship. It is the rule of non-exploitation, an abstention from abusing both others and oneself. For a monk it means celibacy, for a lay person it implies sexual restraint. Celibacy is an ideal goal in a Buddhist world view This comes from the realisation that an attachment to sensual pleasures-with lust and sex as their most powerful forms-only leads to desire, greed, anger and exploitation, thus perpetuating the cycle of selfishness and suffering. A Buddhist's duty, there fore, is to transcend beyond the attachment of sensual pleasure and desires.

Such being the canonical sanction, the actual picture of Thai society is quite different. What seems is that there are some justifications of the sexual exploitation, which are deep rooted in the society. It is in fact the 'culture of power' over Buddhist ideals. It however leads to the conclusion that Buddhism failed to provide a strict sexual code for the society to follow. Religions like Islam and Christianity, control and govern the total life of the adherents including matrimonial relationship. Buddhism can only offer suggestions. Buddhism too believes in openness of mind. Such openness is a kind of weakness in itself. While it fosters tolerance and rids the society of repression and guilt, it at the same time promotes laxity.

How prostitution goes with Buddhism-is a crucial question. The term for prostitute as found in Buddhist Pali texts is *sobhini*, abbreviated form of *nagar-sobhini*, meaning a beautiful woman belonging to the city. In history this term is believed to be first given by the King of Vajji, a republic of 6th century B.C. India and constituted in essence a professional position of state prostitute. To receive the title a woman had to be extraordinarily beautiful, learned and well trained in social arts such as singing, dancing, conversation, poetry and in *kamasutra*,-the art of sexual pleasure. Such women were desires of high-class elites like kings, princes and nobles. Another class of prostitute served the public. They were called *ganika* which simply means a community woman. *Ganikas* were mentioned in the early Buddhist texts but the focus was on the *Sobhinis.*

The early Buddhist texts did not reflect any negative attitude towards prostitution. Lord Buddha himself welcomed these women and gave them opportunity to walk on the path of enlightenment in equality with all people. In Buddhist texts of his own age, we come across a number of *sobhinis* like Ambapali, Salavati, Sirima, Vimalapurana etc. etc. Thus on a primary level Buddhism does not deny prostitutes. Buddha himself accepted invitations from the *sobhinis* and *ganikas.* Lord Buddha himself accepted food from Sujata-the *nagar-nati*-or city-dancer. Similarly Basantasena, the famous courtesan portrayed in Sudraka's *Mrichchkatika* was also a nagarnati ('a woman belonging to the city') in the sixth century B.C.–the age of Buddha. All these prove that prostitution was not segregated in Buddha's teaching.

The oldest compilation of the Buddhist cannons with commentaries in Siamese prose is in the *Traibhumi* of Phra Ruang (The Three Worlds Cosmography) which dates from 1345 A. D. There is evidence that earlier texts existed but were destroyed, but elements of these might have been incorporated in the *Traibhumi* of Phra Ruang. However as a holy text, this Three-Worlds Cosmography has not been exempt from change and adoption. At various stages of Thai history the text has been revised and amended. It is a difficult task to trace the impact of Buddhism on the legal framework governing the male-female relationship in Thai history. Firstly, it is not possible to interpret Thai history as a uniform and linear political succession of different kingdoms for Sukhodaya to Ayuthia to Bangkok and finally to the present form of constitutional monarchy. Modern Thailand is the embodiment of earlier power struggle among many ethnic groups and the cultural vestiges of these groups make what is known today as Thai culture, unified at some level only by Theravada Buddhism. Besides historical records are scanty too. Nevertheless, from the existing data based on epigraphic and documentary sources help us to draw some conclusions about women's position. Scholars of Thai antiquity have suggested that Buddhist universal law *(Dhamma)* was already applied in social organisation.

Let us talk about its application in the Sukhothai and Ayuthia periods. Sukhothai polity is described as relatively simple, compared to the later periods of Ayuthia and Bangkok. The rulers of these states pursued what is often referred to as the personalistic and paternalistic style of leadership. The ideological role of Buddhism was limited to the control of the moral conduct of the people and the legitimization of political rule by kings whose conduct had to be cogent with the ideal kingship stated in the *Dhamma.* Two notable sources which provide insight into the nature of early polity and the class structure are King Ram Khamhaeng's inscription of the state of Sukhodaya and the M*angraisat* and the Peroration which concludes it locate King Mangrai's authority in the Buddhist tradition of royal decrees. The preamble also justifies history according to Buddhist universal law *(Dhamma)* which 'underlies and activates the universe'. As a law-giver, king Mangrai's task was to link Buddhist universal principles to the customary rules and forms of organizations of the people. Such legitimization was less clear in the case of Ram Khamhaeng's inscription. However, evidence suggests that Buddhist universal law *(Dhamma)* was cited and coupled with *Rajasastra* or the legal codes promulgated by King Ram Khamhaeng.

Class structure in Thai society, in conformity with Buddhist principle was not equal for men and women. Buddhism structured the world in such a way that *karma*-the physical, verbal and cognitive actions of past lives-and the accrual or loss of merit in consequence of those actions conditioned the differences between any two individuals in social status, talent, wealth and power. *Karma* relating gender signified that to be a woman and not a man meant that a woman had an inadequate store of merit, and the only way to remedy this situation was for a woman to earn merit through acts of religious devotion. Thus as early as 1399 A. D. at the end of Sukhodaya period the queen Mother founded a monastery and commemorated the event in an inscription in which she requested, "By the power of my merit, may I be reborn as a male ..."

In other ways, too traditional values perpetuated by Buddhist ideals defined a specific role for the Thai women. Many characters in classical literature have exemplified 'right conduct' for a woman. They are admirably set forth, in a 19th century poem *Words of Wisdom for Young Women* or 'Ladies of nobility should keep well within the good traditions and avoid gossips ...A woman is good or bad depending on her husband ... Obey your relative... Tend to your domestic responsibilities and serve your husband well ... Wake up before him. Prepare his toilet articles and his food... Pay respect to your husband at his feet before going to bed... do not argue with your husband and provoke his anger...Be feminine, not half masculine. Be like Sida in keeping yourself above blemishes and gossip'

This subordination is evident in a cosmographic text from Sukhodaya period in the fourteenth century which sets out the Buddhist world-view in a systematic form. It reinforces inequality between men and women. The most discernible example about position of women in traditional society to the ideal marriage between the Universal Monarch and the Queen. The Queen always complements her husband. Their coexistence represents a completeness without extreme. She waits on her husband :

"When the Universal Monarch comes to visit his precious wife, she does not remain seated... she sits lower than him...

when the Universal Monarch gives an order she executes it. She never disobeys her husband and in the smallest action and in her slightest words she pleases him... and she absolutely cannot break away from him."

Talking about palace stories, Anna Leonowens' *Siamese Harem Life* condemns what she claimed was the stifled, repressed, loveless and terror-filled lives of the palace-women whose very meaning of existence had to be for the sole purpose of serving the king's will. Life for women in royal palace was absolutely restricted in all respects. There was a limitation on their movements. They were treated as repository of honour of their families. If palace women *(ying chaowang)* were found as a party to an illicit sexual liaison, the death sentence awaited them. On the contrary in the Siamese harem itself there were numbers of ladies serving in the Inner Palace, Middle Palace and Outer Palace ... as well as ladies in waiting of all ranks, ladies chaperons and chaperons and many palace dancers and concubines."

This being the state of women in Thai society, Buddhist philosophy regarding prostitution i.e. acceptance of prostitution and their non-segregation had good impact on society. Therefore, among a group of Thai women prostitution is not defined as something wrong, but rather it is accepted as a value based system in society. In Thai history as we already, noted prostitution was mentioned for the first time during king Rama I's reign. Throughout Thailand history again, like Indian elite class, it was a common practice for Thai men to visit brothels to prove their virility. Men who did not do so were considered strange and suffered the possibility of becoming social outcaste. Many Thai proverbs reflect the values that relegate women to the status of a commodity or an object of male desire.

According to the analysis of some social scientists, the attitude of Buddhist Sangha is to be considered in this regard.

Consumerism has rapidly planted itself as the Thai people's new religion. According to Buddhist teachings, the main hindrances to one's quest for a chaste life stems from attachment to sexual desires or to other visual pleasures which give rise to greed, anger and delusion. Consumerism creates and nourishes these hindrances. It is based on the pursuit of sensual pleasure, with sex at its core, wealth and success. Given cultural sexism, the flesh trade is therefore exploding because it is endorsed by a new religion that encourages the pursuit of sexual excitement. That is why the Thais feel no guilt or shame about sex trade and it is why the society fails altogether to see prostitution as exploitation. Commercial advertisers are fully aware that sex is the strongest urge. They have always highlighted sexual messages, whether overtly or implicitly in their efforts to persuade people to buy their products. The monastery raised no eyebrow at that. It is therefore not surprising that there exist a big sexual mess in a country that boasts of 250,000 monks and 30,000 temples.

Women, Monastery and Identity

This brings us directly to the question of women's identity in the religious sector. Under influence of Hinduism, Buddhist monks too denied to acknowledge equal role of women. They injected the thinking into the society that women could not in any way become enlightened by themselves. The Buddha permitted ordination of women, but Buddhist monks rejected it. We should bear in mind that Buddhist precepts were initially abused in the olden days by Buddhist monks in India who were deeply influenced by Hindu thinking. In addition, this influence has lasted until the present day in Thailand.

The first serious attempt in modern Thai history to start a community of *bhikkhuni* occured in 1927, two years after the accession to the throne of king Rama VII. Narin Klueng (aka Narin Bhasit) a progressive politician threw a direct challenge to the prevailing system and he denoted a plot of land for the construction of a women-only temple-Wat Nariwong. He arranged his two daughters Sara and Chongdi and some more women to be ordained as samaneri. But the reaction from the society was very strong and women of the Wat were arrested and imprisoned. A year later (1928) the Buddhist Sangha of Thailand, i.e. Sangha Supreme Council passed a law expressly forbidding the ordination of female novice monks.

Yet the struggle for ordination did not stop. In 1957 (B. E 2500) five women were ordained with 10 precepts like novices and they wear brown robes known as 'Silacharini'. Their Centre was at Wat Chanasonggram in Bangkok. Another group wear dark brown robe under the guidance of Bhadraksa-a self ordained female monk. A third group of women started like *Mae chii* wore light yellow robe. Ven Vorami Kabilsingh, mother of Dhammananda received full ordination as *bhikkhuni* from the Sanghas in Taiwan. She lived in the same temple where Dhammananda is staying.

It has been observed by a group of social scientists and also by the present author in her research work on Prostitution in Thailand : Myth and Reality that prostitution in the country to a large extent is a result of social discrimination of women in showing their gratitude to their parents by taking to monkhood. Every man in Thai society takes to monkhood once in his life time and it is believed that this way he brings virtue to the family and his parents gain merits by dint of his monkhood.

The situation was contrary for the women. As religion imposed restrictions on women to enter monkhood, they preferred to show gratitude, love and respect to their families by earning money from any occupation including prostitutes. Many Thai prostitutes interviewed about the background of their occupation confirm to this ideology. It is to be observed that Buddhism in Thailand may be termed as a transformed form of Buddhism. Traditional and deep rooted superiority of the male and female inferiority in Buddhist society, influenced by Hindu thinking is recognised in Thai society. The continuing abuse of Buddhism precepts has created a number of social problems which affect Thai girls and women alike. Many of the Buddha's followers in Thailand have abused his teachings and turned them into a tool to exploit Thai girls and women. Under Hindu influence a woman is nothing, she is valuable only when she becomes a wife or the mother of a baby. In Thai dictionary a wife-*(phanrayaa)* has been defined as 'a person who is dependent on her husband', while a husband *(saa-mee)* has been defined as a possessor. Thus it implies female inferiority to the males. Under influence of Hinduism, Buddhist monks too denied to acknowledge equal role of women. They injected the thinking into the society that women could not in any way become enlightened by themselves. The Buddha permitted ordination of women, but Buddhist monks rejected it. We should bear in mind that Buddhist precepts were initially abused in the olden days by Buddhist monks in India who were deeply influenced by Hindu thinking. And this influence has lasted until the present day Thailand.

It has been further stated that the tradition of pre-marital ordination is considered the greatest activity for sons only. The purpose is to show gratitude to parents. But as Buddhist women are denied to assist their parents on the spiritual path to heaven, they try to find out other ways to show their gratitude. This way gratitude is constantly cited as the main reason that many girls from the north and north east of the country enter both the labour market and the sex trade.

The maximum status a woman can gain in a temple is to become a *Mae chi*. The word Mae *Chii ji* is still controversial. *Mae Chii* in Thai means mother, *Chii* Ji is variously explained. Apparently during Buddha's time Ji was used to mean unordained females wearing white dress, who observed 5-8 precepts. Institute for Thai *Mae Chii* is an administrative body of the Foundation of Her Majesty's Royal Patronage. Social status of the *Mae Chiis* are very strange. They are not *upasika*, but they shave their heads and usually live separated from their families and wordly lives. So they are definitely not laity. A Bhikkhuni holds 311 rules (Theravada) while a *Mae Chii* holds only 8 precepts.

These *Mae Chiis* are not generally accepted in society. According to the Dept of Religious Affairs of Thailand Government, *Mae Chiis* are not 'ordained' into the Sangha and they are not prapagators. At best they are only 'residents' of the Wats. In general *Mae Chiis* are poor and uneducated. 93 per cent of them have only primary education, Because of their poor education, they are very narrow in their understanding of life and society in general. As their religious status is not approved they are not allowed to vote, but they are at the same time have to leave home and worldly concerns. This indicated a double standard for the *Mae chiis*. But after all people say they are aiming at enlightenment.

Currently there are 10,000 *Mae-Chiis* living in thai temples. Dhammananda has broken the traditional system which resisted ordination of women. At present she is staying in Wat Songdharmmakalyani, a temple in Nakhorn Pathom and if she sucessfully completes her two years' apprenticeship she will become a Bhikkhuni-a female Buddhist monk. Her this mission may bring a very big social change-opening vistas of virtue for women. It may be expected that in the near future society to come Thai women will not reflect the lamenting image of sex workers and this image will be replaced by a holy and noble one.

It may happen however, for which there is every chance that women's status as monk remain unrecognised until and unless Buddhist Council law of 1928 is annulled. Many senior and prominent monks still think that ordination of women in Thailand is still a long way away and it is still a very sensitive issue in the country. In this new age of alternative thinking, can we expect that female monks will be a good alternative to social evil. Perhaps the future can only reveal the truth.

Conclusion

One point is very clear from the above noted discussion is that although Thailand is a matrilineal society, here patriarchy dominates in a tacit form and many of the society's ethics, norms and cultural traits, particularly religion has been used and moulded to serve the interest of the patriarchy.

Among Thai Buddhists, the tradition of pre-marital ordination is considered the greatest activity for sons only. The purpose is to show gratitude to parents. But as Buddhist women are denied to assist their parents on the spiritual path to heaven, this leaves a very significant impact on Thai women. They try to find out other ways to show their gratitude. This way gratitude is constantly cited as the main reason that many girls from the north and north east of the country enter both the labour market and the sex trade.

References

A.B. Griswold and Prasert na Nagara "On Kingship and Society at Sukhodaya" in Skinner and Kirsch ed. *Change and Persistence in Thai Society*, London, 1975.

A.B. Griswold and Prasert na Nagara, "The Asoknama Inscription of 1399 A.D." Epigraphic and Historical Studies, No. 2. *Journal of Siam Society*, LVII, 1, January, 1969.

Anna Leonowens, *The Romance of Harem*, Virginia, 1872.

Arnold Wringht, *Twentieth Century Impressions of Siam*, London, 1908.

B. J. Terwiel "The Bowering Treaty : Imperialism and the Indigenous Perspective", *Journal of Siam Society*, Vol. 79, Part 2, 1991.

C. J. Reynolds, A Nineteenth Century Thai-Buddhist Defense of Polygamy and Some Remarks on the Social History of Women in Thailand, paper presented for the Seventh Conference, *I.A.H.A.* Bangkok, 22-26 August 2000.

Chatthip Nartsupha and Suthy Prasartset, 'Proclamation of the Royal Decree regarding Husbands selling wives and Parents selling children in Siam, 1851-1910 : A Documentary Survey", *Southeast Asian Perspective Series, No. 4,* Institute of Southeast Asian Studies, Singapore, 1977.

Chatsumarn Kabilsingh, *Thai Women in Buddhism*, Berkeley, 1991.

E.R. Leach, *Political System of Highland Burma : A Study of Kachin Social Structure*, Boston, 1965.

G. William Skinner, *Chinese Society in Thailand : An Analytical History*, New York, 1962.

______*Recommendations to Combat International Traffic in Women,* Foundation for Women, Bangkok 1995.

Hong Lysa, "Looking at Nineteenth Century Siamese Women Police Files : Between Wang and Muang : Palace Women at the Margins of Social Change", paper presented at the 14th I. A. H. A. conference, Bangkok, 20-24 May, 2000.

Khin Thitsa, "Providence and Prostitution : Women in Buddhist Thailand" *Change : International Reports*, London, 1990.

King Lidaiya, *Les Trois Mondes (Traibhumi Brah Rvan)* trans. G. Coedes and C. Archainbault, vol. Lxxxix in Publications de l'Ecole Francaise d'extreme Orient-Paris, 1973.

Kenneth Perry Landon, *The Chinese in Thailand*, New York, 1941.

Lipi Ghosh, Prostitution in Thailand : Perspective, Problem and Prevention, *The Journal of Women's Studies Calcutta,* Vol. 2. No. 1, April-September, 1997.

Ma Huan, *Ying-yai Sheng-lan.* The Overall Survey of the OCEAN"s Shores [1433]J. V. G. Mills, trans. And ed. (Cambridge : Hakluyt Society, 1970), p. 104 as quoted in Barbara Watson Andaya, "Economic Change and the Growth of Prostitution in early Modern Southeast Asia", paper presented to the 14th IAHA Conference, Bangkok, 20-24 May, 1996.

Malcom Smith, *A Physician at Court of Siam,* London, 1946.

Mayuree Rattanawannathip "Female Inferiority in Buddhist Society", *Nation*, Bangkok, August, 1996.

Mr. And Mrs. Emile Jottrand (trans. and Introduction by Walter E. J. Tips), *In Siam : The Diary of a Legal adviser of King Chulalongkorn's Government,* Bangkok, 1996.

Norman Jacobs, *Modernisation without Development : Thailand as an Asian Case Study,* New York, 1971.

Pasuk Phongpaichit, From Peasant Girls to Bangkok Masseuses, *Women, Work and Development,* No. 2, International labour office, Geneva, 1982.

Salmon M, *History : The Present State of All nations,* London, 1725.

Sanitsuda Ekachai, Buddhism and the Sexual society" *The Journey,* Vol. xlvi, no. 255, section iii, Newzealand.

Siriporn Skrobanech, The Sex Trade in Women in Thailand : Problems and Strategies for Solutions (Thai), *Seminar Proceedings,* Social Research Institute, Chulalongkorn University.

Thanh dam Troong, *Sex, Money, Morality : Prostitution and Tourism in Southeast Asia,* London, 1990.

Wathinee Boonchalaksi and Philip Guest, *Prostitution in Thailand,* Bangkok, 1994.

Wiboon Nakornjarupong "Patronage and the Night Queens", *Business in Thailand,* November, 1981.

WOMEN IN MIDST OF TRADITIONS

13

Japanese Women : Mukoirikon to Modernisation

Purabi Gangopadhyay

Japanese history provides remarkable changes in the status of women in Japan. The changes occurred according to the varied socio-economic trends of the country. Since the ancient period Japanese people used to live in extended families of three or more generations. The whole family relationships were governed by a rigid hierarchical system. The parental supremacy was the main character of Japanese families. The head of the family commanded respect from his children and other members of the family even from his parents. The married women were expected to faithfully obey her husband and in-laws. But with the process of democratization, the status of women in Japanese society improved enormously after the World War II.

Mukoirikon and the Women-centered Society

In ancient Japan (since late Nara or Tempyo period, i.e. 8th century A.D. to 11th century A.D.) the women-centred marriage pattern known as Mukoirikon contributed to social, political and religious supremacy of the women in Japanese society. This Mukoirikon, which is also known as the *Shooseikon* is nothing but the 'matrilocal marriage'. The couple usually hails from the same locality and met at the house of the wife's parents before the marriage.

In *Mukoirikon* the process of marriage starts with the preliminary stage of courtship with very little interference of the family members. Then the future bridegroom formally visits his in-laws' house, which is known as *Hatsumukoirikon*. Then on a sacred day, selected by the family heads of both the houses, the formal marriage ceremony is performed.

In this system the groom was known as *Mukoyoshi* or an adopted son-in-law who moves to his wife's family and assumes its name. This system was prevalent among the court aristocracy as well as in the other social levels. This system continued for a long time and it was popular among the farmer class for a long time. Later the upper class especially the warriors adopted the system of sending the bride to join her husbands family. But this system is still popular especially in the farmers' family where there is no male offspring and among a few communities of traditional labourers, such as fishermen.

Women in Politics and Religion in Ancient Japan

Besides their central role in the families and society, Japanese women also played a prominent position in politics. In the 7th-8th centuries it was acceptable for a women to reign the country as '*Tenno*', i.e. the emperor and there were at least six powerful and prominent women *Tenno* in Japanese history during this period who held a very prominent position in the political history of Japan. These six women *Tenno* were Empress *Suiko* (C. 593 A.D. to 628 A.D.), Empress *Saimei* (C 642 A.D. to 645 A.D. and C 655 A.D. to 661 A.D.), Empress *Jito* (C 686 A.D. to 697 A.D.) Empress *Gemmei* (C 707 A.D. to 715 A.D.), Empress *Gensho* (C 715 A.D. to 724 A.D.) and Empress *Kooken* (C 749 A.D. to 758 A.D. and C 764 A.D. to 770 A.D.)

But after the shifting of the Imperial Capital to *Heiankyo* (modern Kyoto) from *Nara* in 794 i.e. in the *Heian* period, women *Tenno* (emperor/empress) did not appear in the political history of Japan any longer.

Apart from the important role of the women in the society and politics they also enjoyed a prominent role in the religious field especially in the *Shamanistic* practices. Like many other countries of the world, in Japan also women's procreative power was regarded as sacred and the women held a very important position in the agricultural rites especially in rice planting. The importance of Japanese women in religion is also manifested in the designation of *Amaterasu Oomikami,* the Sun goddess as principal deity in the Shinto pantheon. This goddess (sun-goddess) "is thought to have evolved from the concept of a shamaness mediating between humanity and supernatural beings." A princess called *Yamatoshime* founded the famous *ISE* shrine of Japan, which is regarded as the main temple of *Amaterasu Oomikami*. The chief priest of the shrine was also a woman. The importance of women in the Shinto religion is still accepted and continued through a system of shrine-maidens called *Miko* and occasionally the women also serves as female priest the shrine.

Change from Women-centered to Patriarchal form of Society

There were various views regarding the change of Japanese Society from a women-centered one to the patriarchal form of the society. One common factor like any other ancient civilization of the world might be the introduction of agriculture. But in Japan agriculture was introduced in the Yayoi period (i.e. from 300 B.C. to 300 A.D.) with the development of wet-rice cultivation culture. But the women held significant positions till the 7th-8th century A.D.

In 6th-7th Century A.D. the Japanese accepted Buddhism and Confucianism. The acceptance of Confucian and Buddhist views on women's' inferiority was considered to be pivotal for the change of the society into a patriarchal form of society in Japan.

The first constitutional reform of Japan, i.e. the *Taika reform*, which followed the Confucian ideals, took place in 794. As part of the *Taika* reform women were barred from holding any high position in the government and also deprived of the equal share of government distributed land.

Some sects of Buddhism also taught that women were sinful and must be reborn as male before they could attain enlightenment. In spite of all these views in some Buddhist sects, many women of the imperial family advocated the spread of Buddhism and patronized Buddhism in Japan. Even in the 6th century it became a common practice among women of the high-ranking families to take vows as Buddhist Nuns.

But at the same time two evil customs affected the lives of many women of the royal and high-ranking families of Japan. One of those customs was the practice of sending a hostage to the alliance. The other was the political-marriage, which is quite popular in the later periods also. The local chieftains used to send female relatives as hostage *(Uneme* in Japanese) to the Yamato court for maintaining cordial relations with the central power. The women members of the families were bound to accept that inhuman decision of their male family members. To get rid of this custom also many women took vows as Buddhist nuns. This custom was prevalent during C. 4th Century A. D. and mid 7th Century A. D. But after the *Taika* reform this system became more popular among the local chieftains.

In the following period the so-called political-marriage ties controlled the Imperial Court. The members of Fujiwara clan who held very high-ranking official positions in the imperial court of the then Japan had extensive land-holdings though the system of land-distribution of Taika Reform and they also monopolized the highest official positions of Japanese Court and married their daughters into the imperial family. Then they settled the offspring of those marriages as Emperors to get a free hand in the political domain.

But later the rulers of Japan felt that this political-marriage system created many socio-political problems and so they discouraged the system and it was discontinued.

Impact of Warfare

The danger of warfare in Japan from the 12th to 16th century, which changed the custom of inheritance, also effected the women's position in Japanese Society. The Japanese thought it most practical for only one person (the oldest and possibly the ablest son of the family) to inherit the family property. This meant the total loss of property for the women. Previously after the *Taika* Reform the women possessed half the amount of landed property than that of their male counterpart. But during 12th century the system was changed a lot and the women lost all rights of land holding. Naturally, women had to depend on their male relatives for their livelihood. Such altered family patterns and other social changes such as the development of cities etc. led to the growth of prostitution. Brothels were established in the major port-cities and important political centres of the country.

Many warrior families preferred 'strategic marriage', i.e. '*Seiryaku-Kekkon*' for the betterment of their position in the political field. Thus sometimes the women were forced to enter into unwanted marriage ties. Beside this, the custom of sending hostages to the allies also degraded the position of women in Japan.

On the other hand, during 12th through 16th centuries new types of Buddhism such as *Jodo* and *Jodo Shin* sects gave importance to the ladies. They promised salvation for all even for women by mere chanting the name of *Butsu* or Buddha. In the 13th century *Shinran*, the founder of *Jodo-shin* sect, defied convention by encouraging priests to marry.

But in spite of all these social degradation many women especially court-ladies and women of upper class of the society were often highly literate and enjoyed social and political power. *Murasaki No Shikibu,* a noble lady wrote the first novel of Japanese literature in around 1010 A.D. Later also many ladies devoted their times to the literary works and many of them became very famous litterateurs of Japanese literature.

Change in the Position in Edo or Tokugawa Period (1603 to 1867 A. D.)

Again during the Edo period (1603 to 1867 A.D.) the position of women in Japan underwent a remarkable change. In Edo period strictures, considered to be proper for women were outlined. It stressed on the women's obedience to parents before marriage and to her husband and sons in later days. It also stated that a woman could be easily divorced for any of her misconduct or disobedience. Women adultery was punished by death. But the novel or other literary works said that the day-to-day reality of women's domestic lives might not usually have been that much harsh, as prescribed by the strictures.

It could be mentioned here that the women had to live a very tough life in the village side, where they had to work hard with their in-laws family for their livelihood. In the families of the farmers the women were the strength of their family. But at the same time they had to live a very harsh life in their house.

On the contrary, the women maintained a very high position in the religious field during this time especially in the Shinto and Shamanistic folk religion. One lady, called *Nakayama Miki* founded a new religion called *Tenrikyo* in the19th Century.

Women and Modernisation

The vast social changes during the modernization from 1860s to 1940s affected women's lives with regard to their education, their work and in the society. In 1898 the Meiji Civil Code was promulgated. This code granted the traditional family law and ideology. The idea of *Ryosai Kembo,* i.e. the ladies should 'only be the good wives and wise mothers' was still very strong. But at the same time some liberal ideas from the west were campaigned and became popular.

In the Meiji period some leaders like *Mori Arinori* or *Fukuzawa Yukichi* criticized the ideas of women in Confucianism. But the government, while introducing the education for women through *Terakoya* schools, based its education policy on the principal that the girls should be educated as homemakers. That principal continued for a long time.

In 1899 the Higher Girls' School Order or the *Koto Jogakko Rei* stipulated that there should be at least one high-school for girls in each prefecture (an administrative division in Japan, which may be compared with our District) where the girls should be taught only the literature and domestic science.

Later the industrial revolution played significant role in the economic development of the country. During the early phase of this industrialization the tradition became established of employing young unmarried women in the lowest-paid position on temporary or part-time basis and excluding them from management level position. This tradition has continued, making it difficult for the women even today to take the responsibility of any management job.

But article 14 of the Constitution, promulgated in 1946 states "All of the people are equal under the law and there shall be no distinction in political, economic and social relations because of race, creed, sex, social status or family origin."

Thus by and large, Japanese women have achieved legal equality with men, but the belief that men should work and women stay at home still holds sway in Japanese society.

Most of the Japanese believe that housekeeping and child-care is the women's domain, even if she works. Many companies have amended their recruitment policies, but little change has taken place in placement and promotion policies. As reasons for not placing the women in positions of responsibility, companies cited the fact that women on an average work only for a short time and that the women are responsible for house hold works and child-care. Many women must even stop working after a few years to take over the household responsibilities.

Thus it can be concluded saying that the profound changes in the economic, social and political status of Japanese women were set in the modern period especially after the World War II by the constitutional guarantee. Over the decades, since then the prosperity, urbanization, spread of education and many other factors contributed to the development of the position of women legally and constitutionally. But the nature of the family life, informal policies and practices in the employment world and common attitudes towards women's role in the society contribute to the gap that still exists between the legal standard and social equality.

References

Dore, Roland *Education in Tokugawa Japan* New York 1965.

Inoue, Kyoshi, *Nihon Joosei Shi* (in Japanese); Tokyo 1954.

Susan, J. Pharr, *Political Women in Japan*, Tokyo 1980.

Takie, Sugiyama Lebra, *Japanese Women Constraint And Fulfillment* New York (1930).

Vogel, Suzanne H. *Professional Housewife : The Career of Urban Middle-class Japanese Women* London 1978.

The Japan of Today, published by The International Society for Educational Information, Inc. Tokyo 1993.

Kodansha Encyclopedia of Japan-Vol : 9, Tokyo, 1983.

14

Women in Bhutan : Aspects of their Status and Role

Seikh Rahim Mondal

Introduction

The study of women is gaining importance in recent years. Its basic goal is to gather information on women to gain insight about their multifarious roles and problems. The ultimate objective is to empower women in their struggle against marginality and inequality prevalent in the society. Bhutan is a small Himalayan kingdom of South Asia. The women of this country have been playing a vital role in all aspects of Bhutanese life. But with the evolution of time the Bhutanese women seem to lose their important social position and also being victims of some traditional prejudices. But unfortunately we do not know much about the life of Bhutanese women due to lack of sufficient research studies on them.

The present paper is an attempt to present a socio cultural profile of women of Bhutan. The emphasis has been given here to highlight their social status in terms of the roles played by them in Bhutanese society.

The paper is based on facts gathered mainly from secondary sources. Method of content analysis has been used to accumulate the relevant facts. It is to be noted here that, the information on Bhutan is not much available owing to lack of research studies and also due to policy of the monarch. However, relevant literatures were consulted to get the required information. The information has been drawn from various documents and from results of some studies on Bhutan. The most important of them being : Choden 2000, Chetri : 2001, Her Majesty Wangchuk : 2000, Lhamu : 2000, Mondal : 1999, Mondal 2002, Pema : 1989 and Thsering : 1999. The data are both qualitative as well as quantitative and which have been presented in systematic and analytical manner.

Bhutan : Land and People

Bhutan is a tiny, beautiful, land locked, mountainous kingdom located in the eastern Himalayas. The kingdom of Bhutan covers approximate area of 46,500 square kilometers. It is bordered by Tibetan region of China and Indian States of Sikkim, West Bengal, Assam and Arunachal Pradesh.

Population data and census figures of Bhutan have always been kept in secrets. The population of Bhutan is estimated to be 800,000 (1990 statistics). It is considered to be the least populated country in South Asia. The ratio of men to women is almost 48 per cent. Of which 41 per cent are in productive age, i.e., between 20-54 years. Different ethnic and cultural groups are living together in this tiny kingdom. Among them there are three major groups, now termed as ethnic communities. These are Naglop of Tibetan stock in the west, Sharechops of Tibeto-Burman origin in the east, and Lhotshampas of Nepalese ethnicity in the south. Each of the major ethnic groups are further subdivided into various subgroups with distinct cultures and traditions.

Majority of the population in Bhutan, say the Naglops are Buddhist (Mahayana variety) of Drukpa sect.

Lotshampa(s) are mostly the Hindus. While the Sharchop(s) are either animists or Buddhists or Hindus. In addition there are some people of other faiths. The people of Bhutan are mostly composed of indigenous groups or of migrants of neighboring countries.

The Bhutanese nation state as it is today was formed by the seventeenth century when a Monk from Tibet Shabdrung Ngawang Namgyal, Unified the country by bringing numerous chieftains under his control. He was responsible for introducing administrative and legal systems, many aspects of which survive till today. Bhutan began to modernise since 1960's. The King Jigme Singye Wangchuk, the fourth ruler of Wangchuk dynasty, has been on the throne since 1972. The basic demographic and socio-economic facts of Bhutan is presented in Table 1.

Since the Bhutanese society is heterogeneous on the basis of religions, traditions, cultures and social customs, thus the position of women is not homogeneous throughout the country. As a result the women profile which has been presented in this study mostly reflect the picture of dominant, ethnic community. However, ethnic differences of women's status shall also be highlighted on some aspects.

Table-1
Bhutan-Basic Demographic and Socio-Economic Attributes Relating to Women

1. Area	46, 500 sq. kms.
2. Population	800, 000 (1990)
3. Life Expectancy of Birth	66 Years
4. Percentage of urban population	15%
5. Average household size	7 persons
6. Crude birth rate (per 1000 population)	39 (1990)
7. Crude death rate (per 1000 population)	17 (1990)
8. Women of child bearing age as percentage of all women	48 (1990)

(Table-1 Contd.)

9.	Total fertility rate	5.7 (1994)
10.	Adult literacy rate	Male-51 Female-23 (1990)
11.	Primary School enrolment ratio gross	Male-31 Female-19 (1986-93)
12.	Secondary School enrolment ratio gross	Male-7 Female-2 (19986-93)
13.	Percentage of pregnant women immunized against tetanus	60 (19990-94)
14.	Percentage of births attended by trained health personnel	11 (1985-90)
15.	Percentage of contraceptive prevalence	2 (1988-94)
16.	Percentage of pregnant women receiving parental care	63 (1988-90)
17.	Infant Mortality per 1000 live births	70.7 (1994)

[*Source :* Population Reference Bureau, 1988. and World Development Report, 1992; 1994 United Nations Development Programme (UNDP), New York : Oxford University Press]

Bhutanese Women : A Socio-Cultural Profile

Economic Activities

Most Bhutanese still dwell in village. In village economic activities the women have a very considerable role to play. Eighty to ninety per cent of the population live in rural areas and are self-employed. The economy is largely dominated by substance agriculture. Nearly 62 per cent of women are actively engaged in agriculture. Even today, rural agricultural production is driven by family labour. Everything has to be done manually and scope for mechanization is limited due to mountainous terrain. Ploughing is considered as men's job and upkeep of home and farm are treated as woman's job. In most parts of Bhutan, manure handling is strictly a women's task, just as a carpenter, mason and painter is always a man. In some areas men mostly work in small industries and construction companies as wage earners and thereby earn cash. While women are most often burdened with domestic chores and agricultural tasks which is not countable in terms of cash earning. A significant number of rural and urban women are self-employed in weaving, dying, cane and woodcrafts which are off season income opportunities to them. Owing to the tradition of decision making ability in the household, the Bhutanese women have a good knack in business. Even if the business is in the name and hands of men, it is very often noticed managed by women. This may be due to the age-old traditional role of women. They seemed to be better managers than men in general. As far as cottage industries are concerned, say in weaving, the women dominate and manage the activities.

Since the modernization started in Bhutan, men have started dominating incomes from the urban areas. While women still play the most important roles in the rural economic life. They are still involved in agriculture, animal husbandry and village industries. Today a married couple who start their own living away from natal home by making business or trade, it is mostly registered in the name of the wife. Actually the economic role of women in Bhutan is a very significant one. Ownership of land and other assets go to women. Inputs in the house and farm is much more than man and most control of resources remain with women.

The access of women to different types of opportunities are almost equal to men, say trading and credit for employment. Women enjoy full access to credit from all financial institutes, especially from the Bhutan Development Finance Corporation (BDFC). In 1994, 27 per cent of the BDFC loan went to women who comprise 32 per cent of the total clients. Loan recovery rate of women was about 49 per cent as compared to 40 per cent for men. It has become an increasing phenomenon today that more and more women are joining business cycle. They own some of the most modern successful enterprises like hotels, travel agencies, general service stores. Even the best entrepreneurship prizes have been awarded to women. It is relaxed that women have better entrepreneurship abilities than men do. The reason for women entering in business enterprises is due to equal civil/social status of women in Bhutan and also it pertains to the fact that they have been playing a very deminating role in the traditional society of Bhutan. There are hardly any training centers that could provide adequate training for women in enterprising activities. However, in recent times, national Women Association of Bhutan (NWAB) has been working in providing trainings in enterprises skills and self development for women.

Women form 14 per cent of the civil service, where there is no discrimination in pay, compensation of benefits between sexes. The Royal civil service commission provide there months of maternity leave for the first two children. But there is a slight difference in pay for unskilled workers. As a matter of fact women those who work as labourers either in farm or in other works. The women those who engaged in self employment, get less pay then men, very often face some acute problems during winter months, when there is less agricultural work. Weaving is the main activity of women in the central and eastern parts of the country. There are several difficulties in income generation from weaving particularly to marketing. Many women produce fabrics in remote areas where the local market is limited and the transport has not been accessed.

The scarcity of raw material and market outlets of products such as bamboo, wood, and cane crafts considered as major constraints in self employment prospect.

The economic roles played by Bhutanese women is very much recognized by the society, because they carry a substantial responsibility to maintain the family economy. In Bhutanese society women have to work to support their families or to contribute towards the family income. Women are given equal opportunities for choosing careers. But owing to situation, in rural and interior areas women tend to be concentrated more in low paying jobs. There has also been a gap between the earnings of men and women due to their low educational attainments and lack of skills due to poor training facilities. The women entrepreneurs however, face the usual obstacles of limited access to credit and are often handicapped by their own lack of technical training. But in recent times various government projects for training of rural women for gainful activities have been started in Bhutan to help the women for the increase of their earning capabilities.

Access to Resources

In Bhutan the access of women to various resources are quite equal to men, be it is land, livestock, credit, market health and education.

(a) Land

The law of the land does not prohibit women from inheriting land. It is the prerogative of the parents to divide or transfer land as per their wishes amongst the children. Both the matrilineal and patrilineal systems of inheritance co-exist in the country. In northern communities, women inherit all or bigger portion of the parent's property than those of east and south. They also play a more central role in decision making. In the rural areas of western and central Bhutan, it is traditional practice to pass land from mother to daughter. Naglop women or women of west and central Bhutan who inherit land and associated properties tend to play a more central role in the family than women in Sharchop and Lhotshampa communities. A gender study carried out by the planning commission found that 60 per cent of property is owned by women. Property is very often registered in the name of woman, because women are the ones who look after the parents in their old age.

Some Sharchop and most Lhotshampa people follow the patrilineal system of inheritance, thus passing land from father to son. Among Lhotshampa Hindu Communities, female land ownership through inheritance is noticed in case of divorce and widowhood or as daughter in absence of sons. Usually land is divided among sons and in well to do families with large land holding daughter may be given some portion of land. But the case is very rare.

(b) Live Stock

In Bhutan, land and livestock are viewed as two inseparable assets of any rural household. Small livestock purchases are decided upon and carried out by women and they keep income generation from this. But trading in larger livestock, slaughter and sale of meat are normally in hands of men. However, in some Naglop communities, women are frequently engaged in trading of larger livestock's particularly in absence of men.

(c) Credit

The agricultural and rural credit scheme of the Bhutan Finance Development Corporation (BDFC) is the main formal credit scheme, which in 1993 distributed loans to 5099 clients in 10 districts of which 27.2 per cent were women and 72.8 per cent were men. The lower number of women could be attributed to illiteracy of women, lengthy procedures etc. By and large women's access to credit is through male household members because most rural women do not know how to apply for loans. Often applicants have to travel for a long distance to the district headquarters, which women consider waste of time and men even under unsafe for their women. In western Bhutan most of land ownership lies with women but men apply for credit in their wives names and receive cash on their behalf.

(d) Inputs and Technology

In Bhutan agriculture, livestock and forestry training and extension programmes are in general targeted towards farmers and do not specify gender. The extension services in Bhutan are mostly by male staff, while there is no restriction against female members to meet and interact with the male extension agents. But the constraints of female participation are timing, location and duration of activities. But the most interesting fact is that the cultural barriers affecting the contact of male extension agents with female members do not exist at all.

(e) Markets and Handling of Cash

In rural areas cash from sales of milk, butter, cheese and vegetables, small livestock is kept by the women who use it judiciously for the family. But when cash income is in large amount, say form cash crops, sale of large livestock, horse trading etc., men keep the cash, although its use is normally discussed with women. Among Naglop communities, it is mostly women who hold household income, and in other communities it is mostly by men or by both.

Family and Gender Division of Labour

Most Bhutanese still dwell in villages in an extended family system or maintaining strong links with their rural families if they live in urban areas. The average size of the household is estimated to be 7 only.

In general, a rigid gender division of labour is not characteristic of a Bhutanese household. Often the lack of strict division of labour leaves some women with excessive burdens. Men are primarily responsible for more hazardous and difficult jobs. They collect firewood, construct sheds and fences and market the products. While women are often helpers in these areas. It is common to see men helping their women in child care, cooking, milking cattle, washing cloths and other related activities. In the highland mountain household belonging to Tibeto-Bhutanese communities, who are primarily yak harder, nomadic communities, having polyandrous marriage system the women carry out light tasks such as cooking, spinning, dyeing/drying woods etc., while the men take care of all the tasks-heavy as well as light.

In most part of rural areas in Bhutan there are many men whose sole responsibility is to plough the fields and attend meetings trainings outside the village. So they are free most of the time and their women run the entire indoor and outdoor activities. However, Bhutanese men have a fairly accurate perception of their women's workload and appreciate their role both in home and in the farm. Bhutanese women have a most prominent role in natural resource management, agriculture and in household activities.

In Bhutan most activities are carried out jointly by both males and females. There are only few activities that are gender specific such as knitting by women and sharpening of knives by men. On farms men plough and women weed and transplant. In general, in almost all the households, women do more work than men. On an average, women work 20 per cent more than women. The average is 40 per cent for men and 60 per cent for women.

Bhutanese men and women have common as well as separate roles that have evolved over the centuries, and these are strongly influenced by traditions, regions and cultures. Women generally enjoy a equal status in the family, and they are consulted in all affairs which are related to family and household matters. In many households of west, east and central Bhutan it is women who make the final decisions. These are mainly matrilineal or near matrilineal societies in which women inherit land and other property from the parents. In the east among the Sharchops, weaving and bamboo or cane craft making for additional cash income is very common, where women work and men go out to sell the products and purchase good of households needs from the cash earned. However, for most part of the east, men control the household income. The women, however play a great role in saving of this income for purchase of raw materials to continue their business.

Among Hindu Lhotshampa communities of south, men play a major role in decision making rather than women due to strong patriarchal force prevalent among them.

Traditionally women's responsibilities have been restricted to home in cooking, cleaning, child bearing, child rearing etc. Women are considered to be weak, vulnerable and dependent on men, and yet they run the households. While men deal with outside works and assistance only. The women of western and northern Bhutan seem to be very hard workers compared to their counterparts of east and south and this is primarily due to their habitat under which they live in. Cooking meals for the family is a woman's duty, but for big events like festivals and ceremonies services of men play a central and indispensable role.

The available studies reveal that improvement in family welfare by the women have been taking place in Bhutan. There have been a gradual improvement in the position of women through better access to health facilities, education and earning opportunities. The birth spacing, acceptance of small family norms, family planning practices and efficient management of household are in the process of Bhutan. But these are more marked among the urban, literate and elite class than the poor rural masses.

Women and men share the burden of work quite equally in Bhutan although two thirds of the work that women do is unpaid. However, the contribution made by women to the household, the community and the society at large, receive much greater recognition in Bhutan. Traditionally Bhutanese women had more say in the family life than men. Until the recent past, women had the authority to kick the men out of the house if they found them unproductive.

The gender activity profile in a household of Bhutan in presented in Table–2.

Table-2 : Comparative Gender Activity Profile of Bhutan

Features/Activities Religion	*Naglop (s) Buddhism*	*Sharchop (s) Animism, Buddhism*	*Lhotshampa (s) Hinduism*
Social division	Class and status division	Mostly based on economic position	Caste and class
Marriage	Arranged/ Love	Mostly love/ arranged	Mostly arranged
Head of family	Men/Women	Men	Men
Inheritance	Matrilineal	Mixed	Patrilineal
Residence	Matrilocal	Both	Patrilocal
Land ownership	Women	Both	Men
Decision making	Mutual	Men	Men
Access to income	Both	Both	Both
Features/Activities	Naglop (s)	Sharchop (s)	Lhotshampa (s)
Control over income	Mostly women	Both	Men
Off farm employment	Men	Men	Men
Ploughing	Men	Men	Men
Milking	Mostly women	Women/Men	Women/Men
Cooking	Women	Women	Women
Firewood collection	Both	Both	Women
Cleaning	Women	Women	Women
Preferred child	Both	Both	Male
Child care	Both	Women	Women
Participation in public Domain	Men	Men	Men
Self image	Positive self image	Not so low	Low
Saving and managing	Women	Women/Men	Both
Market related works	Both	Men	Men
Nursing	Women	Women	Women
Schooling	Boys and Girls	Boys	Boys and Girls
Craft making	Mostly women	Mostly women	Mostly women

Marriage and Divorce

The status of women under the law of Bhutan is considered to be equal, giving women and men equal rights in all spheres of life say marriage, divorce, inheritance and so on. The laws are applicable to all citizens irrespective of status, wealth and sex. The marriage Act of Bhutan was codified in 1980 and was updated in 1986. Marriage Act was codified in 1980 and was updated in 1986.

Marriage can be contracted according to religious customs or in any other way. Monogamy is the most accepted form of marriage. Customarily, when the situation suits male members of the family, the society does permit polyandry i.e. more than one husband at a time. In some parts of Bhutan even today polyandry is practiced. The concept of polyandry has been well justified because under the pressing environmental situation of the place men could find their means to sustain, while it is very difficult for women. However, the number of such families nowadays are few and found mostly in the north eastern parts of Bhutan and the high altitudes of northern and western Bhutan among the Tibeto-Bhutanese communities. Polygamy is also allowed but it must be with the consent of the women.

In fraternal polyandrous system of marriage where a woman married to several men (mostly brothers) they automatically enjoyed more power over all her husbands and had command over the entire family. From a superficial point of view the polyandry empowers the women, while polygamy disempowers her. But actually in the two forms of marriage-polyandry and polygamy–the overall implications affect women more than men. As a result in contemporary times, the Bhutanese women are not necessarily attracted to entering into either of these forms of marriages as both these complicates their lives.

In Bhutan, it is hard to distinguish between courtship and marriage. A man and a woman come together and decide.

No value is attached to virginity. Men and women are equally free to have sexual relations. Even in the absence of marriage, when children are born, family may also look after such children. There is no hard and fast rule. But among the Hindu Lhotshopas of southern Bhutan, most marriages tend to be arranged by parents following a set of customs and ceremonies that are common to Hindus elsewhere. However, love marriages are also common to them now-a-days. Among the Hindu Lhotshopas, marriage rules are rather very rigid. Bhutanese in general celebrate the wedding with generous offerings of wine and elaborate ceremonies, depending on the family's resources.

In Bhutan greater flexibility in marriage and in separation/divorce given the high degree of promiscuity and adultery and these ultimately affect the women their self steam.

The Bhutanese society does not permit dowry system and organized prostitution is illegal in Bhutan. There is no social taboo against divorce in Bhutan. It can be obtained by either sex either party seeking the divorce has the responsibility to compensate the aggrieved party. The divorce deed is normally drawn up in the presence of witnesses. One of the main causes of divorce in Bhutan is adultery by either sex.

During divorce, personal property acquired prior to wedlock reverts to the previous after wedlock is divided equally among the women, men and children if any. Custody of children under the age of 9 years is granted to the mother and the father contribute in obliged to towards child support until the child reaches the age of 18 years. Bhutanese women remarry without any social prejudice, often with children of first marriage. It is noted that children of previous marriage receive good treatment from their step-fathers. But it may vary from ethnic group to group and culture to culture.

Actually social institution of marriage is not a complex affair. Both men and women are free to select their partners.

Status of the Girl Child

The Girl child is very much favoured in Bhutan. Considering the hard life ahead for females, the girls are more likely to receive greater care and protection than boys during their infancy and childhood. In northern and western Bhutan it is customary among many groups that after marriage bridegroom go and live with the bride's family. In this matrilocal family system, daughters traditionally live with the parents and take care of them in old age. And as a result the girl child is not unwanted to them.

Birth of the girl child is generally considered as degrading misfortune in most South Asian Countries. But this is not the case of Bhutan where it is not looked upon as a doom by the family, rather the girl child is welcomed by the society. A Bhutanese generally prefers, a female child to a male because most likely she is to remain with the family. Males often after marriage go to the wife's house. The parental properties are usually passed to the females and little or none to males. Thus the girl child is considered as very helpful.

Education

The network of educational institution was almost nonexistent in Bhutan prior to 1960. With the establishment of First Five Year Plans, The Royal Government of Bhutan realized that the shortage of working and skilled man powers was the main constraint on the development and thus allocated resources for extending the network of primary, secondary and central schools.

There is an important gender difference in enrolment of boys and girls; approximately 60 per cent are kept for boys and above 40 per cent are meart for girls. Ever since 1950s when modern education was introduced, despite the initial cultural hesitation to send girls to school, today's enrollment of girls in primary schools shows a dramatic change, at 46.6 per cent of the students.

The dropout rate from school is also higher for girls. While the adult literacy rate is 20 per cent, the female literacy is estimated at below 10 per cent. The existence of low literacy rate for women hinders the process of communicating the issues of health, sanitation, hygiene and improvement in income generating programmes. The gender disparity in education is being reduced in Bhutan with the establishment of community schools which are located closer to villages and thus children take less time to reach the school. The parental concerns regarding girls safety has also been addressed.

Although the percentage of educated women is less than men, yet the traditional informal education has added to the positive socio-cultural strength to women that they had since the time immemorial. The village informal education provided the knowledge system which has benefited about 75 per cent of the women population in the country. The comprehensive education system was introduced only in 1961, prior to which only traditional education was imparted by the monasteries to young male monks and few nuns. But over last few decades of development, a drastic change has came due to extensive net work of schools imparting English medium education. Simultaneously, the monasteries continue with the traditional education.

The nature of modern education is widely published in Bhutan and the ratio of girls to boys at enrollment in the primary schools is almost 1 : 1. Even though the education system does not discriminate against girls, yet the percentage of girls moving up the system shows a declining trend, ending up with less female participation in higher education than in primary education. The enrollment rate at primary level is about 43 per cent dropping to 20 per cent at the time of attending junior high level education. The sudden drop in the number of children from primary level to the junior high level is quite notable and this is primarily because of situational as well as socio-cultural reasons.

In a country paper of n Bhutan, 1988, it was noted that the enrollment level of girls appears to be more than half than that of the boys from pre-primary to class VI standard. From class VII and VIII they drop to less than 50 per cent and in class IX and X to 26 per cent respectively. The lower enrollment of girls in schools is due to the reluctance of parents, who do not with to lose the help of the daughters in household and farm works. Lack of appropriate job opportunities for girls is also responsible for the belief that spending money on a girl's education is a sheer waste.

Health Situation

In Bhutan women face a greater health risk than men, particularly during child birth which causes greater stress on women who are undernourished, anemic and suffering from iodine and vitamin deficiencies. Despite impressive improvement in primary health care, the maternal mortality rate remains one of the highest in the world at 7.7 per cent 1000. Majority of women still give birth at home and are not attended by the trained health works, which increasing the risks further. However, there are initiatives for promotion of disease prevention, improved sanitation and hygiene. As a result attendance at mother and child clinics is on the increase. But the low ratio of female health workers, i.e., 69 women to 729 men in 1989 restrict the use of these services by women.

In Bhutan most women still prefer to have babies at home and thus face the consequence of death when complication arises. Pregnant women continue to work till the last months before delivery. The child spacing is also a problem. Rural Bhutanese women who continue to become pregnant every year until they are too old to have babies.

According to UNICEF around 20 per cent of young women and adolescent girls are undernourished and anemic owing to malnutrition caused by low dietary intake, heavy work load, frequent pregnancies and parasitic infection caused by unsanitary living condition. It is said that the health situation of Bhutanese women is improving, but at a slow pace. Traditional spiritual methods of curing and healing are still predominant among rural and even among many urban people. Women are among majority who opt for indigenous forms of treatment.

Women and Tradition

Bhutanese women played a very important role in the retention, growth and development of culture of the land. They are the real protectors of cultural heritage of Bhutan. They actively participate in cultural activities of their respective communities. They used to worship gods, goddesses, and deities and also observe fast on several occasions. Their active participation in local fares, festivals and ceremonies enriched the cultural fabric of Bhutan.

Bhutanese women played a very important role in maintaining traditional cultural heritage of Bhutan. They are the real protectors of cultural heritage of the country which sustain the policy of 'Gross National Happiness' as declared by the His Highness Royal king of Bhutan. Women are the carriers of traditional information of little traditions of Bhutan. In absence of written records, the oral traditions are cultivated by women which helps in continuity of Bhutanese culture pattern. Bhutanese women remain traditional in dress, language, food, ornament and use of resources. They still retain their traditional habitat of growing food crops, diary, poultry, weaving and health care practices.

Women and Social Prejudices

Bhutan is predominantly a Buddhist country. Buddhism is of the viewed that natural inferiority is a history. Discrimination of women is a social practice. Thus advocated to emancipate women through preaching of Buddha's religions of equality. Buddhists on the whole have a more liberal attitude towards women, particularly in respect to their work. Buddhist women do not observe strict seclusion. But discrimination of women is a social practice which has also affected the women of Bhutan.

The social belief system based on the doctrine of *Karma* in Buddhism gives women a ambiguous position, on one hand there is no social stigmatization or repression of women in society at large, while on the other hand there are many sayings and proverbs place women in a lower position than men. There is a popular saying in Bhutan that, 'men are nine lives superior to women'. This means that one has to be born and reborn as a women nine times to be finally born as man. That is why, it is said that, women have to go through painful phases in life such as childbearing and childbirth from which men are free. It is also considered that the women are impure while men are free from impurity. Manure handling, sweeping and cleaning are considered solely as women's jobs, as these will immerse a man in 'impurities' while it seems to be all right to pollute a women.

Self Esteem

In general the self-image of Bhutanese women is high. They are the products of a proud society who do not see themselves to be any less than men and will not tolerate discrimination by their men. Bhutanese women are open and frank. They dominate household politics. Bhutanese women are by nature very modest, but very assertive when things matter to them.

In western and central Bhutan, a husband does not even have the authority to hire his service or land out tools or any household items to others without his wife's permission. While among eastern and southern Bhutan, men are the principal decision makers but women participate equally because they have a good degree of influence and authority over matters affecting the household economy and welfare. Bhutanese men across the country do value their women highly and as a matter women have good self image in this country. But the most notable thing is that the customs and traditions have created a social environment in which the women consider that the man is omnipotent and hence they are dependent on them. Hence the women treat men as superior to themselves. Perhaps this is one aspect of Bhutanese culture in which women allow the men to feel superior and hence gain control over them. Actually in matters of tradition the self image of Bhutanese women in comparison to men is low.

Women and Violence

Women in Bhutan generally enjoye a relatively high status. The Government of Bhutan also accept that discrimination against women is socially unacceptable for various reasons. The women of the country are not free from violence. Alcohol consumption and unfaithfulness to wedded partners are same of the causes of violence against women and men. Heavy consumption of alcohol by both men and women is prevalent in the country, especially in the eastern Bhutan.

Wife beating is not an uncommon phenomenon in Bhutan. It very much exist, but on a lesser scale. Many divorces and quarrels occur out of it. Equally common, however, is husband battering, and this is perhaps very peculiar to Bhutan.

Rape in its classical sense had never been a cause of concern in Bhutan. But with rapid modernization and changing attitudes and values, crimes closer to rape have begun in this country. The Royal Government has drawn up a specific legal tool called Rape Act passed by the National Assembly in 1993.

Sexual harassment and abuse of women and girls in the work place and educational institutions are also been reported in Bhutan. A very important area which seems to be alarming is that of increase of domestic violence which occurs in Bhutan now a days and there tends to be a culture of silence. The problem of AIDS is also reported in Bhutan recent times.

Representation in Decision Making Bodies

Bhutanese tradition has no restrictions against a woman being promoted to any high level post. But the customary practice is to appoint a male, despite the absence of any intention to discriminate against women. National Assembly public representatives are normally selected by the people from amongst the active numbers of the village. In the past it was normal to see only men being chosen to participate in the National Assembly. However, in recent years few women have been selected for National Assembly.

In Government service participation of women clearly diminishes as the grades rise, resulting in an absence of women at the highest decision making levels. 29 per cent of teachers are women and among health workers women constitute about 20 per cent only. Women are not seen in army but some women are working in police force. Employment regulations do not discriminate against women, yet the number of women clearly diminishes as the grades rise, starting at 15 per cent at the lowest level in civil service to 1 per cent at the highest decision making level. It was reported that there were 9 women members *(Chimis)* to the 142 male members in the National Assembly.

For various reasons Bhutanese women in general are isolated from active organizational and political participation.

They lack proper or formal and even informal political bodies. Politics and organization of women is still a concern of educated elite and aristocrat sections of the country.

Bhutanese rural society is still regulated by the informal council of village elders which is under the control of men. Only in absence of male members of the household owing to male migration for trade and service, a women can represent her family. Thus her role is secondary in public affairs and in community decision making.

Male Migration and Women's Responsibility

Bhutan has a tradition of male migration, owing to ecological and socio-economic reasons. Men are engaged with trade and service and habituated to travel a long distance on foot carrying goods on their backs. Sometimes men would be away from home for long periods. Beside migration, traditionally the people led a fairly nomadic or semi-nomadic life. In northern parts there are some nomadic Tibeto-Mongoloid groups who led a pastoral life. They normally have two establishments-winter home and summer home. Polyandry is prevalent among these groups. So the men or families moved from winter pastures to summer pastures to feed and keep their live stocks. In recent times the migration of males from rural areas to urban centers is also very common in Bhutan as like as other places. The male migration has a lot of consequences and this ultimately affects the women.

Many rural male move out in search of off farm employment to urban and industrial areas or for trade leaving their women to take care to family, farm and livestock. It is not unusual to find out that there are many households in Bhutan those are run by women who take care of family, farm, and livestock. This means that the women make decisions and enjoy control over resources of the family. But these increasing number of female headed households in Bhutan may have negative impacts on women in near future, as they became excessively burdened with more tasks, whole were traditionally assigned to men. This encourages young couples for monogamy and to move to urban places for setting up nuclear families by breaking the tradition of extended households. The lack of rigid division of labour by gender has its advantages, but it may create disadvantages to women by increasing workload in the context of male out migration.

Changing Gender Relations in Bhutan

In contemporary times various policies and programmes, specially the women focused programmes, have made a serious impact on life of the Bhutanese women. Influx of new values has also lean gradually propagating. New values bring new aspirations. Significant number of Bhutanese women are now working to earn a living to support the families. Parents are now sending girls to attend school with a belief that education can free their daughters from being trapped at home. Traditional social practices relating to marital issues are also changing. The ethnic communities who had the traditional system of polyandry now allow different brothers to marry separately. With growing awareness, pressure on girls to marry early is decreasing. Unmarried girls engaged in education or occupation are now criticized but appreciated by the society in general. Thus polyandry is being replaced by monogamy or polygamy. Traditional notion of big family of extended nature is now replaced by nuclearization of family with small size. The concept of planned family is gaining popularity. The traditional experience of the extended rural families has suddenly been replaced by the urban nuclear families. The most negative consequence of change out of urbanization and globalization of economy which is affecting the position of women is monetarization.

Much of women's economic value in the family is now defined by amount of cash that she can contribute and which has changed the traditional barter system with which women were mostly involved. Further, the male out migration for trade or business or service which is very characteristic to Bhutan has increased the work load of women. The most significant change which is very often reported in Bhutan is the education of the girl child and awareness of women. Their participation in development process is gradually increasing but they face serious constraints of getting infrastructural facilities owing to remoteness of the places in Bhutan.

Bhutanese women continued to grow food to feed, and fibers to clothes, nourish and nurture their families; while men enjoyed opportunities beyond farming, by seeking religious education and practice or by trading, or joining in the service who feuded and fought for control of territory and power. There are no sharply defined male/female domains. Therefore, rather than being segregated, women are now entering main stream development process without major hindrances. Looking specifically at least last two decades changes have reached to women of all sections of the Bhutanese society. The changes can be largely attributed to education system, maternal and child health care services and rural to urban migrations for new socio-economic opportunities. The transition from the rural subsistence lifestyle to the emergent multifaceted urban lifestyle has changed the women's life in various ways. Empowered by literacy, education and exposure, women are redefining their cultural roles from feminine domesticity to assertive mobility and professionalism. Not only did the physical world change, but the women's self image changed too a great extent. Women's traditional status and power as a viable contributor of economic well being of the rural household changed to her recent position of economically dependent on men's earning in urban areas. No doubt her life has become easier in terms of less hard work on farm with more leisure time, but her own economic power and self steam diminished obviously. Women in Bhutan have been playing a vital role in all aspects of rural Bhutanese life since the time immemorial. But with the advent of time the women seem to loose their important role.

Today men seem to have taken opportunity to avail the urban as well as modern opportunities and leave their farm responsibilities. While majority of women have remained at their rural home and are engaged to look after the farms.

Times are changing and today's young Bhutanese women are not just satisfied with their traditional roles of housekeeping, farm managing and trading. They want more' and are ambitious. The younger generation of Bhutanese women are more career oriented than their predecessors. They are making impacts on once male dominated areas like engineering, administration and finance. But owing to tradition one of the biggest challenges faced by Bhutanese women is managing the balance between career and the family, personal decisions and prioritizing the needs. In spite of very positive role played by women in the Bhutanese Society, there are many problems that affect women to a considerable extent. The most notable problems are illiteracy, poor education facilities, emerging sex violence, monetarization, and status degradation.

Conclusion

It is very difficult to make generalizations about the status of women in Bhutan because of differences found in society between ethnic groups and places of the country. Although, there are differences in the position of women at the macro level, depending on ethnic groups and regions, Bhutanese women in general are known to have a comparatively favourable social status. They do not suffer many of the gender-biased discriminations those are faced by the women of neighboring south Asian countries. But to say that the Bhutanese women are completely free from all gender-related prejudices would be an over generalization.

There is a culture of acceptance of some prejudiced differences in the societal beliefs and norms that influence gender-related attitudes and practices.

Bhutanese women have a fairly visible role in the economy and the family as well as in natural resource management. The socio economic role, which the women play is recognized, valued, appreciated and acknowledged by men of the Bhutanese society. Position wise, Bhutanese women are, with out a doubt, have better status, but further improvements are very much needed. Therefore, it would be better to give due recognition to the contributions of women through specific gender free policies. Throughout all of Bhutan, women are over burdened with indoor and outdoor tasks. This needs to be recognized at the policy and planning levels of all the development sectors of the country.

By analyzing the overall aspects of gender relations in Bhutan it may be ascertained that, the position of women in Bhutan is very ambiguous one. It is very true that there is no significant difference between men and women in this country. But at the same time it is untrue that Bhutanese women are not affected and victims of discrimination. Bhutanese women and men have common as well as are separate roles that have evolved over the centuries, and these are strongly influenced by religions, traditions, cultures and varied environments of the country.

So far the socio-religio-philosophical values are concerned Bhutanese women may have lower place, but for practical purposes they have the say in every domain. Despite the practical and visible favourable position enjoyed by the Bhutanese women, in religio-philosophical matters men are granted a higher position. Since religion and philosophy is a way of life and influence the day to day living, there is a feeling of superiority of men over the women in spiritual sense. Thus it may be interpreted that, in matters of socio-economic cultural roles the Bhutanese Women's position is high, while in matters of tradition and values the self image of them in comparison to men is low.

References

Choden Kunzang, *Bhutanese Women and their Changing world : Swiss-Bhutan Partnership in a Changing World,* Helvest; Bhutan, 2000.

Chetri Saamdu, "Women in Bhutan", An un-published research paper (Personal Communication), 2001.

Her Majesty Ashi Sangay Choden Wangchuk, "For Women's Rights and International Peace" in *Kuensel,* 11th March, 2000.

Lhamu Thuji, "The Changing Role of the Modern Bhutanese Women" in *Kuensel,* 11th March 2000.

Mondal Seikh Rahim, "Status of Himalayan Women", in *Empowerment,* Vol. 6, pp. 41-56, 1999.

Mondal, Seikh Rahim, "Ethnic Groups and Ethnicity in Bhutan : An Appraisal", in Girin Phukan (Eds.) *Ethnicity and Polity in South Asia,* New Delhi, South Asian Publishers, 2002.

Pema, L., *Women in Development : Bhutan,* Thimpu, Asian Development Bank, 1989.

Tshering, Phuntahok C. "Case Study in Bhutan" in Jennette D. Gurung (Eds.) *Searching for Women's Voices in the Hindukush-Himalayas,* Kathmandu : International Centre for Integrated Mountain Development, 1999.

Upreti, Sonia, "Status of Women in Bhutan" in Ramakant and P.C. Misra (Eds.) *Bhutan-Society and Polity,* Jaipur : South Asian Studies Centre, 1996.

Index

A

ACWF (All China Women's Federation), 71-73
Administration and Managers, 59
Administration System, 231
Adult Mortality Ratio, 49
Advertisements, 211, 213, 215-16, 219
  Commercial, 219
  Industries, 221
AIDS, 49, 277
Al-Bireh, 122
Anglo-Saxon Philosophy, 183
Arab Women's Union, 119
Arabic and Central Asia, 12
Arabism, 114
Arab-Jewish War, 117
Ashoka Mehta Committee, 82
Asian and African States, 56
Asian Development, 11-12, 14, 16
Aung San Suu Kyi, 71

B

Balwant Rai Mehta Committee Report, 82
Bangladesh, 47-49, 58-59, 68, 70, 107, 109
Bangladesh's Society, 68
Baul
  Community, 184, 186-92
  Philosophy, 190
  Society, 188
  Songs, 192
  Spiritualism, 187
Bhutan, 52, 257-83
  Agriculture, Livestock, Forestry Training, 264
  Development Finance Corporation (BDFC), 261, 264
  Rural Society, 278
  Society, 270
Bhutanese
  Community, 265
  Nation, 259
  Women, 257, 260-62, 266-67, 270, 273-77, 279-82
  Economic Roles, 262
  Society, 257, 262, 275, 280, 282
Birzeit University, 130, 136
Brahmanism, 228,
Buddhism, 228, 232, 234-37, 251-53, 275
Buddhist(s), 258
  Kings, 229
  Monks, 242
  Nuns (Japan), 252
  Philosophy, 234
  Philosophy, 239
  Rituals, 227
  Sangha, 70, 239, 241

Society, 242
Teachings, 240
Universal Law, 237
Women, 275
Burma, 71

C

Central Asian
Republics, 173
Society, 141, 173-74
Women, 146, 151, 153, 157, 160, 176
Chinese Women, 71
Chinese Women Movement, 73
Civil Administration Law, 132
Colonialization, 70
Committee on the Status of Women in India, (CSWI), 82
Communist China, 71
Communist Party of Palestinian, 117
Community Schools, 272
Confucian Ideals, 252
Confucianism, 251, 255
Crash Programme, 68
Cultural Socialization, 211
Custom of Inheritance in Japan, 253
Customs and Trade, 12
Customs and Traditions, 171

D

Darjeeling Hill Council, 87
Democratic Front for the Liberation of Palestinian, 117
Dhaka University, 186
Dharmasastra, 228-29
Discrimination of Women, 275-76
Drupka Sect, 258

E

Economic
Development, 60
Globalization, 279
Policy, 217
Reforms, 99
Economy, 11, 100, 260, 276
Edo Period, 254
Education and Employment, 40
Employment, 27, 42, 56
Enrolment Ratio, 43
Ethnic Communities, 258, 279

F

Family Planning, 68, 267
Fatah, 117
Female
Child Prostitution, 226
Infanticide, 69
Labour Force, 25
Slaves, 230
Fetus Sex Selection Abortion, 41
Fidayeen, 129
First All Women Panchayat, 89
Five-Year Plan (4th), 69
Five-Year Plan Documents, 68
Flying (Prostitute) Women, 195, 197, 199-202
Freedom Movement in India, 77, 80
Fujiwara Clan, 252

G

Garment Industry, 107
Gaza Strip, 117, 131
GEM, 60
Gender
Development Index (GDI), 43-45, 52

Disparity, 39-40, 43, 45, 47, 53, 55, 60-61
Empowerment Measures, 26, 44
Parity Index (GPI), 53
Global
Development, 11
Economic System, 64
Globalization, 11-12, 16, 27, 30, 32, 99-100, 104, 106, 108
Gram Panchayat, 83, 86-87, 89-92

H

HAMAS, 117
Hindu and Buddhist Cultures, 225
Hindu Communities, 264
Hinduism, 227, 234, 242
HIV/AIDS, 109
House of Chakri, 232
Human Development Index (HDI), 44-46
Human Development Report on South Asia, 36
Human Rights, 40, 44

I

Illiteracy of Women, 264
India—Bhutan, 13
Indian Ass. and Pacific Studies—Calcutta Univ., 13
Indian Immigration, 228
Indian Womenhood, 219
Indian Women, 77-78, 219
Industrialization, 100, 255
Inheritance System, 263
Matrilineal, 263
Patrilineal, 263
International Women's Day, 127
Iran, 64, 66, 69
Iranian Women, 66-67
ISE Shrine (Japan), 251
Islamic
Fundamentalism, 159
Laws, 144
States, 64
Islamification, 67
ISM (International Solidarity Movement), 135
Israeli Army, 127
Israeli Women, 131

J

Japanese
Society, 249, 251, 253, 255
Women, 249-51, 255-56
Jewish Immigration, 117, 119
Jigme Singye Wangchuk, 259
Jodo Shin Sects, 253
Jordanian Rule, 121

K

Karnataka Panchayat Act, 82
Kerala, 53, 60
King Mongkut, 233

L

Labour
Laws, 107
Market, 66
Markets, 28-29, 32
Lahore, 66
Legal Reforms, 217
Literacy, 43, 52-53, 55, 58, 79, 89, 126, 280
Adult, 272
Female, 53, 55, 58, 272

M

Mahar Zila Parishad and Panchayati Samitis Act, 82

Maldives, Malaysia and Thailand, 100-101
Male Migration, 278
Manu, 228-29
Marginal Economic Sectors, 30
Marriage Act of Bhutan, 269
Matriarchy, 191
Meiji
 Civil Code, 255
 Period, 255
Migration, 168-69, 278
Migration of Rural Labour, 93
Modernization, 63, 70, 261
Monogamy, 269, 279
Muslim
 Feudal Society, 144
 Society, 144, 152
 Women, 69, 153
Myanmar, 70

N

Naglop, 258, 263
 Communities, 264-65
 Women, 263
National Association Bhutan, 277
National Perspective Plan, 83
National Women Association of Bhutan, 262
Nepal, 52
NLM (National Literacy Mission), 89

O

Occupational Segregation, 28-31, 33
Oslo Accords, 130
Ottoman Empire, 114
Oxus-Pyrenees, 114

P

Pakistan, 15, 48-49, 52-53, 58-60, 66
Pakistan and Bangladesh, 69
Pakistan, Bangladesh and Sri Lanka, 39-40, 44, 46-50, 55, 59
Palestinian
 Liberation Army (PLO), 117, 123, 132
 Women, 116, 122-24, 126-27, 129-30, 133, 137
 Women's Movement, 113, 118-19, 131
 Women's Union, 118-19, 123
Palestinian's Women Health Coalitions, 132
Panchayat, 78, 82, 84, 86
 Raj, 16
 Raj Institutions (PRI), 77-78, 82-83
 Samiti, 89
Patriarchal, 199, 212
Patriarchal Social Structure, 102
Political
 and Social Movement, 36
 Participation of Women, 82
Polyandrous Marriage System, 265, 269
Polyandry, 269, 279
Polygamous Marriages, 67
Polygamy, 142-43, 232-34, 279
Poverty Eradication, 27

R

Rape Act, 277
Reservations, 78, 80, 93
Royal Civil Service Commission, 262
Rural Bhutan Women, 274
Russian
 Cultures, 165

Education, 172
Migration, 168-69
Population, 173-74
Women, 144, 163, 168-69, 176-77

S

Sakdina System, 230-32
Samarkand, 175
Sangha Supreme Council, 241
SC/ST Population, 89
Self-Help Groups, 91, 93
Sex Industry, 226
Sex Ratio, 78-79, 94
In States, 79
West Bengal, 79
SGRY Scheme, 91
Shabdrung Ngawang Namgyal, Tibetan Monk, 259
Shamanistic Folk Religion, 254
Sharia, 67, 69
Shariyat Law, 143
Shinto Pantheon, 251
Shinto Religion, 251
Sikkim, 258
Siliguri Sub-Division Council, 87
Sishu Siksha Kendra, 91
Social
Changes, 14
Empowerment, 27
Structure, 211
System, 129
Socialist China, 71
Society, 12-13, 40, 47, 142-43, 156, 185-87, 190, 209, 219, 234, 225-28, 238, 250-51, 262, 279
Civil, 70, 199
Indian, 77, 184
Matrilineal, 244
Multi-Cultural, 184
Palestinian, 117-18, 124-25, 131, 133
Patriarchal, 251
Society and Sex, 234
South Asian
Countries, 48, 100, 271, 281
Women, 36-37, 102
Soviet
Central Asian Women, 141
Economy, 150
Education, 146, 148
Union, 141, 145, 163, 168-69, 171, 177
Sri Lanka, 15, 47-49, 52-56, 58-60
State Institute of Panchayat and Rural Development (SIPRD), 84
Status of
of Girl Child, 271
Women, 78, 225, 269
Women Workers, 101
STD, 109
Sufi Saints, 157
Supreme Soviet of the Union Republics, 146
Swadeshi Movement, 127

T

Talk Reforms, 252-53
Tapati Singh, 90, 93
Tashkent Institute of Communication, 176
Tenno
Empresses, 250
Women, 250-51
Thai
Buddhist, 244
Culture, 237
Society, 225, 227, 229, 233, 235, 239, 242

System, 230
Women, 229, 238, 239
Theravada Buddhism, 234, 237
Third Regime, 71
Third World Countries, 27
Tibeto-Bhutanese Community, 265, 269
Tokigawa Period, 254
Tomb of Sultan Vais Baba (Turkmenistan), 157
Turkification, 114
Turkmen Women, 145

U

UNDP (United Nations Development Programme), 43-44
Guidelines, 26
UNICEF, 274
USA, 101, 109, 122
USSR, 117, 143, 148, 151
Uttar Pradesh, 61
Uzbekistan, 163-64
Uzbek Women, 145, 147

V

Vaishnavism, 187
Village Industries, 261
Violence of Women in Society, 40

W

Wangchuk Dynasty, 259
WATC, 132
Wat-Nariwong, 241
Weaving, 262
West Bank, 117, 122, 125, 134
University, 136
West Bengal, 77-80, 84, 87, 89, 93
Assam and Arunachal Pradesh, 258
Panchayat Act, 82
Women and Sex Sector, 225
Women in Politics and Religion, 250
Women,
Activism, 63-64, 74
Activism in Asia, 16
Affairs Centres, 130
Asian, 13
Decision Making Positions, 59-60
Economic Empowerment, 26-27
Educational Status, 85
Health, 80
In Administration and Managerial Positions, 36
In *Baul* Community, 184
Labour Force, 14, 58
Legal Aid Society, 130
Liberation and Equality, 71
Ministers, 59
Monastery and Identity, 240
Movement, 72
Movement in China, 72
Of Asia, 63
Organizations, 71
Panchayat Leaders, 84-85
Participation, 102, 126, 129, 150-51, 225
Political Committee, 128
Position, 16
Position in Central Asia, 147
Rights, 230
Saints, 157
Social and Economic Status, 14
Social Identity, 13
Social Status, 14
Status of, 13
Studies Centres, 130
Workers, 99, 105-09

Women's
  Economic Value, 279
  Equality Summit, 101
  Movements, 118-19, 215
  Organizations, 118, 121
  Role in Society, 256
Working Women, 196-97
  Committee, 126-27
World War II, 114, 116, 169, 249, 256

Y

Yangtze Basin, 12

Z

Zila Parishad, 82
Zionism, 114-16
Zionist
  Immigration, 114
  Movement, 115